QUEER MAN ON CAMPUS

A HISTORY OF NON-HETEROSEXUAL COLLEGE MEN, 1945–2000

PATRICK DILLEY

RoutledgeFalmer
New York and London

A portion of Chapter 3 was adapted from "Queer theory: Under construction," in *International Journal of Qualitative Studies in Education, 12*(5), 457–472.

Published in 2002 by
RoutledgeFalmer
29 West 35th Street
New York, NY 10001
www.routledge-ny.com

Published in Great Britain by
RoutledgeFalmer
11 New Fetter Lane
London EC4P 4EE
www.routledgefalmer.com

RoutledgeFalmer is an imprint of the Taylor & Francis Group.
Printed in the United States of America on acid-free paper.

10 9 8 7 6 5 4 3 2 1

Library of Congress Cataloging–in–Publication Data
is available from the Library of Congress.

CONTENTS

ACKNOWLEDGMENTS

Over the past seven years, a number of individuals aided me in completing this project. First, I want to thank the participants of this study; without the fifty-seven men who volunteered their time and their stories, the data of their lives and identities, I could not have produced this book. Although I had room to include extensive narratives from only twenty-two of the respondents, I learned immensely from each of them.

Michael Schiavi, Michelle Knight, James Koschoreck, Martha Soto, Delores Akins, Shereen Fogel, Sherri Bayouth, and Eric Moore listened to my rantings and ravings about the process and the product of graduate education, as well as my conceptualization, research, and analysis of theories of identity development and things queer. I am grateful to Benjamin Baez and Susan Talburt, who both encouraged me to write this book and to work with the fantastic editorial staff at Routledge, including Joe Miranda. And Kristen Renn, my frequent partner in writing and in bourgeois tragedies, has the most remarkable polka-dotted mind and merited extra credit for her willingness to listen to many paragraphs of disembodied text.

From the University of Kansas, I want to thank Cindy Sanders Derritt, David Hardy, and Ruth Lichtwardt for their friendship, encouragement, and sharing of memories and materials. I appreciate the assistance and encouragement of the faculty advisors to the *University Daily Kansan*, Tom Eblum and Malcolm Gibson. I also benefited from the help of the reference staff of the Spencer Research Library at KU; Kathleen L. Neeley and Barry Bunch from the university archives provided outstanding service.

While I studied at the University of Southern California, I gleaned a great deal of insight and technique from its stellar faculty, including Marjorie Becker, Paul Knoll, and Gretchen Guiton. Linda Hagedorn showed such faith in my work: she invited me to speak about my research in almost all of her classes for several years. I want to thank Estela Bensimon, who taught me so much by challenging my thoughts on diversity; she continues to inspire me to be a better teacher.

If I know anything about qualitative research, I learned it from Bill Tierney. While I wrote the original dissertation, he brought me to new understandings of veracity, validity, and vitality. (But as he might tell you, any mistakes in the data or analysis remain mine.)

Finally, I want to acknowledge two family members: my mother, Marsha Dilley, who never dreamed when she would tell her young son that he would go to college that he would never leave; and our cousin, Patty Workman, who, as my fourth grade teacher, made me believe that I was limited only by the constraints of what I could imagine to ask and to learn.

FINDING MY WAY

CHAPTER 1

Calling Names, Naming Tales

When I was in the fourth grade, sitting alone at home one afternoon, I was perusing the *World Book Encyclopedia* set we kept in the den. I looked up *sex* and read about the physiological facts and functions. I dutifully studied—a prospective researcher even then—each cross-reference. I came across an entry in the *H* volume. As I read it, I thought, "that is talking about me and why I like boys." That moment, for me and for others first naming of a part of themselves that they could not convey before learning new names, was a powerful experience.

Three years later, the winter of my thirteenth birthday, my family vacationed in the Florida Keys. A grandson of one of my mother's friends arrived a few days later. Karl was dramatic in a 1940s Joan Crawford way, dressed a la Truman Capote (long knitted scarf and gloves, even in Florida), and a year older than I. I knew, immediately, he was, like me, "not like the other kids," but I did not understand how or why I knew that. We found a fast rapport. Although the details of our lives were dissimilar, we shared a particular meaning of the world in which we felt trapped: snared by high school bullies, by small towns and minds, by our inability to replace those bourgeois tragedies with the dramas and comedies we wanted. That night was the first time I ever stayed awake the entire night, as we lay on the floor, watching and listening to the waves of the ocean, telling our stories about our Midwestern adolescence in the dark.

The researcher I have become recognizes the patterns that form my life evident in those moments. I continue to study identity, particularly of people "not like the others," who are sexually and emotionally drawn to members of the same gender. I still listen to their stories, asking questions, comparing and contrasting the tales I gather. College life—the extracurricular activities in which I participated, the topics I chose to study, the professional focus I developed—built upon both aspects of my identity—as a non-heterosexual male and as a scholar of identity and higher education. The two aspects are intertwined: without one, the other makes little sense on its own.

"Common" Sense and "Queer" Sensibilities

How, then, I wondered, do other men who do not identify as heterosexual make sense of their lives in college? How do they understand who they are? What impact did their postsecondary experiences have on those understandings? What elements of postsecondary education contributed (or detracted) to the identities and experiences of non-heterosexual males?

One goal echoes Hesford's call (1999) "to explore multiple articulations of authority and identity and to discover how authority and agency shift from one pedagogical context to another" (1999, p. xxix). Another aim is to document and examine experiences previously hidden (McLaughlin and Tierney, 1993), while a third harkens to Talburt's challenge to move beyond simply representing voices and making lives visible, to convey "the relations of voice to visibility within circulations of knowledge and ignorance—what is revealed, seen, and heard, by whom, how, and with what effects" (1999, p. 536). Ultimately, I question existing notions of what we know about "gay college students": their experiences, their identities, and their history.

I proffer a theory of how non-heterosexual males—and their identities—can be understood during their college years. The theory is typological, providing classifications for identity based upon the patterns of how individual students thought of their identity while in college, what activities they engaged in while a student (and the motivations behind those actions), and how their self-concepts and actions related to other concepts of identity (both heterosexual and non-heterosexual). In much of the research on the lives of these students, a paired master category (akin to those of power and subservience in Marxism, or male and female in feminism) exists: one is assumed to be either heterosexual or not, with few (if any) gradations between the two. The typology I provide, however, moves beyond the binary definitions of "straight" and "gay," or even "straight" and "gay, lesbian, or bisexual."

Although recent research has advocated separate theories for development for those identities (Brown, 1995; de Monteflores and Schultz, 1978; Esterberg, 1997; Fassinger, 1998; Henderson, 1984; Jenness, 1992, 1998; Weinberg, Williams and Pryor, 1994), the latter three terms are usually paired collectively against "heterosexual." Because of the compelling evidence of the differences in experiencing non-heterosexual contexts and concepts for women and for individuals who identify as bisexual, I limited my study to the experiences of men. In addition, I was able, due to my gender and my identification as a non-heterosexual man, to talk to men about the intimate details of their early lives, thus decreasing barriers against obtaining trustworthy data (Coffey, 1999; Denzin, 1989; Fontana and Frey, 2000; Gergen and Gergen, 2000; Glesne and Peshkin, 1992; Merriam, 1998; Warren, 1998).

While I was conducting the interviews, I began to discern patterns of identification and experience, which I eventually developed into a typology, or sets of patterns, of identity (outlined in Figure 1.1). Resisting the temptation to simplify my understanding by using existing, agreed-upon yet amorphous terms and definitions was not easy. For instance, the incongruity of what the

---

FIGURE 1.1: **Non-Heterosexual Collegiate Male Identity Typology, Late Twentieth Century**

YEARS MOST EVIDENT	IDENTITY TYPE
1940s to Late 1960s	**Homosexual**—acknowledged feelings/attractions, but did not necessarily tell others; sex and identity viewed as a very private matter. Clandestine socialization with other non-heterosexuals, if at all.
Late 1960s to Present	**Gay**—publicly announced/acknowledged feelings/attractions; often involved within institutional systems to create change. Public socialization with other non-heterosexuals.
Late 1980s to Present	**Queer**—very publicly deployed identity, in opposition to normative ("straight") culture; often tried to create change from mores.

IDENTITIES EVIDENT ACROSS DECADES

"Normal"—identified as heterosexual ("just like everyone else"); homosexual activity did not have an effect upon self-identity, and the dissonance between self-concept and deeds was not recognized.

Closeted—recognized feelings/attractions to other males, and acknowledged to self the meanings of those feelings and attractions. Did not tell many others of his feelings (if anyone at all). Tried to avoid social contexts that might reveal his feelings/attractions.

Parallel—identified and experienced as "straight" (non-homosexual) while within those situations and contexts, and as non-heterosexual in non-straight situations and contexts. The cognitive and emotional dissonance, if experienced at all, was compartmentalized, so long as the two worlds were kept separate.

Denying—rejected affectional and erotic feelings for and attractons to other males.

men told me to what was I knew or learned before did not negate the validity or veracity of what they told me, even if the information did not fit into previously proposed theories. Theorization about identity formation—particularly for a typological theory—must be open to multiple paths of development, even within discernable patterns or types.

I strove to keep my thinking as unsettled as possible while talking to and about the very distinctly different life stories I collected, collated, constructed, and dissected. *A priori* research is particularly troublesome in work concerning identity; after all, we must know *something* about our research topics in order to know what questions to ask, and of whom. But those of us who investigate *how* and *why* people identify in particular ways must guard against the initial evaluative response that so often occurs: "That answer does not reflect my experience; can that response be true?" Even after many interviews, I sometimes asked myself, while I was in the midst of talking with a respondent, *That story does not fit into the patterns you have recognized so far; can it be true, or even relevant?* The key to working through these impulses, I believe from this study, is not to ignore that voice, that questioning impulse, but to do two things when I hear it: one, to utilize the recursive and/or compare/contrast techniques, to probe the respondent further and (with luck) glean information that will help with later analysis (including of veracity of the data); and two, to note (preferably within observational and field notes) the thoughts of the potential discrepancies for consideration during the analysis of the entire project. The confounding data should not be discounted out of hand, however.

From this basis of classifying actions and self-concepts flows the typology, comprised of: *homosexual, closeted, gay, queer,* "*normal,*" *parallel,* and *denying.* Taking into account Bravmann's call for "new investigations of the varied histories of gay men and lesbians [that] include looking at how queer subjects have made and made sense of their cultures" (1997, p. 38), I provide the typology as a pattern of understanding non-heterosexual collegians' identities evident in their educational life histories. The patterns show not only the differences of the identities but also the relational and historical natures of those identities; changes in the last 55 years of the very notions of what was considered a non-heterosexual identity can be seen in this progression.

Those changing notions, I found, were based upon formations of common components of identity development: *experiences* (what happened to these students in college), *senses* (how the students perceived what happened), and *sensibilities* (the meanings they ascribed to those experiences and perceptions). Few, if any, theorists of identity seek to convey the meanings individuals make; most concentrate upon either experiential or self-perceived aspects of students' lives and identities. Further, for non-heterosexual male students, none of those three qualities of collegiate life have been studied extensively; indeed, in the bulk of the research, a "gay" student is defined either exclusively through self-contemplation (an ephemeral nature), or through self-action (physical homosexual experiences). To read the research literature on "gay" college students, one would assume that all men in college who do not identify as heterosexual have a fairly homogenous, unified pattern of experiences and understandings. Moreover, no study has placed the concepts of such an identity in a historical context. I feel the narratives in this study convey complexities that escape current theories of development.

Gay identity theories are also incomplete and inadequate for comprehending non-heterosexual collegiate identities. As I demonstrate in chapter 2, such development models rarely, if at all, address collegiate experiences; one would think that achieving postsecondary education had no bearing upon the development of a non-heterosexual man. As the stories of the respondents in this project demonstrate, such representations are facile and misleading: the participants in this study spoke frankly about love and sex (both public and private), relations with other non-heterosexuals on campus, demonstrating for change on campus (in manners unauthorized and official), and perceptions of how their self-concepts compared to those of their peers (both straight and not).

Defining Desires

Like those issues, many of the terms in this study might seem to overlap, if not be synonymous; several appear to have multiple, sometimes conflicting, meanings. Does *homosexual* differ from *gay*? The data, in the form of narrative responses from the men I interviewed, show the answer was, paradoxically, yes and no. In some instances, terms like *gay* and *queer* might be interchangeable in the stories of the men, but at other times each will have distinct meanings. I have endeavored to use the terminology with discrimination, to correspond to the *sensibilities* of the narrators' use when presenting their words, as well as my own when discussing theoretical constructs of identity based upon those distinctions.

Consequently, I offer a few clarifications. Most of the meanings I utilize have historical distinctions (Chauncey, 1994; Dilley, 1999; Jagose, 1996). While within the context of the narrators' stories the meanings might differ, I offer the following as my working, contemporary definitions.

IDENTITY DEPLOYMENT: the conscious acts—physical and vocal—of displaying (or not) aspects of one's identity to others; one could conform (or perform) unconsciously or without consideration to contexts, but deployment requires some consideration of audience and self.

HETEROSEXUAL: sexual and/or affectional relationships with members of the opposite gender; also, a person exhibiting those qualities.

HETERO-SEX: actual physical sexual activities between members of opposite genders.

HOMO-EROTIC: pertaining to sexual desire of one person toward a person of the same gender.

HOMO-SEX: actual physical sexual activities between members of the same gender.

HOMO-AFFECTION: intimate and/or romantic feelings (but not necessarily enacted physically) from one person toward a person of the same gender.

HOMO-EXPRESSION: an identity deployment, of a physical nature or intent, that is homo-sexual and/or -affectional in nature, but not outright homo-sex; such a deployment could be "a delight in one another's physical proximity, an awareness of each other's bodies, a sort of excitement that overtook them at the prospect of spending time together" (Gustav-Wrathall, 1998, p. 57), or it could be extensive, sexually charged conversation about matters homo from someone who identifies as not.

HOMOSOCIAL: a different form of identity deployment than homo-expression, with less emphasis upon sexual communication or action and more upon socializing and living with other men. This, then, is a relational aspect of non-heterosexual identity (Mann, 2001, p. xx) rather than a physical aspect.

HOMOSEXUAL: sexual and/or affection relationships with members of the same gender, but usually indicating that the acts or relationships have some marker of influence upon the actor's personality (i.e., someone identifying as the oppositive of—or other than—heterosexual at least in part because of those actions and relationships); also, a person exhibiting those qualitites.

GAY: having homosexual and/or homo-affectional relationships with members of the same gender (by the late 1970s, usually, but not exclusively, referring to gay males); more specifically, used to describe men who identify socially and/or politically in such ways.

QUEER: in current context, a collective, inclusive adjective (incorporating gay, lesbian, bisexual, and at times transgendered people and perspectives), as well as a political adjective (in opposition to the norm of heterosexuality); often the two go hand in glove. In previous contexts (prior to the 1980s), the word did not have overt political connotations but instead was an invective slur.

CLOSETED: denying to others homo-sexual or -affectional feelings while recognizing within oneself those feelings.

DENIAL: denying homo-sexual or -affectional feelings for others while also not recognizing, or denying, to oneself those feelings.

NON-HETEROSEXUAL: sexual and/or affectional relationships with members of the same gender, but not necessarily indicating that the acts or relationships have any marker or influence upon the actor's personal identity (i.e., someone engaging in sexual activity with another of the same gender, but not identifying himself with a label or term because of the action).

In this study, I utilize the term "non-heterosexual" from the viewpoint of the men whose lives I draw upon; they uniformly conceptualize heterosexuality as a fixed, monolithic quality, which was separate and different from their own sexuality. What the respondents' narratives will show is that identities apart from heterosexual are not fixed but are fluid and contextually based. Their comments, however, explicitly relate only to their own identities; through using the inclusive (if contrapositive) term "non-heterosexual" in this study I do not intend to make statements about heterosexual identity nor bisexual identity (a concept that encompasses its own body of scholarship, research, and theory). As I discuss in the next chapter, language contains our very ability to express, investigate, and talk about sexuality and identity; that could be the reason previous researchers concentrated only upon experiences or self-perceptions.

Different Voices, Different Lives

This project is an attempt to map out the intricacies of being a student and a man who is not heterosexual. I explore, on the one hand, the nexus between what researchers have shown as ways students develop and change while in or because of attending college, and, on the other, how the experiences and qualities of men who identify as non-heterosexuals bring them to such an understanding. I combine interview data with historical documents and scholarship; the interviews provide the data for the typology, while the historical material provides a context for understanding how and why differences exist in the data—and in the self-concepts and -identities—of the respondents.

I hope my thoughts continue the fairly recent examination of gay and lesbian issues and experiences as topics of inquiry in higher education, history, and identity development of students (cf., Tierney and Dilley, 1998). I frame my attempts to answer those questions within four bases of knowledge: historical and empirical works concerning non-heterosexuals on college campuses, student identity development theory, gay identity development theory, and queer theory. A number of goals influenced my decision to undertake this project and to make it a qualitative, typological study. Queer theory provides the critical lens of my thinking. As Carlson pointed out, "queer is among the slipperiest of terms, and its meaning glides back and forth between affirming and disrupting identity categories—often in the same text" (1998, p. 113). I utilize queer theory analytically, to examine how the concepts, the "norms," of identity were formed in relation to the master categories of heterosexual and non-heterosexual, and to other concepts of "non-heterosexuality." In doing so, I attempt what Talburt would label a "queer project . . . shift[ing] ethnography's purposes from representation of gay and lesbian subjects and experiences to an analysis of practices as they are constructed in social and institutional locations" (Talburt, 1999, p. 526). I also expand upon Rhoads's challenge for those working with non-heterosexual identities to resist the dominant developmental inclinations of portraying a monolithic "homosexual" identity without acknowledging that "significant differences exist among lesbian, gay, and bisexual students" (Rhoads, 1997b, p. 461), as well as their conceptions and constructs of whom they are. Indeed, identity for non-heterosexual men in the United States over the latter part of the twentieth century was as much a matter of accepting that one was not one "name" or label instead of another, a process as much of unbecoming as it was of becoming. For many men, the college years were a peculiar twilight time between what was considered "normal" for heterosexuals and what was often considered "normal" for non-heterosexuals. To understand what these men thought they could become in their lives, one must understand both concepts of "normal" and how those concepts meant to the lives of these men.

As their narratives in chapters 3, 4, and 5 exhibit, male collegians viewed their sexual activity, self-identity, and campus roles and participation more recursively, more bound by the contexts of participants and settings, and paradoxically more and less dependent upon the judgments of others' views of their identity. Some men knew, at relatively early ages, that their feelings of difference placed them in a category juxtaposed to "straight." In the mid-century, their ideations of how they could live, their relations to other people (both straight and non-straight), and their personal goals were conscripted by the secretive and penalized nature of their non-straight identities. Homosexual collegians could find others whose feelings and experiences mirrored theirs, and with whom they could socialize more freely, but not necessarily openly: private gatherings and parties were the main form of socialization, and if sex were found, it was usually quick, anonymous, and secret. The consequences for transgressing these boundaries—being too open sexually, socializing too frequently with homosexuals "known" by straight authorities—could be dire. Expulsions from college were not uncommon, either for being caught *in flagrante delicto* or simply being associated with those who were. In almost all cases, homosexual collegians considered their sexuality a private matter, at most important only to close friends (but rarely family). And in this, their identities were juxtaposed to the public lives and emotions of heterosexuals; homosexuals not only were opposite in their sexual affections but also in their ability to deploy or enact those identities.

By the 1970s, the precepts of what it meant to be non-straight had changed: some forms of visibility were encouraged, and non-heterosexual collegians began to socialize with others who identified as gay. The concepts of self-identity and life goals transformed accordingly: in the politics of the time, "gay is good" represented a paradigm shift from the clandestine and whispered to the visible and spoken. For students viewing themselves and their lives as gay, the integration of sexual orientation into their identity fostered a need to become involved in the local community; others brought their sexual identity to the fore of their campus experience through work in collegiate organizations and/or political movements. Some gay collegians, however, maintained the homosexual collegian's separation of social activities and scholastic endeavors during their undergraduate years.

In the late 1980s and early 1990s, queer came into prominent use not only as a marker of difference from normal (which the term had been, evident in the experiences and the sensibilities of students as early as the 1970s) but also as a political and social rallying cry. Not just visible, queer students confronted social mores and traditions; not just spoken, queer ideology—and students— was often shouted. Queer students tended not simply to join campus or community organizations, but instead to attempt to subvert or to reinvent the structures of those very institutions. Whereas gay students working for change on a college campus might become involved in university governance, student politics, or campus activities, queer students formed coalitions to protest many of those very elements of campus life, or to plan events that highlight the social stigmatization they felt in a non-homosexual environment. It is also possible, in a historical analysis, to see that the type "queer" was visible long before the term emerged in its current use.

Throughout these decades, closeted individuals realized their non-heterosexual feelings but consciously and actively avoided addressing and/or reconciling those feelings with their self-concepts. Closeted collegians might act upon their desires, but never very often and rarely within their own social circles. For still other men, there was a sense, during their college years, of leading parallel lives: they had one set of self-concepts and behaviors for straight contexts and friends, and another set of for non-heterosexual contexts. Also consistently throughout the periods, some men were denying their feelings, either consciously or unconsciously choosing to avoid even admitting to themselves their attractions and/or emotions.

During each of these times, a significant number of collegiate men defied the norms of both the straight and the non-straight cultures. They did not identify socially or politically as gay, homosexual, or queer; indeed, they did not seem to undergo the process of "finding" or "establishing" an identity, the "unbecoming" that many of their non-heterosexual peers experienced, an act that those who are non-homosexual (or not a member of other minorities) often never experience. Yet at the same time as they were not questioning their identities, these men were engaging in homo-sex, often quite frequently. While they were not denying to themselves that they enjoyed the sex, it had no correlation to their sensibility of who they were, to how they viewed themselves in relation to their (straight) peers. Many of these peers were their (secretive) sexual partners. These men found, at the time, no dissonance between their actions and their "selves": they were "just like everybody else"; they were, in their own estimation, if not that of others, "normal."

What Lies Ahead

Six of the seven identities types—all save one—are explored in the narratives within the data section. Chapter 3 explores the experiences of men whose experiences place them into the homosexual (corresponding primarily to the years 1945 to 1970) and closeted types (also beginning in the 1940s but applicable through the 1990s). Chapter 4 covers identities that came afterward, gay (starting from the late 1960s), and queer (starting in the 1970s, but more public from the late 1980s). Chapter 5 examines two identities evident across the entire second half of the twentieth century that are not covered in earlier studies: parallel and "normal." The aspects of denial are covered in relation to all of the other identity types in the historical analysis of chapter 6.

Chapter 6 is key to contextualizing the changes in non-heterosexual sexual identity, the concepts that represent what one might be in relation to the meanings one makes of his experiences and senses. My determinations about the meaning of identity are as much dependent upon understanding the social history of non-heterosexuals in the United States as it is about understanding the educational life histories of the men with whom I spoke. Much of the historical literature I draw from—memoirs and autobiographies, oral histories, diaries, histories—relates differing ways of how people who are homosexual (or bisexual) have identified their different experiences as individuals and groups to themselves and others. As Jenkins wrote, "all classes and groups write their collective autobiographies. History is the way people(s) create, in part, their identities" (1991, p. 19). Yet when it comes to queers and the meanings of their lives, history is as much about the ways people did not create their identities. To quote William Mann, "Writing gay histories requires a revaluation of traditional rules of 'evidence.' Learning to read between the lines *without reading into them* is an acquired skill, as is learning to discern the truth as much by *what isn't said* as what *is*" (2001, p. xx).

Historical analysis is one way to explore non-heterosexual identities, as is typological analysis of identification; but in combining the two, I feel I understand the development of non-heterosexual identities—and can demonstrate how and why I understand them the way I do—better than if I delimited my thinking. Chapter 6 includes an analysis of the development of each particular identity type, as well as how each type relates to the other identities. It is also a fairly traditional historical narrative, focusing primarily upon how those identities can be seen and understood through events at one campus, the University of Kansas.

Examining the changes in student identity as demonstrated in campus experiences at one traditional, Midwestern institution shows how what experiences and deployments of non-heterosexual identity was considered normal (and who considered it so). Consequently, I center this chapter on KU to provide historical context for the changing culture of the United States over the latter half of the twentieth century. Finally, in chapter 7, I offer seven major findings from the narrative data that provide challenges and guidance for identity development theorists as well as postsecondary educators, policymakers, practitioners, and programmers.

Without meeting these challenges, neither student identity development nor gay identity development theories will truly reflect the formation of non-heterosexual identity for males through their collegiate experiences. Further, the differences outlined through the typological model in this study calls into question the validity of the dominant developmental models as progressive stages and/or static models of a singular identity. If the understandings and presumptions of educators, administrators, and programmers are incorrect, then the services and guidance they can offer to their non-heterosexual students are faulty. If identity development theorists do not incorporate the incongruities of this student population, not only will theories not be as valid as they could (and should) be but what theorists teach educational practitioners, programmers, and administrators will continue to be disconnected from the reality of non-heterosexual students, perpetuating the problems of representation and education.

Before the data chapters or the conclusions, though, I present information on prior research and theories that framed my thinking, which should aid the reader to understand the contexts into which I placed the data, as well as the typology. (I provide more detailed information on the methodology I utilized in this work, answering who, how, when, where, and why I conducted the research and the analysis for the typology, in the appendix.) Chapter 2 summarizes the four bodies of relevant scholarship pertaining to my research: previous studies of non-heterosexual college students, student development theory, gay identity development theory, and queer theory. My summation of these distinct disciplines illuminates the benefits and deficits inherent in the existing literature.

The limitations of "the utility of developmental models of gay identity, such as stages theories" (Rhoads, 1997b, 461), became clear to me as I talked with the men who agreed to share their memories of their collegiate experiences, senses, and sensibilities with me. As I listened to them, I was not only a researcher completing a study but also someone who believes strongly in the ability of theory to guide student affairs practice and programming, so long as theory is valid and representative, descriptive rather than prescriptive. I also remained, in many ways, the teenager listening to others who somehow didn't fit into straight cultures tell their stories of how they figured out who they were, who they are, and what those senses of identity affected (or, in some instances, effected) their collegiate experiences and sensibilities.

CHAPTER 2

Queer Theory,
Identity Development Theories,
and Non-Heterosexual Students

Just as human lives have many components that influence identities, any understanding of non-heterosexual student identities draws from several areas of scholastic research. In this chapter, I outline four areas of research that inform my understanding. In some ways, the narratives of the men I present in this study are snapshots of campus life over five decades, fitting into that category. But just as frames require material (data—which I offer in chapters 3 through 7), tools are needed to construct a frame. These works frame my thinking about what is known—or not—about the lives of these students.

The frame built by research and theory, then, is ontological—a study of "being"—as well as epistemological—how we know what we know about "being." To help us to ask and to know about the verisimilitude of being, theories become the instruments through which we implement our craft. Consequently, in addition to the previous studies of experience, in the rest of this chapter I review the three analytic tools I utilized most frequently. In this chapter, I first summarize the earlier descriptive and analytical studies of collegiate gay and lesbian experiences. Next, I briefly cover student identity development theories, paying particular attention to two widely utilized and studied models of understanding college student identity. I focus on psychosocial works because the corpus of gay identity development theories, to which I devote a bit more attention in this chapter, are also psychosocial models. Finally, I outline the tenets of queer theory; the critical lens of "normal" and "deviant" of queer theory focuses the organization and questions and structure of this historical study, my analysis of the narrative and historical data, and the resulting typological theory. One queer work in particular relates to identity as I came to understand it through investigating collegiate lives, and I will use its analytic motif throughout the narratives and analyses in later chapters.

What Do We Know about Non-Heterosexuals in College?

A number of researchers provide insight into the experiences, senses, and sensibilities of non-heterosexual college students; these form the first side of my frame of thinking. Often, these researchers investigate the publically unseen as well as the seen, positing the "queer" experience of people who identified as something other than heterosexual (be that *gay, lesbian, queer,* or another term relating to sexual and/or affection status) against the "normal" experience of those who identify as heterosexual. Few, however, address identity—at least not in ways that go beyond essence or experience.

Several of the (male) subjects of Nardi, Sanders, and Marmor's (1994) collection of life histories reflected on college life before the 1970s. Fellows (1996) also compiled a group of recollections from gay men, from the Midwest, who came of age during the twentieth century; almost all of the men attended college, and mention their collegiate lives at least in passing. Marotta (1982) presented interviews he conducted with gay men from Harvard's class of 1967; similarly, MacKay (1993) collected reminiscences from lesbian and gay Vassar alums from the 1930s to the 1990s. D'Emilio's (1990, 1992) essays on gay life in higher education spanned the 1950s to the 1980s. Perhaps what is most evident from these studies is that non-heterosexual students were on college campuses throughout the twentieth century; they did not always identify along collective social or political identities on campuses, but rather often had lives (positive and negative) that were different from their heterosexual peers.

Non-heterosexual students from more recent years, however, related experiences and identities unlike those of their earlier peers: they organized more openly and collectively, often around issues of social and political reform, to provide equity for non-heterosexuals. Teal (1995) outlined the origins and actions of many of the early gay student organizations, as part of his history of the beginning of the gay liberation movement in the United States. Chandler (1995) and Due (1995) portrayed lives of gay youth, several of whom were in college in the 1990s, while Howard and Stevens (2000) collected personal accounts of lives of non-heterosexuals in college in the last two decades. The most theoretically advanced of these efforts to detail campus life for non-heterosexual students was Rhoads's (1994) findings from a two-year ethnographic study focusing on their "struggle for a queer identity." Again, it is important to remember that these studies were not necessarily about identity, but about lived experiences; consequently, they are primarily journalistic in approach to the questions of non-heterosexual lives. Changes in how non-heterosexual students were thinking of their relation to their campuses, to each other, and to their concepts of who they were are represented, although not deeply questioned or analyzed in these efforts.

In addition to these studies, a growing number of memoirs in the late twentieth century by non-heterosexuals addressed their recollections of life in college, from the 1940s to the present (Boyd, 1978; Duberman, 1991; Helms, 1995; Kantrowitz, 1977; Louganis with Marcus, 1995). Gay service people, whose collegiate environments are very different from civilians', reflected upon higher education within the military (i.e., Staffan, 1992). Fraternity members who were gay also depicted vivid portraits of living with multiple dimensions of identity (Windmeyer and Freeman, 1998), as did sorority members (Windmeyer and Freeman, 2001). Perhaps most uniquely, primary source materials, such as the diaries of Jeb Alexander (1993) and Donald Vining (1996), provide insight into non-heterosexual experiences during college at the beginning of this century. But again, while these works convey valuable information about individuals' experiences and self-reflection, the authors addressed more *what it was like* to be non-heterosexual rather than *how they were* non-heterosexual.

Tentative investigations into the experiences and beliefs of ethnic minority non-heterosexuals have appeared only since the late 1980s; perhaps not surprisingly, researchers of these lives with multiple minority identities were more analytical, bringing in social and race theories to help to understand the experiences of such folks. Loiacano's (1989) interviews with black American non-heterosexuals indicated their need for validation from both the black and the gay communities. Chan (1989) reported that Asian-American homosexual college students perceived a choice—or a refusal of choice—between ethnic identity and gay or lesbian identity: One chooses to emphasize sexual-orientation aspects of one's self-identity at the expense of one's ethnic identity, or one refuses to choose to do so. Espin (1987) reached a similar conclusion from her subjects' lives: the desire to identify as both lesbian and Latina can be a fundamental dilemma. These studies of the multiple identities found within members of multiple subcultures support an idea of multiple, contemporaneous, and/or potentially conflicting aspects of identity.

A few researchers have also begun to define and to demonstrate aspects of community, within general populations and college student populations of non-heterosexuals. Davies' (1992) observation of gay male communities echoed Herdt and Boxer's (1993); he stated that the crucial point for gay men coming out is that they choose new lifestyles, companions, and social structures. Rhoads (1993) posited a theory of gay male student contraculture, a set of socialized communities that reflected differing values, interests, and ideologies of gay students. One such community was centered around a concept of queer identity, which Rhoads (1994, 1995) defined (using his subjects' responses) as a political exposition of personal identity to challenge prevalent heterosexual norms.

How Postsecondary Theorists Make Sense of Student Identities

Obviously, from my earlier comments, I had more questions than answers after reviewing the literature on gay collegiate experiences. *How were those students' identities affected by their experiences? How did their self-concepts change—or not—as a result of being non-heterosexual in college? Was such a self-concept fairly universal or contextually specific?* This thinking brought me to the second piece of the frame: studies of college students' identities and the resulting theories of how students develop as a result of their collegiate experiences.

Brown (1972) first coined the term "student development theory" in reviewing a number of theoretical perspectives on interpersonal student change in college as a result of college policies and practices. Student development theories have been produced from a number of perspectives, including psychological, sociological, and cognitive development (Moore and Upcraft, 1990; see Renn, Dilley and Prentice [forthcoming] for a more detailed examination of studies of identity and student development in postsecondary education). The concept has proved quite useful for postsecondary educators and administrators to use, either to understand or to promote and encourage student socialization and learning. Evans, Forney, and Guido-DiBrito (1998) classify the theories into three general clusters:

1. psychosocial and identity development theories (combining personal development, the effects of personal qualities, and some theories of growth and change)
2. cognitive-structural theories (enveloping cognitive development, campus environmental effects, and the remaining theories of student growth and change)
3. typology theories (finding association patterns based primarily upon personality traits)

Although all these sets guide postsecondary research and practices to some extent, to understand non-heterosexual students of the past half-century, I concentrate upon the first and last. Despite the strengths of typological theories to help understand student cultures and collective identities (a large part of the scope of my investigation), more commonly utilized are psychosocial theories of student identity development.

Typologies

Typologies examine dissimilarities within specific (similar) populations, mapping identifiable trends and characteristics that denote differences within those populations. "Typology theories reflect individual stylistic differences in how students approach their words" (Evans, Forney, and Guido-DiBrito, 1998, p. 204). In this manner, typological theories are inclusive, expansive, and represent a variety of experiences, serving "as a framework within which psychosocial and cognitive-structural development takes place, and . . . [influencing] the manner in which students address development in these aspects of their lives" (Evans, Forney, and Guido-DiBrito, 1998, p. 204). As such, typological theories are descriptive rather than prescriptive.

One of the strengths of typological models is the ability to "give us important information about sources of support and challenge for students who are otherwise developmentally similar" (Evans, Forney, and Guido-DiBrito, 1998, p. 204). Moreover, that information is not used to classify people as "good" or "bad," but rather as different (and how): "Each type is seen as contributing something positive and unique to any situation" (Evans, Forney, and Guido-DiBrito, 1998, p. 204). Beyond describing individual or group characteristics, typological models limn the methods and manners of interpersonal interactions within and across types.

A number of well-known psychological and developmental theories are typologies, including Kolb's (1984, 1985) theory of experiential learning, Astin's (1993) theory of student involvement, Clark and Trow's (1966) theory of collegiate student identities, Holland's (1958, 1992) theories of vocational personalities and work environments, the Myers-Briggs (Myers and McCaulley, 1985) adaption of Jung's (1923/1971) theories of types of personality, and most recently Kuh's typology based upon student activities (Kuh, Hu, and Vesper, 2000). Particularly relevant to my thinking is Tierney's (1997) typology of gay men in present Western society: Passers, Castro Clones, Queer Nationals, and Cultural Citizens are the four categories that Tierney suggested are "cultural stances that are available to us," each "a collective response rather than one that tells individuals how to cope" (Tierney, 1997, p. 39). Still, even Tierney is suggesting a typology based upon actions and cultural responses, rather than a theory of identity (collective or personal).

One might notice that these examples are primarily concerned with experiences and identities apart from educational settings; moreover, most of these typological theories present individuals as maintaining a (fairly) fixed identity, not open to much fluctuation, let alone change. Most theorists who study college student development do not utilize typological models, perhaps in part because mapping *change* is a vital component of student identity development. I believe the same to be true for those who work in gay identity development, as well. But the typological model offers a broader context for conveying experiences, and how those experiences affect (and effect) changes in identity for individuals, over time and in particular contexts.

A Model Model: Campus Life. Helen Lefkowitz Horowitz's *Campus Life* (1987) is a typological study that served as a model for my thinking and analysis. Her work, which is both qualitative and historical in methodology, provides a clear typological model of various student identities contextualized historically. She "attempts to describe the variety of ways that undergraduates have described themselves, viewed their professors and fellow collegians, formed associations, and created systems of meanings and codes of behavior" (Horowitz, 1987, p. ix). In doing so, she proposed a system of student identities utilizing three basic classifications: *college men, outsiders,* and *rebels.*

College men (and later, females Horowitz termed *college women*) forged their collective identity through struggles against the faculty of the earliest colleges in the United States. From the end of the eighteenth century on, they created clubs, associations, and extracurricular activities for themselves, in part to relate what they were learning in college to the world they perceived, and in part to provide support (numerical and emotional) for reform efforts aimed at their college. College men did not expect to take interest in their instructors, nor much in their studies; the purpose of college, in their minds, was to discover how to operate in society and make contacts for life after college. College men could be viewed as *insiders,* working within social and campus structures to create a privileged (and privileging) social system.

Outsiders, the second type of student to appear in Horowitz's schema, are evident within the same time periods but are perhaps more evident in the early to mid-nineteenth century. Outsiders were typically poorer than the college men, often attending institutions on scholarships and reliant upon faculty for their continued sponsorship. Rather than looking to their collegiate peers for role models, outsiders turned to faculty members for examples of how they saw themselves fitting into society after college. Because of their ethnicity or religious beliefs (often not matching the religion of the majority of their peers), outsiders were excluded by college men from many of the associations and fraternities; by the mid-nineteenth century, some outsiders tried to form their own extracurricular activities (usually study groups or literary societies), but for the most part outsiders studied, tried to remain on neutral if not on good terms with their instructors, and prepared for a "serious" life.

Unlike the college men and the outsiders, *rebels* perceived that life was not confined to the college or its campus: "Outside its gates stood a vital world of economics, politics, and the arts, more real than the fun and games of football" or the "grind" of simply studying (Horowitz, 1987, p. 86). Rebels combined the studying of the outsiders with the nonacademic aspirations of the college men, and applied both to the world in which they planned to enter after graduation. They felt more ties to current political and artistic movements than to traditions of either students or institutions, and they used college as a training ground, testing their abilities to effect change upon their immediate world, the campus. By the early twentieth century, rebels created their own associations, and more importantly, their own publications, if they could not be active in the established ones.

Using these three types of collegiate identity, Horowitz traces the history of student life from the late eighteenth century through the mid-1980s. Along the way, she describes the changes each group experienced, including the institutionalization of the traditions of college men, the changes of peer and public attitudes toward outsiders in the 1950s and 1980s, and the cultural and political importance of the rebels, particularly in the 1910s and 1960s. Horowitz's analysis is largely based upon how students defined or understood themselves and their actions, which is often quite different from the definitions institutions or researchers might place upon the students and/or their actions.

Psychosocial Theories

As I noted, though, typologies are helpful for understanding identity through a cultural lens, but not necessarily through a personal one. Leaving what can be learned about student cultures and identities from typologies, I now turn to the more widely utilized set of theories to understand identity in higher education. Psychosocial models are among the most prevalent theories utilized in college student advising, programming, and study (Evans, Forney, and Guido-DiBrito, 1998; Pascarella and Terenzini, 1991; Renn, Dilley, and Prentice, forthcoming). Structurally, psychosocial models of student development are often stage models, with clear points articulating paths of progression from is-sues facing entering freshmen to challenges confronting graduating seniors. During one's time in college, one progresses—or at least is believed should move—positively toward more mature, developed ways of relating to others and comprehending one's role in society.

Erickson (1968, 1980) first outlined such a series of progressions of issues at various times in a person's life. Particular issues become so important at those times that how a person responds reflects how a person conceptualizes himself and his role in society. These interpersonal or intra-social matters pose "developmental tasks, [that] arise and present compelling questions that must be resolved" (Evans, Forney, and Guido-DiBrito, 1998, p. 32). The concerns are grouped into stages of development, in each of which a "developmental crisis, or turning point" (Evans, Forney, and Guido-DiBrito, 1998, p. 32) oc-curs. How a person answers those questions, responds to the presses, resolves the crises, is indicative of his development and identity, as well as how he will approach and resolve other issues in later stages. Stemming from the work of Erickson (1968, 1980), Chickering and his later colleagues (Chickering, 1969; Chickering and Reisser, 1993; Thomas and Chickering, 1984) applied the idea of psychosocial development to college students.

In conceptualizing how to understand student collegiate identities in this project, I keep returning to Chickering. Before the publication of *Education and Identity* (Chickering, 1969), few works on postadolescent development had been proffered; afterward, although researchers explored cognitive, moral, and ethical development, until the 1990s, "not much attention was paid to feelings and relationships, which seemed to occupy center stage in the lives of students" (Reisser, 1995, p. 506). Further, despite the simplicity of Chickering's model, is-sues of establishing interpersonal relationships, and establishing identity based upon emotions and relationships, are the crucial components to Chickering's theory—as well as to the gay identity development models that later followed.

Chickering's Vectors. Chickering's theory of student development (Chicker-ing, 1969; Chickering and Reisser, 1993), is primarily a psychosocial model. The theory identifies seven stages, or vectors, of human development, a con-secutive (although not necessarily strictly sequential; the theory allows room for overlap and repetition, in certain circumstances) series of changes that col-lege students (and presumably others the same ages) experience (figure 2.1). There is a hierarchy to the vectors, presuming a transformation from less to more developed senses of identity; however, a baseline of development (al-though not necessarily full resolution of the developmental issues in that vec-tor) can lead a student to begin developmental processes in other vectors.

Movement along any one [vector] can occur at different rates and can interact with movement along the others. Each step from "lower" to "higher" brings more awareness, skill, confidence, complexity, stability, and integration but does not rule out an accidental or intentional return to ground already traversed. (Chickering and Reisser, 1993, p. 34)

The seven vectors each represent an area of personality and identity, each increasing in specificity. Growth and development requires stimulation—either physical, mental, social, or emotional—to move the student to change (Chickering referred to this stimulation as a "developmental press"); each vector has one or more "developmental challenges," or goals, to be addressed and, if successfully met, resolved. Development depends upon and comes from the ability to symbolize the events and objects (the presses) causing stimulation to form a meaning or pattern relevant to the student's life (that would presumably complete the student's progression through the vector).

Any experience that helps students define "who I am" and "who I am not" can help solidify a sense of self. Colleges and universities provide a myriad of opportunities for students to explore the different rooms in the house of the self and to understand how the interlocking parts—

FIGURE 2.1: **Chickering's Vectors of Identity Development**
(Chickering and Reisser, 1993)

Vector One:
Achieving Competence

Vector Two:
Managing Emotions

Vector Three:
Moving through Autonomy toward Interdependence

Vector Four:
Developing Mature Interpersonal Relationships

Vector Five:
Establishing Identity

Vector Six:
Developing Purpose

Vector Seven:
Developing Integrity

body, mind, feelings, beliefs, values, and priorities—all constitute a coherent sense of self with a continuity of experience. Personal stability
and integration are the result. (Reisser, 1995, p. 509)

Through encountering and comprehending more complex situations and
thoughts, the student integrates and organizes the different perceptions (the
different patterns and meanings), beliefs and behaviors of others (and himself) into a more coherent view of himself and his place in the world. By the
time he reaches the final vector, the student should have discovered and resolved questions of identity and purpose in life.

Vector One: Achieving Competence. The challenges of the primary vector stem
from intellectual areas, physical and manual skills, and relationships with others. One's perception of competence is at the heart of vector one: "confidence
in one's ability to cope with what comes and to achieve successfully what
[one] sets out to do" (Chickering, 1969, p. 9). Although physical competence
is important, intellectual and interpersonal competence are more influential
upon further development. This vector stresses changes in the behavior do-
main, in learning how to become more competent at college-level activities,
and in developing a strong sense of self-competence about one's abilities and
competencies.

Vector Two: Managing Emotions. Sexual and aggressive emotions are, or at
least were, for Chickering's predominately male sample populations, the two
emotions most in need of resolution and most apparently operating within
the second vector. The second vector deals with learning to handle these and
other emotions, personally and socially: conscious choice in behavior and expression of emotions in varying contexts. The main goal of this vector is "to
develop increasing capacity for passion and commitment accompanied by increasing capacity for passion and commitment through intelligent behavior"
(Chickering, 1969, p. 53). Students undergoing the presses of this vector often
begin to examine reflective controls, such as parental rules and societal norms.
Students can respond to these presses by understanding, maintaining, or re-
placing adopted standards and controls with internally adopted standards and
controls, or by any combination of the three.

Vector Three: Moving through Autonomy toward Interdependence. College life
allows increasing independence for students, a situational independence due
to the lack of proximity to parental control and the increase of responsibility
for maintaining academic and social status. Beyond this is "the independence
of maturity . . . emotional and instrumental independence, and a recognition
of one's independence" (Chickering, 1969, p. 12). Away from parental guid-

ance and regulations, students have less reassurance for, and approval or dis-approval of, choices and actions. This, in turn, allows the student a better understanding and appreciation of his abilities.

One of the main developmental challenges of this vector is learning to manage time, commitments, and priorities. Relationships for students in this vector take on new meaning, based on mutual respect, benefit, and cooperation. Other people might increase in importance to the student, creating for the student the paradox of newfound personal (instrumental) independence and tentative personal interdependence.

Vector Four: Developing Mature Interpersonal Relationships. After becoming comfortable with themselves, students must increase their ability to interact with others. The developmental goals at this stage of personal development are "increased tolerance and respect for those of different backgrounds, habits, values and appearance" (Chickering, 1969, p. 94). Tolerance refers not just to the ability to endure unpleasant people or events but to the ability to have a greater openness and acceptance of diversity.

In vector four there is an increased shift in the quality of relationships with close friends and intimates (Chickering, 1969, p. 94). This reflects the development of the student's capacity for intimacy, resulting from the acceptance of the self in vector three and the new perceptions of relationships emerging from vector two. Students must learn the differences between types of, and levels of, relationships; next, they must work out their attitudes about those relationships; and then they must develop relational behaviors to match their knowledge and values. This vector was originally the fifth vector in Chickering's (1969) theory, but Chickering and Reisser retitled and moved it "primarily to recognize the importance of students' experiences with relationships in the formation of their sense of self" (Chickering and Reisser, 1993, p. 39); however, they "kept the two components of the vector on developing relationships: tolerance and capacity for intimacy" (Reisser, 1995, p. 509).

Vector Five: Establishing Identity. The fifth vector is pivotal to Chickering's theory. Growth, or progression, among the first four vectors influences the ability to accomplish the challenges and meet the goals of vector four; vector five itself fosters and facilitates the last two vectors. Students must think about self-identity component issues, discover or create attitudes and self-concepts that are realistic and positive, and match their behavior to acknowledge these attitudes. The key challenges here are gaining confidence in one's self and recognizing one's core qualities.

To establish a positive identity, one must clarify and become comfortable with one's conception of one's physical characteristics and personal appearance. Further, one must accommodate to appropriate sexual behaviors and roles to fit one's identity. Other factors influencing identity might include how one incorporates the changes encountered in the previous vectors into one's personality, how one chooses to be a part of society after incorporating those changes, and how one compares one's self to others.

Vector Six: Developing Purpose. The challenge of this vector for the student is to gain a sense of future direction and a purpose in living. Students in this stage will often need to develop plans that integrate personal interests, vocational goals and aspirations, and lifestyle choices. This cognition about one's interests, abilities, and opportunities leads to behavior changes to match those interests for "[m]ore sustained, focused, rewarding activities" (Chickering and Reisser, 1993, p. 39), as well as attitudinal changes to strengthen family and interpersonal commitments. These tasks help to refine students' values and lifestyles.

Vector Seven: Developing Integrity. The final vector harbors "clarification of a personally valid set of beliefs that have some internal consistency and that provide at least a tentative guide for behavior" (Chickering, 1969, p. 17). Developing integrity requires humanizing and personalizing one's values, discovering a sense of social responsibility instead of only self-interest, and changing actions to discard discrepancies between values and actions in favor of congruency between values and actions. The task is to reexamine one's values (through understanding, organizing, and integrating everything that one has learned from experiences in the previous vectors) into a comprehensive whole that reflects one's values through actions and perceptions. In reconsidering, one becomes aware that no absolute rules exist, and all rules and their purposes must be considered realistically.

Although in their revisions of the theory Chickering and his colleagues reference differences in gender and sexuality upon identity development, those variations would appear to have little or no effect upon a student's progress or general challenges to identity development. Such a presumption, though, is disproved by theorists who research the experiences and identities of nonheterosexuals.

How Theorists Make Sense of Gay Identities

I arrive now to the third arm of the frame of this study: Contrasted to research conducted on the lives and development of (presumably heterosexual) college students, very little has been produced about gay, lesbian, or bisexual college students. In terms of homosexual identity development theory, most researchers have produced works that address gay and lesbian youth more generally, rather than specifically on changes occurring during college. What is known or theorized about gay male students' identity development and experience is not extensive, but some research and theories exist.

Levine and Evans (1991) found that most gay identity development models fall into either the psychological or the sociological perspectives. The psychological "concentrate on internal changes experienced by individuals as they come to identify as homosexual" (Evans, Forney, and Guido-DiBrito, 1998, p. 91), while the sociological "tend to focus on the impact of community, development of social roles, and managing stigma" (Evans, Forney, and Guido-DiBrito, 1998, p. 91). In this section, I outline the thoughts of the prominent researchers in both the psychological (Cass, Troiden, and Goode, Savin-Williams) and the sociological (D'Augelli's lifespan schema) approaches to identity theorization.

Cass's Stage Model. Cass's (1979, 1983/1984, 1984) psychological model of homosexual identity formation is undeniably similar to Chickering's theory and was seminal in the field of researching non-heterosexual identity, particularly as a primary source for understanding gay identity development among college-aged people (Evans and Levine, 1990, pp. 51–55). According to Cass, through increasing tolerance of one's own homosexual identity and increasing socialization and identification with other gays, one forges identity pride, a recognition of the incongruence between one's homosexuality and society's rejections of homosexuals, and reconciling this discrepancy into one's personal self-concept. To depict this, Cass proposed six developmental stages (figure 2.2) that "all individuals move through in order to acquire an identity of 'homosexual' fully integrated within the individual's overall concept of self" (1979, p. 220).

Cass's model supposed a subject who has a socially-supported self-image as heterosexual and non-homosexual. Homosexual identity formation begins in *Stage One: Identity Confusion*, a "conscious awareness" that homosexuality is relevant to his behavior, either overt (as in kissing) or internal (thoughts, emotions, or physiological responses) (Cass, 1979, p. 222). This self-awareness is important, for the process begins only when the subject is able to label his own behavior as possibly homosexual (Cass, 1979, p. 222).

After this acknowledgment, "'Who am I?' becomes the burning question. Feelings of personal alienation are paramount" (Cass, 1979, p. 223). These feelings are characteristically addressed through one of three ways: a search for more information about homosexuality and homosexuals; the curtailing of all behaviors that the subject perceives as homosexual, the avoidance of informa-

FIGURE 2.2: **Cass's Model of Homosexual Identity Formation**
(Cass, 1979)

Stage One:
Identity Confusion

Stage Two:
Identity Comparison

Stage Three:
Identity Tolerance

Stage Four:
Identity Acceptance

Stage Five:
Identity Pride

Stage Six:
Identity Synthesis

tion about homosexuality, and the denial of its relevance to him and his life; or the personal redefinition of the behavior or emotions within a non-homosexual context: it is discounted as simply what the subject's peers are doing, or as due to the effects of intoxicants.

In *Stage Two: Identity Comparison*, the subject accepts the possibility that he might be homosexual. The increased congruity between the subject's sense of self and his behavior creates greater incongruity with others' concepts of the subject. The developmental task of stage two is how to handle social alienation, including the lack of models and guidelines for behavior, ideals, and expectations for the future (Cass, 1979, p. 225).

Stage Three: Identity Tolerance marks the passage from the possibility that the subject might be homosexual to the probability that he is. This stage is characterized by the subject's acknowledging social, emotional, and sexual needs, and conversely by a heightened alienation between the subject and his non-homosexual peers. To alleviate this alienation, subjects at stage three seek out other homosexuals and their subcultures for a sense of place and belonging.

The ability for the subject to say *I am a homosexual* marks the passing of stage three and the entry to *Stage Four: Identity Acceptance*. Continued and increasing contacts with other homosexuals "validate[s] and 'normalize[s]' homosexuality as an identity and a way of life" for the subject (Cass, 1979, p. 231). Groups within the gay subculture influence how the subject restructures his interpersonal environment and how he progresses through the remaining stages. To alleviate the burgeoning dissonance between his self-concept and how others perceive him, the subject might begin to "selectively disclose [his] homosexual identity to significant heterosexual others" (Cass, 1979, p. 232).

Stage Five: Identity Pride consists of the process of recognizing the incongruency between the subject's homosexuality and society's rejection of homosexuals, and reconciling the incongruence into the subject's personal self-concept.

> In order to manage this incongruency [the subject] uses strategies to devalue the importance of heterosexual others to self, and to revalue homosexual others more positively. This program allows [the subject] to give less weight to a perception of how heterosexual others see [him] and more to how homosexual others see [him]. (Cass, 1979, p. 233)

"Commitment to the gay group is strong, generating a sense of group identity ('These are *my* people') and of belonging" (Cass, 1979, p. 233). Subjects become angry with heterosexual norms and proud of their sense of selves, and can become activists against established institutions. "The slogan 'How dare you presume I'm a heterosexual' is indicative of feelings at this stage" (Cass, 1979, p. 233). The rejection of established norms gives the subject less concern about how heterosexuals perceive him and more freedom to disclose his orientation.

The final stage is *Stage Six: Identity Synthesis*. Positive reactions from heterosexuals prompts the subject to reevaluate his attitude of opposition with heterosexuals. The subject "accepts the possibility of considerable similarity between self and heterosexuals, as well as dissimilarity between self and [other] homosexuals" (Cass, 1979, p. 234). The sexual identity component of the subject's self-concept is integrated with the other aspects of self. "Instead of being seen as *the* identity, it is now given the status of being merely one aspect of self" (Cass, 1979, p. 235).

In later revisions, Cass augmented her theory (1983/1984, 1984) and allowed that "there is no such thing as a single homosexual identity. Rather, its nature may vary from person to person, from situation to situation, and from period to period" (Cass, 1983/1984, p. 111). Still, Cass's theory is a progressive, psychosocial developmental model. Movement from early to later stages is motivated by incongruity between one's prior understanding of feelings, thoughts, or behavior, and newly assigned homosexual meanings to those feelings, thoughts, or behavior. That progression, though, does not always occur; one's experiences within any of the stages might cause foreclosure of the process.

Also in her later writings (1983/1984, 1984) Cass noted the difference highlighted by other researchers between *homosexual identity*, describing one's sexual orientation and focused on explicit sexual acts and coincidental behavior, and *gay identity*, which reflects an affiliation with a community in a cultural and social sense (cf., Cheseboro, 1981; Warren, 1974). This distinction has continued within the past fifteen years, offering researchers and theorists new ways of conceptualizing the entire process of sexual orientation and identification (including, as outlined earlier in this chapter, queer theory). I also find it important to note that Cass's subjects were Australian men interviewed in the late 1960s and early 1970s, were older than most of the participants in the other studies reviewed here, and were incarcerated at the time of the interviews. Such details of Cass's sample population, often neglected in reviews of her work, in my mind must be taken into account when considering the transferability and generalizability of her theories.

Other Psychosocial Gay Identity Models. Despite her prominence, Cass is not the only psychological/social theorist of gay identity development. Troiden and Goode (1980) investigated variables related to the acquisition of a gay identity. They identified three—age cohort, high school heterosexual activity, and high school homosexual activity—which relate to the age at which respondents first self-recognize and self-identify as gay. A trend appeared in these later studies, for younger (i.e., college-aged and younger) identification as non-heterosexual, which were earlier than in Cass's findings. I believe this reflects both changes in the cultures between Australia in the mid- to early 1970s (Cass) and the United States at that same time (Troiden and Goode), as well as differences in the population samples of the two studies. Troiden and Goode's subjects demonstrated a specific sequence of identity acquisition starting in the teen years:

> First, they suspected they might be homosexual (mean age 16). This was followed by the decision to label certain feelings as homosexual (18). Next (coincident with or shortly after initial interactions which committed members of the gay subculture—mean 19), our respondents labeled themselves homosexual (19). The last step was to enter into their first homosexual love relationship (mean 20). (Troiden and Goode, 1980, p. 387)

Obviously, these activities occur during traditional years of college attendance in the United States, and others have also observed sociological phenomena of how gays of this age group identify and socialize. Browning

(1993), in constructing a depiction of gay (primarily gay male) culture, utilized the life experiences of college-aged men in the late 1980s and early
1990s. Herdt and Boxer (1993) reported on a multifaceted longitudinal study
of non-heterosexual teenagers involved in the youth group of Horizons, a
Chicago gay and lesbian community center. From multiple interviews and observations of the youth, Herdt and Boxer presented an argument for viewing
coming out—acknowledging and incorporating a gay (or non-heterosexual
identity) into one's self-identity—as a rite of passage into homosexual culture;
in doing so, they examined the common experiences of coming out, the affects and effects coming out had for the youth, and how the youth interacted
with the older gay society. Herdt and Boxer believed that "[I]n American society . . . 'coming out' is a polarizing process that leads to social roles being
more clearly defined as 'gay' and 'lesbian' than in other societies"; they feel
their "study shows how important it is to understand individual development
in cultural context as a system of interpretation" (Herdt and Boxer, 1993, p. 3).

Herdt and Boxer argued that cultural context, in both the homosexual cultures and the dominant culture, was changing. For the current cohorts of
youths, increased access to information about homosexuality and homosexuals created better (although not complete) ideations—conceptualization
models or categories for potential self-identity—for gay youth. This was a shift
from the ideations, beliefs, and actions of many of the older cohorts.

> The great majority of youth come of age self-identifying as gay or les-
> bian, and thus expecting not only to live their lives openly, but to tell all
> of their family and friends, and their employers of their desires and
> lifestyles. (Herdt and Boxer, 1993, p. 12)

Much of the existing theoretical work was based upon gays' and (more
rarely) lesbians' shared or common experiences of interactions with heterosexual, majority communities. Savin-Williams (1990) was one of the few gay-
youth identity theorists to include lesbians (at least in his earlier studies). His
theories stress the commonalities of gay and lesbian youth due to their status
as a group oppressed by the majority society; these commonalities are compounded by the majority's joint classification of youth based on their sexual
orientation. He did not, however, address possible distinctions, or lack of societal perceptions of distinctions, between lesbians and gay men.

Savin-Williams's more recent work (1998) depicted "young men's stories"
of their lives, placed within the context of gay identity development theory.
He did this to expand his earlier notions, "to account for this richness of

diversity in the lives of gay and bisexual youths is *differential developmental trajectories*" (Savin-Williams, 1998, p. xii). This was Savin-Williams's attempt to create a more detailed map of different (yet still progressive) ways gay men develop their concepts of self-identity and incorporate their sexuality into those concepts of self-identity.

> [A] differential developmental trajectories approach proposes that the task of developmental research is to investigate the ways in which sexual-minority youth are similar to and different from all other adolescents, as well as the ways in which they vary among themselves throughout the life course. . . . [This] heightens the focus on diversity within sexual-minority populations, recognizes continuities and discontinuities in development, and highlights the turning points in individual lives. (Savin-Williams, 1998, p. 10)

Through conveying the "personal stories" of gay men's youth—from first sexual attraction through experiences of final self-identification—Savin-Williams attempted to correct misconceptions of both the sexual experiences of young people and how those experiences are (un)related to identity development:

> [T]he young men interviewed . . . were asked to recall their developmental progression from first memories of being attracted to other males—which for some was as early as their first memories of life—to a subsequent integration of their sexual identity with their personal identity. This chain of feelings and events often included labeling feelings as "homosexual," first having sex with a male, first having heterosexual sex, labeling self as gay/bisexual, first disclosing this information to another, and first having a same-sex romantic relationship. (Savin-Williams, 1998, p. 1)

While the respondents' narratives are illuminating (particularly in regard to adolescent sexuality), Savin-Williams's main contribution is in the depiction of the broad range of developmental markers or presses within his (progressive) categories of gay identity development. While not every marker might be experienced by a non-heterosexual youth, nor might the markers always be in this particular order, Savin-Williams (1998, p.15) noted the most common pattern of these markers (figure 2.3).

Despite the similarities of development patterns in general, distinct differ-

---

FIGURE 2.3: **Savin-Williams's Pattern of Gay Identity Development**
(Savin-Williams, 1998)

1. Identifying feelings of "difference" from gender norms of other males.
2. Identifying attraction to other males.
3. Understanding definition of "homosexuality."
4. Labeling feelings as "homosexual."
5. Experiencing sex with another male.
6. Experiencing sex with a female.
7. Labeling self as "gay" or "bisexual."
8. Disclosing that self-labeling to others.
9. Experiencing a romantic relationship with another male.
10. Integrating self-concepts and experiences into a positive identity.

---

ences often exist in individuals. To understand these differences within similarities, Savin-Williams proposed using "differential developmental trajectories" (1998, p. 8) that name

> the variability within and across individuals, and . . . refers not only to specific events during particular moments of time but to the full range of milestones and processes that occur throughout the life course. (Savin-Williams, 1998, p. 9)

Hetrick and Martin (1987; Martin and Hetrick, 1988) reached similar conclusions, and proposed that "the primary developmental task for homosexually oriented adolescents is adjustment to a socially stigmatized role" (1987, p. 25). They did not, however, suggest any approaches to deal with that task. Herdt and Boxer (1993) spent two years observing several teens involved in a youth group for gays and lesbians in Chicago. Coming out, the process of identifying as gay or lesbian to oneself and to others, was viewed by Herdt and Boxer as a ritual rite of passage into a new culture, a new community apart from, and yet existing within, the heterosexual community.

D'Augelli: Social Construction of Gay Identity Over the Life Span. D'Augelli (1989a, 1989b, 1991, 1994; D'Augelli and Rose, 1990) also investigated the stigmatization of non-heterosexuals that homophobia causes, as well as the experiences of homosexual and bisexual youth in college. He noted in analyzing the responses of gay youth to his questioning that they "may seek to explore their sexual orientation in what they presume to be a more accepting context"—institutions of higher education—than they had previously known (D'Augelli, 1989a, p. 546).

> The late adolescent and early adulthood years of college and university life are culturally conceived of as a time for identity exploration, with the result that major career and relationship dilemmas are (at least temporarily) resolved. For lesbian and gay college students, these normative expectations are rendered much more complex because of the additional identity components they must manage. (D'Augelli, 1991, p. 140)

He also denoted the primary developmental challenge for gay college students is a process of *identity transformation*: "negotiating exits from heterosexual roles," developing an identity with a gay context, and learning socialization skills within the context of sexual orientation: "relating to lesbian and gay people, becoming involved in lesbian and gay communities, and integrating lesbian and gay status into all domains of personal life" (D'Augelli, 1991, p. 140). D'Augelli concluded that for the college students in his studies,

> gay identity is in transition although they have long known they were gay. Many other aspects of gay identity—among them the most challenging—are in flux. . . . Not fully hidden nor fully disclosed, these men experienced worries and fears related to the dilemmas they have yet to confront. . . . (D'Augelli, 1991, p. 145)

Rather than accept the assumptions of sequential stages of developmental models, D'Augelli based his theory of lesbian, gay, and bisexual identity development (1994) on life-span models of identity development (i.e., Baltes, 1987). His model also utilized postmodern concepts to posit homosexuality and gay identities as social constructions rather than essential identities (or components thereof), "shaped to varying degrees by social circumstances and environment and changeable throughout life" (Evans, Forney, and Guido-DiBrito, 1998, p. 95). Accordingly, this life-span model accounts for "the complex factors that influence the development of people in context over historical time" (D'Augelli, 1994, p. 317): for instance, fifty or seventy-five years ago, a person might not have had any concept of how to "be" anything, any social role, other than he saw in his own environment, and consequently probably identified as no different from anyone else.

This differs from previous models that did not really address social factors contextualizing identity, yet it is certainly akin to what Chauncey (1994) and Loughery (1998) found in (some of) their analyses of non-heterosexual lives in historical contexts. Conversely, within the past thirty years, different conceptions of non-heterosexual lives and roles have proliferated and have consequently been available for consideration and/or adoption by individuals (Blasius, 2001; Dilley, 2002; Evans, Forney, and Guido-DiBrito, 1998, p. 95; Talburt, 2000).

D'Augelli (1994) identified three sets of interrelated variables involved in identity formation, accounting in various ways for the societal pressures and barriers to developing a positive self-identity as a gay, lesbian, or bisexual person. *Personal subjectivities and actions* include a person's sexual behaviors, the meanings ascribed to those behaviors, and perceptions and emotions about the person's sexual identity. *Interactive intimacies* incorporate influences of family, peers, and other social/emotional intimates, as well as the meanings a person ascribes to them. *Sociohistorical connections* are "the social norms, policies, and laws found in various geographic locations and cultures as well as the values existing during particular historical periods" (Evans, Forney, and Guido-DiBrito, 1998, p. 95).

Instead of stages, D'Augelli posited six "interactive processes" that affect gay and lesbian identity development. Rather than occurring sequentially or during particular times of one's life, any process might take prominence depending upon the social and/or cultural contexts the person is in. Although not posited as a stage, each process presumes degrees of internal progression necessary to achieve a fully integrated gay/lesbian/bisexual identity across processes. The processes are outlined in figure 2.4.

D'Augelli also stressed the importance of the individual within and upon his own development, both in understanding the social construction of his identity as well as choosing (or not) to address the interactive processes. In that regard, he echoed somewhat Astin's (1993) notion of student involvement—engagement with one's contexts and environments, to consciously choose to accent or develop particular skills, functions, or roles. In arguing for this change in understanding how identity for non-heterosexuals is formed, D'Augelli stated,

A revision of our operational definition of sexual orientation must occur, allowing for study of the continuities and discontinuities, the flexibilities and cohesiveness, of sexual and affectional feelings across the life span, in diverse contexts, and in relationship to life and culture. (D'Augelli, 1994, p. 331)

FIGURE 2.4: **D'Augelli's Interactive Processes Affecting Non-Heterosexual Identity Development**
(D'Augelli, 1994)

1. Recognizing that one's attractions and feelings are not heterosexual, as well as telling others one is not heterosexual.
2. Summarizing self-concepts, emotions, and desires into a personal identity as gay/lesbian/bisexual.
3. Developing a non-heterosexual social identity.
4. Disclosing one's identity to parents and redefining familial relationships afterward.
5. Developing capabilities to have intimate gay/lesbian/bisexual relationships.
6. Becoming a member of a gay/lesbian/bisexual community.

Despite this call for reframing concepts of sexual identity, gay identity development theory and student identity development theory do not move beyond the normative presumptions of heterosexuality. Most gay identity development theories have presumed a fixed non-heterosexual identity fitting within the binary distinction between "normal" or heterosexual, and "different" or homosexual; one is either heterosexual or one is gay (or lesbian or bisexual). Both types of theories depict students (straight or not) as developing from one identity (or understanding of their lives and relation to society) to another. But the path is singular, the outcome unquestioned, and unquestionably either achieved or not. Queer approaches to identity, such as the one Mendelsohn (1999) deployed and I outline later in this chapter, question those presumptions, paths, and identities in relation to the norms of heterosexuality and non-heterosexuality.

Making Sense of Queer Theory

As I mentioned earlier, while Rhoads (1993, 1994, 1995) and Tierney (1997) utilized theoretical perspectives to examine and analyze non-heterosexual lives, most of the other researchers did not. In this study, I employ queer theory to examine and understand those lives, and I examine it next. Queer theory is not the only theory to be exercised to be sure, when studying the lives of either non-heterosexuals or college students, but it forms the final piece of the framework: juxtaposed to the earlier tradition of studies of gay experiences, bridging student and gay identity development theories.

So, what is queer theory? For that matter, what's *queer*? The answers are neither as definite nor as simple as I would like them to be. The state of *queer* and *queer theory*, ever the post-postmodern concepts, is as elusive to nail down as mercury. Like that element, we can contain queer theory, but the concept will fill—even overflow—our container; we can also use it as a gauge (or a guide) to the climate of lives and experiences.

What is Queer? The flexibility of the English language, compounded by academics' transformation of general words into jargon, necessitates a few definitions. *Queer* can be an adjective, a noun, or a verb. In general use, it is most commonly an adjective, meaning "not normal," or, more specifically, not heterosexual. The word historically held a negative connotation, particularly in school settings (D'Augelli, 1989a, 1989b; D'Augelli and Rose, 1990; Herdt and Boxer, 1993; Rhoads, 1994; Chandler, 1995; Due, 1995; O'Connor, 1995). *Queer*, as operationally defined by Doty (1993), "is a quality related to any expression that can be marked as contra-, non-, or anti-straight" (p. xv), which serves not to identify people as much as forms of communication, and the positions that afford and inform that expression. In this usage, *queer* reflects the work of Foucault (1979, 1980), who demonstrated that one's sexual identity is formulated and judged within larger cultural themes of normality (with which heterosexuality is aligned) and deviance (including homosexuality).

Whereas sexual practices once had no direct effect upon identity, Foucault demonstrated a shift in thinking, by the late nineteenth century, to a view that identity was determined and defined by sexual practices (see also D'Emilio and Freedman, 1988; Greenberg, 1988; and Katz, 1995, 2001).

> Sexual difference had become neatly describable in terms of a hetero-homo binary, with each term in the binary dependent for its meaning on its opposite, which it excluded. Hetero implied healthy, homo implied sickness; hetero represented control of sexual desire and impulses, homo represented the sexual outlaw controlled by his or her desires. All of this worked to support an elaborate system of motivating conformity to the highly repressive norms of modern culture. (Carlson, 1998, p. 114)

Prior to the analyses of Foucault and his followers, sexuality—and sexual identity—was viewed accordingly. (For a more detailed analysis of Foucault, see Halperin, 1995).

Within the past decade, however, those of us looking at how our modern Western society identifies (and is identified by) sexuality have noticed another shift, even further away from the performance of particular sexual activities as the marker for difference, toward the notion of the relationship and position between what was considered normal (hetero) and abnormal (homo). The grouping into abnormal has grown past the (simple) act of having or wanting to have sexual relations with someone of the same gender. Consequently, the adjective *queer* has been used in increasing frequency as a substitute for *gay and lesbian*, and to include others whose sexuality and/or gender places them outside of society's idea of "normal" but yet not on either side of the hetero/homo dichotomy: bisexuals, pansexuals, and transgendered people (Penn, 1995; Rhoads, 1994; Warner, 1993).

But queer developed a meaning beyond its use as an inclusive categorization; as a noun, the word can be used to refer to one included in the marginalized group: a queer. Often there is a political ideology or intent in the use of this word, based in part upon a decision to confront what is experienced as discrimination and to commit to a collective identity based upon being marginalized because of one's sexuality, rather than simply identification because of one's gender and object of one's affection (Rhoads, 1994, 1997a; Jogose, 1996). In a sense, such a definition of queer is not about a lack of something (a lack of heterosexuality) (Hocquenghem, 1978), but a presence of something: a desire for same-sex experiences, a position outside of the normal trope of daily life that affords perspectives apart from the norm. Queer is a term that by its very use questions "conventional understandings of sexual identity by deconstructing the categories, oppositions and equations that sustain them" (Jagose, 1996). As Honeychurch (1996) summarized, "It is perhaps in the more expansive term 'queer' that the most possibilities emerge for denominating and declaring a range of differences and positions arising from the gamut of sexual diversities" (p. 341).

Ettinger (1992) viewed these transformations as "discursive strategies that reject and transform the categories produced by a hostile and hegemonic heterosexual discourse" (p. 53). Indeed, Abelove's (1995) descriptions of his queer students showed the effects, intentional or not, of postmodern reflection upon positionality and the power of naming by many of today's non-heterosexual students: "[Q]ueer students think that there is not and cannot be such a thing as authenticity, and that there certainly is not and cannot be such a thing as an 'authentic lesbian sexuality'" (Abelove, 1995, p. 52).

Furthermore, over the past two decades, students not identifying as straight have experienced lives that differ in varying degrees from those of their predecessors, and the result is that while not being straight might not be a terrific experience for many of them, such lives and experiences are no longer considered entirely abnormal, or without precedence.

Queerness has also challenged the gay credo, "we're just like you," and proudly and defiantly asserted the right and even importance of being different. It is a bold assertion from the margins, a declaration that we do not want to be normalized. (Carlson, 1998, p. 110)

Whether the result of better research and writing about growing up non-heterosexual or a solipsism of Generation X, today's non-heterosexual students have found the transformation of queer from adjective to noun empowering (Escoffier and Berube, 1991).

[Queer undergrads] do not typically experience their own subjectivity as marginal, even at those moments when they feel most oppressed by homophobic and heterosexist discourses and institutions.

Marginalization isn't their preferred trope. It doesn't seem to them to be cogent as a narrative device for organizing the telling of their own lives, or, for that matter, of their history. What these queers prefer to say and believe or try to believe instead is that they are both present and at the center. (Abelove, 1995, p. 48)

Such a transition from the margins of concept and study to the center creates a queered position for reflection, expression, and action. From that position, analysts change *queer* into a verb. In academic circles, to queer something is to analyze a situation or a text to determine the relationship between sexuality, power, gender, and conceptions of normal and deviant, insider and outsider. As Honeychurch observed,

A queered position requires an ontological shift comprehensively resistant in its exceptions to dominant normativity. A queering of standpoint in social research is a vigorous challenge to that which has constrained what may be known, who may be the knower, and how knowledge has come to be generated and circulated, . . . [and] queers participate in positioning themselves through both authoring and authorizing experience. (1996, p. 342)

These analysts in queered positions developed queer theory.

What is Queer Theory? To understand/imagine queer theory, one must make distinctions between queer as a quality (essentialism) and queer as an attribute (constructionism). The former posits sexual orientation (not necessarily identity) as immutable and unchanged across time and culture: people did—and do—desire and have sexual relations with others of the same gender. The latter defines "sexuality as a product of social relations and thereby suggests the history of sexuality to be 'the history of the subject whose meaning and content are in a continual process of change'" (Penn, 1995, p. 26). The construction of those meanings and contents, along with the power and concurrent identification of and with them, is at the heart of queer theory (Britzman, 1995, 1997; Seidman, 1995; Slagle, 1995).

The most conspicuous strain of queer theory draws heavily on French post-structural theory and the critical method of deconstruction (Seidman, 1995; Slagle, 1995). Deconstruction, simply stated, is a social analysis of who, why, and what produced a text; an analysis of what is said—and unsaid—through the language, form, structure, and style of a text (a written work, a film, art). Queer theory enlarges that definition of text to include any form(s) of communication utilized to convey an understanding of one's world; it could be a book or a film, obviously, but a text could also be a conversation, a life story, a memory, sexual activity, history, a gathering place, or a social trend. This is, to say the least, something of a stretch for postsecondary educators and researchers who were trained to think of themselves as social scientists: whither empirical evidence—let alone validity and rigor—in queer research and theory?

Queer theory supposes a position if not within the marginalized then at least outside of the margins of "normality" (Britzman, 1995). This new standpoint creates unique ways of looking, new paradigms of analyzing, and new methods of representing queer data. It represents a change from how and why the experiences of non-heterosexual people are studied, a "shifting theory away from its present grounding in identity concepts to a cultural or epistemological centering" (Seidman, 1995, p. 130). Even the very language used to conceptualize and to relay our thoughts and inquiries is questioned:

> Queer theory might better remind us that we are inhabited always by states of desire that exceed our capacity to name them. Every name only gives those desires—conflictual, contradictory, inconsistent, undefined—a fictive border. . . . (Edelman, 1995, p. 345)

This process is not a question of "*who* is queer" but "*how* is queer"; not so much "*why* are they queer" but "why are *we* saying *they* are queer?" The key to answering those questions is through examining the binarism of homosexuality and heterosexuality, in response "to the damaged lives and suffering engendered by a compulsively heterosexual society" (Seidman, 1995, p. 134). Much as Marxist theorists utilize the opposition of bourgeois and proletariat as a master category for social analysis, and as feminists do with masculine and feminine, "queer analysts claim for the hetero/homo binary the status of a master category of social analysis" (Seidman, 1995, p. 132).

In some ways, queer theory is a logical extension of ontological philosophy. If modernism and empiricism are about objectively researching and reporting what we see/know, and postmodernism and constructivism are about investigating and reporting how the positions between researcher, researched, and research construct what we see/know, queer theory is about how both the knowledge (found and produced) and the positions (also both found and produced) create a new body of knowledge, a delimitation of the space between position and product, investigator and investigation. Queer theory inverts the notion of outsider giving voice to the insider as well as the notion of insider information being untouched by outsider information.

Postmodern constructionism serves as the obvious structural framework of queer theory. As the queer undergraduates in Abelove's courses demonstrated, sexuality is important and provides a focal point for understanding the relation of individuals (and groups) to what others (individuals and groups) consider "normal." While sexuality is not the only dimension of human experience that define queer, it is one that informs all others.

> Sexual orientations are not a private matter that impacts only personal sexual practices, but are dimensions of subjectivity that infuse all human experience, including higher cognitive functions; are imbricated in that sexuality, gender, class, etc.; are layered and interimplicated and therefore cannot be read monolithically; and are viewed as identities coherent enough to be recognized, but fluid enough to be interrogated. (Honeychurch, 1996, p. 345)

Not every study of gay lives is queer, or benefits from queer theory. Indeed, in many ways, queer theory contradicts traditional studies that do not question the very framework of the investigation. The shift in viewpoint necessitates a shift in sensibility, style, tone, values, and commitments. Britzman (1997) argued against examination of gay lives as overly simplistic; the questions should regard why, how, and who determines that those lives are queer. "The study of why gay rights are so difficult to achieve requires not a look into the lives of gays and lesbians but into the questions and conditions of why sexuality must be regulated, outlawed, and fought for" (Britzman, 1997, p. 36).

Duggan posited that queer theorists critique three elements of research and representation: (a) humanist progressive narratives of gay identities and gay liberation against repressive forces; (b) empiricist methods claiming to present "reality" through simple and objective events, dates, and motives; and (c) "stable, unitary, or 'authentic' identity categories" (Duggan, 1995a, p. 181). Indeed, Seidman believed

> Queer theory is less a matter of explaining the repression or expression of a homosexual minority than an analysis of the hetero/homosexual figure as a power/knowledge regime that shapes the ordering of desires, behaviors, and social institutions, and social relations—in a word, the constitution of the self and society. (Seidman, 1995, p. 128)

Queer theory is not easily understood partly because it challenges basic tropes used to organize our society and our language: even words are gendered, and through that gendering an elliptical view of the hierarchy of society, and presumption of what is male and what is female, shines through. Queer theory rejects such binary distinctions as arbitrarily determined and defined by those with social power. As Edelman's earlier quote hinted, if all of these concepts are constructed out of whole cloth, it becomes difficult to explain what queer is if it is not in opposition to straight—or even to gay.

Historian Lisa Duggan (1995b) related a funny story of a fact-checker for *Rolling Stone* trying to ascertain from literary critic and queer theorist Eve Sedgwick whether Sedgwick was straight or gay. The fact-checker dogged Sedgwick with questions like, "Are you straight? If you're not straight, you must be gay? But if you're married, you're straight, right?" Sedgwick sidestepped answering through a series of Socratic responses: "Did I say I was straight? Did I say I was gay? Did I say I was married? In some ways, I might be considered queer."

The fact-checker's questions were based in the essentialist language of facts, of course, while Sedgwick was responding from a very consciously constructed position. This problem is but one example "to illustrate the difficulty of communication across the gap between the predominantly constructionist language of queer studies and the essentialist presumptions of public discourse" (Duggan, 1995b, p. 183). If queer is so troublesome to use as a word that means something personally and can be easily understood by the public, it is even more difficult to explain in plain language what queer theory is.

Queer theory, then, comes from queered perspectives of the researcher and the researched. The sexual dimensions of a subject become the central site of investigation, primarily in juxtaposing the queer to the norm. This positioning represents both a change in the interests of researchers and theorists, and in those about whose lives we report. In Abelove's estimation, queer students desire a shift in the lens of study of non-heterosexual lives:

> [F]ocus not on the margins, but on what was "queer" in the center, such as musicals, or comedies, or films by or with homosexual (or bisexual) creators. "What could be queerer? . . . All these cultural productions were central rather than marginal. By ignoring or neglecting them, we misconceive the past and unwittingly reduce our presence in and claim to the present," they say. (Abelove, 1995, p. 49)

Such actions and ideas go against much of what is thought, and believed, in both the academic and the lay worlds—and in doing so call into question the very concepts of those thoughts and beliefs (Penn, 1995; Honeychurch, 1996; Seidman, 1995). Who is making the claim/determination of what is normal and what is queer? What are his agendas? What are her politics? The text (broadly defined, in social sciences, as analyses, theories, identities, and discourses) is our source of knowledge, but like that text, knowledge is constructed by constructed people. In questioning such conventional wisdom, both gay and straight, queer theory is all the queerer for its subjects and its subjectivities. As Britzman stated,

> Queer Theory signifies improper subjects *and* improper theories, even as it questions the very grounds of identity and theory. Queer Theory occupies a difficult space between the signifier and the signified, where something queer happens to the signified—to history and to bodies— and something queer happens to the signifier—to language and to representation. (1995, p. 153)

In many respects, queer theory might offer the most qualitative of methodologies for collecting and analyzing data. As queer theory questions, even defies, notions of objectivity and the historical essentiality of fact, queer theory opens more "texts" for study, and more bodies of knowledge to compile, compare, and evaluate. "[I]t mobilizes a radically wide range of knowledge—modes of understanding from science to gossip—to reconstitute information about queerness, thus transforming the range of reference 'queer' has by multiplying its specifications" (Berlant and Freedman, 1992, p. 153). Again, the flexibility overflows the delimitations of words to contain what queer theory could be.

Queer theory is not simply about the studying of people whose sex lives are not heterosexual, or even the positionalities of those people in relation to the "center" or "margins; at its core, it is about questioning the presumptions, values, and viewpoints from those positions (marginal and central), especially those that normally go unquestioned. In regard to identity, queer theory provides a tool to examine how experience as well as personal contemplation and interpersonal relationships work in conjunction to shape, contain, and name identities. As Talburt challenged those who conduct queer cultural research, "Rather than reifying experience as self-evident or continuous with identity and difference, researchers must attend to social and historical processes that shape experience and subjectivity and inquire into *what counts as experience and why*" (Talburt, 1999, p. 257).

Elsewhere (Dilley, 1999), I have posited that queer theory is more *transdisciplinary* than *interdisciplinary*: the concepts and the methods can be, and are, utilized by a number of researchers in various disciplines, but the particular product or analysis in one discipline might not have any impact or influence upon another discipline. In other words, while the results of, say, a queered investigation of film studies might not interest or be applicable for educational research, the methodologies of investigation, analysis, and representation might be very relevant and provocative. And, as Britzman's (1995, p. 155) three-part methodology—studying limits, studying incongruence, and studying reading practices—implied, analytical reading in areas in which one does not normally read—itself a reading practice—can in itself be a queer method.

Regardless of the discipline of the researcher, three tenets are evident in queer research:

- Examination of lives and experiences of those considered non-heterosexual.
- Juxtaposition of those lives/experiences with lives/experiences considered "normal."
- Examination of how/why those lives and experiences are considered outside of the norm.

Not all queer research considers equally each tenet, but at minimum at least one is emphasized. In addition, researchers using queer theory also often try to find novel, creative ways of representing in print data that aid in fulfilling those tenets. In doing so, the texts become queer as well.

I stated that queer theory is transdisciplinary; the body of literature of queer theory reflects this, showing connections between disciplines, and advancement of the theory's development across the disciplines, while the works produced remain tied to particular disciplines. Consequently, I categorized queer research into four categories: language, literature, and the arts (where the concepts and tenets of queer theory were first formed); history; queer life histories/stories; and queer praxis (Dilley, 1999). In this study, concerned as I am with the changes in non-heterosexual lives and identities over time, I concentrate upon how queer theory impacted the process of analyzing data about peoples' lives as part of conceptualizing and writing history.

Queer Theory in Historiography. Although the study of literature and film were the flashpoints of queer theory, history is surely the discipline that has applied queer theory in a practical sense; as Abelove pointed out, "this change has apparently produced a partly new way of reading and thinking history" (1995, p. 44). Duggan (1992, 1995a, 1995b) has been one of the proponents for a queer historiography, trying to energize practice through queer theory; Bravmann (1990, 1998) also called for use of queered (and other nonconformist) manners and methods of depicting gay lives. The histories that have resulted from queer methods are important. Katz's (1995) recounting of the "invention of heterosexuality" used the same type of analysis that had previously been used to place historically the construction of homosexuality. By inverting that procedure, Katz showed that, in this case, the margin, the queer, was used to define the center. Prior to construction of categories of homosexuality and heterosexuality as components of identity in the late nineteenth century, the "norm" of sexuality did not reside in identity.

Chauncey (1994) showed that sexual actions did not always determine the identities within sexual relationships of men who had sex with other men (the definitions were not based upon specific actions), but rather that gendered roles sometimes created an identity based upon social roles within the relationship and the community, no matter who did what to whom. Chauncey's pathbreaking work was also queer, in a sense. Conventional wisdom held that social and personal definitions of gay or homosexual did not begin until after World War II, and that the history of public "gay" lives started after the Stonewall Riots of 1969. But Chauncey countered one of the "norms" of gay and lesbian studies, unveiling a publicly social world of gay life in New York City from 1890 to 1940, documenting its public status, and presenting gay— and queer—identities as stated through interviews with members of that subculture. Kaiser's (1997) more recent work also examined New York City; although not necessarily queer in its concept (the work examined non-heterosexual lives, but did not consider the relationship of those lives to the norm), it moved beyond the historiographical norm, drawing from published reports of people we now know had same-sex relations, from gossip, from popular culture, and from more traditional historical sources as diaries, interviews, and printed accounts. Howard (1999) similarly does so, using Mississippi as a model for queer southern history.

Perhaps the most queer of all of the recent histories is Sadownick's (1996) history of *Sex Between Men*. In it, Sadownick attempted to find a locus between sexuality, identity, and spirituality, using qualitative data about men's sexual lives and experiences, the places they lived and had sex, their thoughts and feelings about those events, and how all of those concepts changed for those men over the past fifty years. These lives of the past come sharply into focus through queer application of qualitative and ethnographic methods. Beemyn's (1997) edited volume of community histories illustrated how, for several generations, non-heterosexuals in communities large and small responded—personally, collectively, and politically—to the dominant perceptions of what normal was; Higgs's (1999) collection similarly covered urban histories since 1600. Using qualitative ethnographic methods in addition to traditional historical methodology, the historians in Beemyn's collection demonstrated how historiographical methods can be used in conjunction—and in opposition—to discover and (re)present lives of queers.

To study things queer(ly) is more than researching homosexual lives, whether those lives were lived on the margins or in the forefront of public conversation and consciousness; it is researching/theorizing why/how/when lives are homosexualized, "queered" outside of the norm. This queering is the result of someone, either the subject, the researcher, or the audience, determining that the senses, sensibilities and experiences of—the data derived from—the subjects are not what an audience, or a writer, thinks the data "should" be.

Queer theorists attempt to show the structures and concepts created by those limits and borders, and how the people involved in creating theory effect and are affected by those concepts. They challenge—and sometimes reject—the notions of epistemological certainty, normal and abnormal, inclusion and exclusion, homosexual and heterosexual. And the questions, once posed and answered, must continue to be re-examined, for, if nothing else, queer theory has taught us the inefficiency of language to convey so complex a notion as identity, especially an identity based upon sexuality.

As I have displayed, much of queer theory in historical research pertains to identity; still, it is far from overused, or lacking in potential. As the positions of non-straight identities become less shadowy, if not less marginal, new understandings of where the spotlight of normality shines—and whom it illuminates—can inform our understanding of (and outreach efforts to) queer(ed) people *and* those we currently consider "straight." In this respect, queer theory demonstrates that constructionism is a two-way street, and that identities are fluid and descriptive rather than prescriptive. Theorists who work with non-heterosexual identities and cultures must take into account the tenets of queer theory; as Rhoads noted, for "lesbian, gay, and bisexual people, their struggle to develop a positive sense of sexual identity takes place within a larger cultural frame that situates heterosexuality as the norm and homosexuality as a deviant expression" (1997b, p. 462). The queer binary of hetero/homo cannot be avoided in trying to understand and depict non-heterosexual identities. But what if the binary were confronted? What if the queer dichotomy were operationalized to understand how such identities were formed?

Mendelsohn: Men and De of Queer Lives. Although not a full-fledged theory or developmental model, Mendelsohn's autobiographical examination, *The Elusive Embrace: Desire and the Riddle of Identity* (1999), provides provocative insight into gay male identity formation. His work is troubling to my attempt to understand identities (particularly gay male identities), for it both refutes and affirms traditional student development theories and gay identity development theories. The trouble, however, is quite informative: as Mendelsohn expressed, identities are neither consistent nor constant; gay men inhabit multiple realities (sometimes contiguously, sometimes simultaneously) that both contradict and depend upons the other for definition.

In the grammar of the ancient Greek language, sentences were constructed between two halves, the *men* (in a manner of speaking, the idea of the sentence as subject) and the *de* (the idea of the sentence as object). The "untranslatable monosyllables—particles, they are called, not really full-fledged words at all—whose presence in any given sentence tells you about the balance of that sentence, what its rhythm, and, ultimately, its meaning will be" (Mendelsohn, 1999, p. 25) are in juxtaposition to each other: "on the one hand *x*, but on the other hand *y*" (Mendelsohn, 1999, p. 25). Both are necessary to understand the full context of ancient Greek sentences.

Mendelsohn comprehended his life, and the experiences of other gay men, through this understanding of constant connection to both the *men* and the *de* of their lives, the comfort of conformity and the desire for (or to be) the "other." For Mendelsohn, the attraction to the *de* of gay life (often found in or symbolized by urban gay ghettos) leads one away from the *men* of one's past (the sense of place and priority found in the circumstances of one's childhood). He told of a young man he met in New York City, who was leaving New York to return to St. Louis. After the two had sex, as the young man was leaving, he relayed to Mendelsohn a telling statement: "I came here to find myself . . . but instead, I got lost" (Mendelsohn, 1999, p. 13). This was the conflict, at least for that man, between the *men* of the life he observed, learned, and felt he did not belong in St. Louis (suburban, heterosexually oriented), and the *de* of the life he lived, experienced, and felt he did not fit in in New York City (urban, gay oriented, with a "dizzying nightlife, [and] the sheer, confusing superabundance of opportunities" [Mendelsohn, 1999, p. 13]).

The attraction to those opportunities is, for Mendelsohn, contrapositioned to the suburban life of his past and his present. Reflecting upon his discontent with either life in suburbia or life in the gay ghetto, Mendelsohn ". . . thought [he] had to be one thing, a man who could wholly possess the thing he wanted in a way that was continuous with who he was. And this, it was clear, was impossible" (Mendelsohn, 1999, p. 203).

In *The Elusive Embrace*, Mendelsohn chronicled how he divides his time between the city, where he socialized primarily with gay friends, and the suburbs, where he established a relationship as a father to the son of a female friend. He was being and feeling gay in the city, heterosexual in the suburbs, and consequently occupying a queer position in both places because of the relationship of both identities to his sensibility, to the meaning he made of his life. This compromise, to "move between two places" (Mendelsohn, 1999, p. 204), fulfilled both of his concepts of identity, both of his desires of whom he wanted to be. The concession is the actualization of the paradox of gay identity:

> Gay identity, as we actually experience it, so many of us who live here, is, in the end, nothing if not structured by paradox and conflict, by the mysteries of *men* and *de*. You can be two things at once; you can life in the middle voice. You can, some of us have learned, to be "queer" and "mainstream" at the same time, someone equally committed to your family in the suburbs, *men*, and to the pleasures of random encounters with strange men in the city, *de*. (Mendelsohn, 1999, p. 34)

One could not be one's self, a complete self, a real self, without acknowledging that both aspects of gay male identity are simultaneously at work (and play) at all times.

It is conceivable, though, that the two aspects—queer and mainstream—could be something other than gay and straight, but the concept of one notion of (sexual) identity being juxtaposed diametrically to a different notion of (sexual) identity is key. Neither notion is complete without reference to the other concept, just as a Greek sentence was incomplete without both parts: the general idea could be understood, but the true meaning of the expression (or of the identity) is partial, at best, without knowing both the *men* and the *de*. Mendelsohn's work is a queer move, from a linear approach—identity as a process from one concept to another, both based upon the binarism of heterosexual or not—to a recursive, paradoxical integration of seemingly contradictory concepts.

Making Sense of My Framework

Two years after devising the three-part theoretical tool for examining identity (sense, experience, sensibility), I discovered the work of qualitative researcher Brian Pronger. *In The Arena of Masculinity* (1992), Pronger examined male sexuality as seen through the lenses of sport and meanings of sex. He posited that "Rather than defining a person, 'homosexuality' and 'heterosexuality' describe modes of being in the world, fluid ways of perceiving or interpreting oneself and others in gendered culture" (1992, p. 8). He used many of the same terms and concepts that I do, separating sense from experience; I was both excited and distraught that someone else had developed so similar a way of examining identity as I had.

But as I read further, I found that while Pronger and I might use similar language and methods, we are not talking about the same thing. He argued for a "change from the concept of identity to sensibility" (1992, p. 8), based on a relation of one's self to cultural "myths" of sexuality and identity.

> For the last hundred years or so, homosexuality has been understood as an essence; more recently, under the influence of popular social science, it has been conceived as an identity. As I will suggest . . . people do not experience homosexuality as an essence. It's not an identity; it is, rather, a way of being and understanding. (Pronger, 1992, p. 8)

Well, no and yes. No: non-heterosexual identities do exist, as self-concepts and -deployments in specific contexts and situations; yes: part of non-heterosexual identity is a way of being and understanding, the physical deployments or performances that reflect one's integration or dissonance among one's sense of self, experiences, and the meanings they make of those concepts and deeds.

The clarity of my thoughts (and my confidence in citing the limitations of Pronger's useful approach to exploring non-heterosexual experiences) comes from my study of the four bodies of thought and research that frame my project. Student identity development theories do explore how experience relates to self-concept; gay identity theories do convey particular senses of self based on sexuality; studies of campus experiences of non-heterosexual collegians bridge experience and essence, but queer theory is needed to understand the how and why those meanings are constructed in the particular contexts surrounding sexuality.

After reviewing the tenets of and assembling my framework, I was left with a number of questions that the existing research did not answer. My uncertainties fell within six broad areas that the previous research and theories outlined but that were not systemically applied to non-heterosexual collegiate populations.

- *Experiences and thoughts.* Within the past five decades, what experiences or thoughts influenced how non-heterosexual male college students conceived of themselves and their sexual orientation, particularly in relation to their collegiate experiences? How might have those experiences, thoughts, and/or self-concepts differed, if at all, over time?
- *Influences.* How did those experiences influence the actions and beliefs of these non-heterosexual students? How might have collegiate experiences contributed to—or detracted from—identification based upon sexual orientation? In what contexts—places, times, social settings—has this type of identification occurred?
- *Interaction.* How did those students behave, interact with other students, and/or socialize with other non-heterosexuals?
- *Campus.* What elements of the institution of higher education contribute(d) to the identities and experiences of these students?
- *Implications.* How can these patterns of identity inform educators' understandings of, and practice for, this student population?
- *Theory.* What patterns of identification for non-heterosexual male college students exist in those contexts and through those experiences?

Although I provide answers to the questions in the chapters that follow, the responses are more formative than summative, less definitive than evocative. The typology of this project, then, is ideal for this mapping of areas and aspects of college student identity development and non-heterosexual identity development, for it is an overview of multiple patterns, each with its own set of characteristics and complexities.

Perhaps the greatest criticism of stage development models, both those describing homosexuals and those pertaining to college students, is that if one does not fit the model, one is, by necessity, flawed. A student whose experiences bring him to different sensibilities of how he views himself in the world in ways that differ from Chickering would, by implication at least, be classified as not as fully developed (since the student did not achieve mastery over the particular challenges of one or more advanced vectors). Similarly, as Rhoads pointed out, "Cass implies that queer students . . . need to work through their hostile attitudes and achieve a less radicalized sense of identity" (Rhoads, 1997b, p. 477). The theories do not allow for diversity of experience or sensibility, and only account for it in terms of deviance from the norm of the model.

Such a viewpoint highlights how fertile to our understanding of students and of identity the relatively unexplored field of non-heterosexual collegiate identity is. Issues of normality and deviance frame (and are framed within) queer theory; "Thus, by decentering norms we move away from a politics of identity that situates analyses within individuals and we struggle to move toward an understanding of institutional and cultural practices that frame sexual orientation in a particular manner" (Tierney and Dilley, 1998, p. 65). Consequently, theorists can benefit from applying queer theory to student and to gay identity development theories, to explore how what is not considered "normal" is understood, situated in the developmental theories, expressed in the literature, and utilized for student advisement and programming.

I believe that the identity models are not as discrete, nor as self-contained, as a "straight" reading would impart. Further, despite their grounding in psychosocial identity development theories, in some respects the gay identity development models are somewhat typological; that is, each theorist posits a progression of identity development in which an individual views himself— and his relationship to society—as a particular role or quality of person. A gay youth who in his identity management is consciously closeted, could be said, broadly, to be a particular "type" of gay person. The same could be said of the Queer Nationalist, or the gay activist. As Evans, Forney, and Guido-DiBrito (1998) noted,

Typology theories reflect individual stylistic differences in how students approach their worlds. . . . Typology, then, serves as a framework within which psychosocial and cognitive structural development takes place, and it influences the manner in which students address development in these aspects of their lives. (Evans, Forney, and Guido-DiBrito, 1998, p. 204)

I contend that these two epistemologies of personal identity development are not mutually exclusive, no more so than Mendelsohn's *men* and *de* make sense without understanding the relation of one to the other (and other to the one). Rather, particular contexts create environments where specific identities are fostered or discouraged, but those identities are neither static nor permanent; one can "be" a type in certain contexts, at certain times, but can also display the qualities and sensibilities of another type (as Mendelsohn's conflicting self-concepts demonstrate).

Indeed, the binary division between queer and normal, or homosexual and heterosexual, is, to an extent, arbitrary. Human identity is rarely so clear, for gay and straight people interact and they (often) share some common cultural values. Moreover, other aspects of personal identity are always present, perhaps even competing (or complementing) against the label of straight or gay. This study seeks to begin to map those manners, in those differing contexts, for men who attended college over the past fifty years. Certainly, as their narratives will demonstrate, men who engaged in non-heterosexual behavior or emotions managed their identities in different ways, during different times and in different conditions.

In the three chapters that comprise the next section, I present the recollections of men who attended college in the United States since the mid-1940s, who recognized their collegiate experiences as fitting within six categories of conceptualization. In chapters 3 and 4, I discuss four classifications of experience and identity for non-heterosexual students; chapter 5 is concerned with two distinct sets of experiences and sensibilities of non-heterosexual students not discussed in the existing literature. I have arranged the narratives chronologically, to demonstrate the consistency of the classifications over time, as well as how cultural changes might (or might not) e/affect those ideations. The men's individual experiences and responses to the concepts highlight the differences as well as the similarities of their non-heterosexual experiences on campus, and, always, the juxtaposition of their lives and sensibilities to those of the (presumed) norm of heterosexuality.

PATTERNS OF NON-HETEROSEXUAL LIVES

CHAPTER 3

Tearooms and No Sympathy: Homosexuals and the Closet

The earliest classifications of non-heterosexual student identities was evident by the 1940s and continued, perhaps surprisingly, at least through the 1980s: those who identify (or are identified by others) as "homosexual," a clinical term denoting sexual activity as an (or the) indicator of identity (Greenberg, 1988; Katz, 1994), and those whose sexual and emotional lives are led secretly, "in the closet" (Signorile, 1993; Tierney, 1997). These labels are in direct opposition to what was considered the norm in American culture: the open and visible heterosexual who has no questions or qualms about his sexuality.

Homosexual

Although, as other scholars have noted (including, among others, D'Emilio, 1983; Howard, 1999; Loughery, 1998; Marcus, 1992; and Sears, 1997), *homosexual* as a collective social identity did not really resonate among many non-heterosexuals until the late 1960s, the term was nevertheless used as early as the 1940s to distinguish certain people (distinct from certain *acts*) from the norm. The U.S. Army's use of questions pertaining to homosexual acts and "tendencies" to eliminate non-heterosexuals from military service, as mentioned in Sam's narration in this chapter (and in Berube's *Coming Out Under Fire*), focused on "tendencies," not specific actions; indeed, the psychological rationale behind the question itself shows the clinical origins of the idea of what meaning must be connoted not in carnal activity but in "tendencies," ideations, or preferences for those behaviors. Government officials were less concerned about whether a man got off with another man than to what extent he liked it (or thought he would like it).

Collegians in the mid-twentieth century held similar views: the actions could be overlooked if a man appeared to "like" girls. Despite this, social conformity to sexual roles did not prescribe the self-concepts of non-heterosexuals as it might have to their heterosexual peers. As Arnie Kantrowitz, who in 1970s New York City was on the one hand a gay activist and on the other a college English professor, wrote in his memoir of life in the closet:

> Socially, I was a heterosexual. During the [high] school year I escorted the daughters of Newark to movies and bowling alleys and restaurants, to dances and hops and proms. Every date was ended with interminable tongue kissing in the back hallway. I don't know if my attentions turned my dates on, but they didn't do much for me. It was just that I knew everyone else did it, and there had to be something to brag about the next day; but I couldn't escape the feeling that I wasn't the only one for whom it was done out of obligation rather than desire. Whatever their reasons, everybody was pretending to have a good time. We were all afraid not to: it would have seemed un-American. (Kantrowitz, 1977, p. 48)

Although he continued to date women during his years at Rutgers University (which were his late teens, as he matriculated at an early age), Kantrowitz ultimately admitted his same-gender affections and desires. Beneath that revelation, however, was resentment of those who were, like him, feeling (if not necessarily living) outside of the norm.

> I finally confessed to myself that I was a homosexual. I confessed to my best friend, Leslie, too. And he confessed to me. The same confession. We suffered the blow fate had dealt us in the years of prolonged telephonings of mutual self-pity. We referred to our common vice by the code name "Peanut Butter," because there was a bar near school named Skippy's that was reputedly gay, even though we were both afraid of being seen there. Although we commiserated, we really felt contempt for each other's sexuality, because we saw disquieting reflections of ourselves in it. Ultimately I could no longer endure the waspiness we engendered in each other, and I asked him to stop calling . . . . He was the only homosexual friend I had until I was twenty-nine. (Kantrowitz, 1977, p. 57)

For Kantrowitz, his identity was formed as much by the dissonance he experienced between his desires and the cultural norms he perceived as it was by those desires. He was sure of this identity, and confided it to another, before he ever had a sexual encounter with another man (which happened at age 20, just after he graduated from Rutgers) (Kantrowitz, 1977, p. 58). As is true for other homosexual collegians, the intent, the emotional investment, of the desire to have sex with another man primarily determined the homosexual identity.

Other aspects were ascribed to the concept as well, although a preponderance of those traits was usually deemed necessary to be considered truly homosexual (as opposed to just temperamental or not conforming to social norms). Debauchery, effeminacy, and passivity were perceived traits of the homosexual male. Even if one displayed two of the three, a single trait could be enough to convince one's self (or perhaps others) that one was not unnormal. A passage from the autobiography of noted Episcopalian priest and peace activist Malcolm Boyd conveys how one could separate the homosexual act from the actor:

Once when the four of us [high school friends, in Denver] were at a drive-in, somebody pointed out several truck drivers walking out of a parking-lot men's room. They rubbed their crotches and laughed. A captive "queer" inside had "gone down" on them, we were made to understand. So, I thought, *that* was homosexuality. It would take a devastatingly long time before a concept of gay life as something furtive and melancholy would change for me into healthy, life giving realities. (Boyd, 1978, p. 44)

Consequently, homosexuality was equated not to the genital contact between two men but the importance and lack of enjoyment of the experience. The "furtive" and "melancholy" were not the boys who forced the homo-sex or enjoyed having their dicks sucked, nor those who displayed homo-expressive crotch rubbing. A homosexual was obviously someone who didn't enjoy such things. As a teen, Boyd felt homo-erotic and homo-affectional stirrings but, while he recognized the difference between himself and most of his peers, Boyd's sensibility was both hidden and not "homosexual." He did not see the similarity between himself and the public definition of homosexuality he had observed.

The private definition, however, could expand to include others to whom one felt an affinity. Homosexual men gathered socially, if discretely, as Fellows's (1996) narrators from the Midwest and Howard's (1999) from Mississippi demonstrate; indeed, as early as the 1930s, non-heterosexuals formed social networks—including house parties, public gatherings, and scholarship—were evident (to those who knew or chose to look) at the University of Nebraska at Lincoln (Loughery, 1998, pp. 77–78). Throughout the twentieth century, in smaller towns as well as larger cities, homosexual men met for dinner, threw parties, and created webs of connections that stretched across states and social strata (Chauncey, 1994; Fellows, 1996; Howard, 1999; Loughery, 1998).

But these meetings were always at risk of being discovered, the men of being identified by those outside of the group as being a part of the group. The meanings students made from those experiences—and the definitions the men placed upon those meanings and actions—were placed in opposition to the norm of heterosexuality. As both of the following narrations from homosexual collegians convey, meeting and gathering with others who identified as homosexuals became a part of their collegiate experience (although it also took them both away from their campuses, in two distinctly different ways).

Walter

Adolescence. Walter grew up in Chicago, living with his mother and grandmother. "I was shy, didn't know anybody." He recognized his attraction to other males—and his dislike of females—at an early age; his emotions were apparent to his family: "My grandmother once, when I was about ten or eleven . . . gave me a bear hug and said, 'You know, I hope someday when you grow up you find a nice man to live with and be happy. I know you hate women but I love you anyway." I said, *Yeah, I think you're right, but I don't know why.*"

Early College. Walter received a Catholic education and completed two years of study at the University of Illinois—Navy Pier, in Chicago. In 1950, he enrolled at the University of Illinois in Urbana, living alone in an apartment off campus. From Walter's studies of history he felt he was "born 200 years late. I knew I was gay, always would be. . . . [But thought] there aren't many people like me. At the time, it was harder for me to study, to plan for my life" because of this.

"I didn't have any [non-heterosexual] friends or any acquaintances. The only place I can vaguely remember is a sort of gay cruising area in a park, at night. I don't recall any other places where gay people were congregating, although I did meet two or three professors. I'm trying to think of how I became acquainted with them; maybe at the library or on campus or something. . . . I would be at their apartment, and they would—I guess they had little, quiet parties, social gatherings, dinner parties occasionally. That was about it.

"They had what we would call an open relationship. After a while, it [Walter's relationship to the professors] wasn't sexual, it was social: we would discuss literature and all sorts of things. One of them eventually moved to New Jersey, and the other moved to Washington, D.C. They both had other lovers after that. We wrote over the years.

"At the time, this was about 1951, maybe, they [the University of Illinois] had what they called the 'pogrom,' like the Russian deal. One of the professors told me, *You have to be very careful.* He even had his telephone disconnected because they were investigating everybody, and they said the college at that time had a quota system. The college could have no more than five percent Jewish students, no more than two percent blacks, and zero tolerance for gays. These two people that I knew [the professors] were discovered in the investigation. Ultimately . . . they were given a transfer instead of just being fired. They were told to leave, and they [each] transferred to another university."

During this time, Walter also came under the scrutiny of campus authorities. "I got a call one time from the security police, and they asked me if I knew somebody. I can't even remember his name, either. I don't know how I met him, but I did know him; I think I might have met him at one of the dinner parties. He was a rather outwardly gay person: promiscuous a little bit, I guess. So I just mentioned that I knew him and that was all. Then after that, I was being investigated. Over the Christmas holidays I might have been in a gay bar that was raided, in Chicago. It was on Division Street. And I don't know whether that might have gone on my record. They [the Chicago police] asked what I was doing, and I had to admit that I was a student at the university. Without much of a hearing or a lawyer or anything, [the university] just sent me a letter. They had a regents' meeting at the school; I was dismissed for conduct unbecoming a student. It was a civil rights matter then, as it is now, but that's what happened.

"At that time, I made up my mind I was going to get my degrees, and I had to find out how. I didn't get a lawyer, which people would have done now, I suppose. I had to tell my mother what happened; I had to come back home, give up my apartment. Then I went to a short time to a psychoanalyst in Chicago. This was maybe going to help me being dismissed, but it didn't. The psychoanalyst said, *Well, you certainly should go on with your college career,* and he gave me a names of several colleges that would take gay people. There were only three or four that would ever let anybody in as a student in those circumstances, and one of them happened to be Roosevelt College, now Roosevelt University. They were more than happy to have somebody with a good academic background; whether they were gay or not had no effect whatsoever. So I managed in the next year or two to get my degree from there. After that, I went on and took a graduate program at Northwestern University in Chicago, and I went for my M.B.A. at that point."

Recalling the other names on the list of schools accepting students after dismissal for homosexual conduct, Walter remembered, "Northwestern I think was one of them, and there was another university in Ohio (it might have been Oberlin), and it seems to me there was a journalism school at the University of Missouri, but I'm not certain of that." But the list provided by the psychoanalyst proved to Walter that there were institutions of higher education at the time that were not averse to homosexual students.

Later College. After leaving the University of Illinois, Walter maintained a private, interior life: "I didn't think there was any point in saying anything one way or another." At Roosevelt, "they didn't really have a gay and lesbian group there, either." Nonetheless, Walter did not feel he had to be as discreet as he had been at Illinois and continued to have sex with men. "I was looking for a long-term relationship, but because of the nature of context . . . it didn't crystallize into a long-term relationship." Although he had a car, "I had a very limited social life. I didn't know where to go, really. I just have vague remembrances of parks or places like that to meet people, and that was a rather limited encounter. There were certainly, as I recall, no gay bars or restaurants."

Compounding Walter's isolationism was his disconnection from his family. His father had moved away from Chicago when Walter was very young, and Walter did not seem to be emotionally close to his mother. They only discussed his sexuality, his "private matter," once. "When I told my mother, *Well, I have to come home, I'm being expelled,* and I told her why, she said, *You should have told me all those things. Why didn't you tell me?* And I said, *It's none of your business.* She wasn't upset, and she didn't have any feelings about it. I never mentioned it to the rest of my family, and they never knew."

Over time, Walter's conception of how his sexuality impacted his self-concept changed. The physical acts were no longer paramount to his understanding of his identity: "Sex was very important, but the identity—social, intellectual—was the most important." Being homosexual was "a private, personal matter—but the political aspect—political and social power" held forth as Walter went on to complete graduate work at Northwestern.

Duchess

Early College. Duchess enrolled at a large university in Los Angeles in 1979. Originally from the Tropics but from a Western-educated family, Duchess felt constrained by the reception he felt from his classmates. He "didn't want to be just stereotyped with the ethnic population. I wanted them liking me as an individual, not as an ethnicity." He recognized his interests and feelings for other boys before coming to the United States at age eighteen, but had neither the opportunity nor the inclination to act upon them. "For me, [homosexuality] wasn't even real when I was growing up in the Tropics. It didn't exist. I never could see that it actually existed in real life."

Even after matriculating, Duchess found it difficult, if not impossible, to express himself. "I had a very limited number of friends, certainly nobody I could talk to. I was so naive, I didn't even know that a community existed, that social places existed, that there were books about gay people."

He also did not have a vocabulary to convey his desires or emotions, but that changed during his first year in college. In his second semester, Duchess answered a classified advertisement in the campus newspaper, from a photographer searching for male models, "all types, for print work and runway work. It was a legitimate ad, very short." Duchess called the number listed, made an appointment, and then rode the bus to meet the photographer. "The bus happened to go through West Hollywood. . . . I remember looking down and seeing these guys, and thinking *There's something very*—excuse the word—*'odd' here.* I guess it was a start to make me think that there's an actual life that revolves around that." The photographer became Duchess's first non-heterosexual friend, who introduced him to gay social life in Los Angeles in the early 1980s.

Later College. Duchess stopped out of course work to explore his social life, choosing to explore cultural settings more accepting and to associate with others more akin to his burgeoning self-concept. When he returned to campus a few semesters later, he found it difficult to feel as comfortable in scholastic settings as in socially gay contexts. "I wanted to seek out what the university had as far as meeting other people, what kind of support or social programs. So I heard about the gay and lesbian student union. It was a very loosely-held organization. I think it received enough support from the student senate to make the student senate look politically correct, but nothing more than that. I wanted to be a part of something more, so I became more active." He was executive director of the organization in 1986–1987, "but unfortunately it was more in title than anything else. I was still feeling very closeted in school, and finding it difficult to really be active and open at the same time." Others on campus were displeased with Duchess because he was not open on campus or in classes about his sexual orientation; his involvement with the gay and lesbian student union dwindled.

Although he might have used the term gay at the time, and although he became increasingly involved in Los Angeles' gay society (and less involved with campus life), Duchess's sensibility—his understanding of the meaning of his actions and emotions—was more akin to the homosexual identity than to gay identity. "I guess back then, especially considering being nineteen, twenty years old, I think more than anything it was about the sex. It was the fact that I could have sex with another guy. But I don't want to say that was what it was all about; I met my first lover when I was nineteen, and I had no idea that two men, I couldn't fathom the idea that two men could live together like a married couple, like a heterosexual couple."

Despite the changes this insight created for Duchess, his concept of who he was, and how that concept affected his behavior, was compartmentalized. His sexuality "was an attachment to my life. My life didn't revolve around it. I think I still identified with having a heterosexual existence: work, professionally; the way I lived, socialized. Even when I was out with someone I liked, I became very straight-passing. That's the way I lived back then. Even when I was out with someone I liked, with people who knew we were a couple, we would still behave very hetero: not hold hands, not show any signs of affection, not address each other in endearing terms."

Closeted

While some students were cautiously open about their sexuality during college, others feared the social disapprobation more than the isolation necessary to avoid society's stings of denigration. The term "living in the closet" served as a metaphor for denying, suppressing, or hiding one's non-heterosexual feelings or activities (Signorile, 1993; Tierney, 1997). As the narrators in this section show, some closets were larger than others, some were deeper, and some appeared to have revolving doors. Closeted men felt distanced from classmates, despite their efforts at joining social and living organizations. Some dated and even married women, to prove (or to disprove) their sexuality to themselves and peers. Still others found sex, or at least symbolic substitutes, in the most conspicuous and seemingly heterosexual places. But the men in this type, who spent their college years evading, avoiding, or lying about their sexuality, were living, in the words of an undergraduate in the late 1970s, a life "on the fringes."

The reminiscences of Malcolm Boyd (1978) of life in college in the 1940s again illustrate this experience:

> In college, I dated for appearance's sake, and because I like to dance and be in the social company of others. I made obsessive efforts to achieve

acceptable sexuality via the fraternity life. I joined the jock fraternity, dated a number of girls, and hung my Greek pin on two or three at successive intervals. (Boyd, 1978, p. 44)

Boyd "lived constantly in a kind of hell, a world split down the middle between hard social contradictions and insoluble personal dilemmas" (1978, p. 46), "playing the masquerade, trying to find some way to express the affection that other boys expressed so easily and enviably with girls" (1978, p. 39). If the social norm were heterosexuality, Boyd and others classified as closet types believed so firmly in its power that they hid their emotions, actions, and identities.

The five respondents in this section convey similar responses to the duality they felt the closet imposed upon them during college. These narratives show how closet life was similar, and yet varied, across the United States. The narrators' self-reflection, afforded by distance from the collegiate experience, also created a richer depiction of the ramifications of living in the closet. Although four of the five stories concern college life in the 1950s, the final story illustrates the closet remains the identity of choice or necessity for some non-heterosexual students later in the twentieth century.

Paul

Adolescence. Paul grew up in a town of 2,300 in central New York state. "Everybody knows everybody there. I had the notion that once I got out of my hometown, it [life and feeling unpopular] would be different. I certainly made that so. The first thing that was different [upon leaving for college] was that I was called by my first name, instead of by my middle name." He attended Fordham College, a Catholic institution in New York City's Bronx borough, in the early 1950s, where he majored in sociology. "The freshman year was the happiest time of life, up to that point. I was totally accepted. I was in the 'in' crowd. I had been a kind of social leper in high school, up until senior year. It was a big adjustment, to go from being on the out to being on the inside. At college they didn't base social acceptance on whether you were on the basketball team or the football team."

Early College. His religion influenced both Paul's choice of school and his concepts of his sexuality. "I was very much a *Catholic* young man. . . . I thought I was straight, with homosexual tendencies. While I knew that I had gay tendencies, I didn't acknowledge to myself that I was in fact gay until ten years, at least, after college. It was, for me, an identity crisis."

The crisis was not so much about his feelings toward others but in his response to their attraction to him. "I realized that I was attracted to other men, and a lot of them were attracted to me. During college, I was really rather upset, quite upset that other men were attracted to me. I didn't have as much of a problem with my being attracted to other men, because I didn't think it was that serious," unlike their interest in him. "When men were attracted to me, it scared the shit out of me. I put them down as gently as I could. It bothered me that I attracted men. Had I been attracted [to those I attracted], I probably would have succumbed, because there were a couple of guys that I was attracted to."

In his mind, his attractions were normal, or at least not sinful, while the unwanted attention of other men to him signified both Paul and the others as not normal. "All of the guilt about sex was related to females, because they told you how wrong it was to pet or to have sex before you're married. But they never mentioned having sex with friends from the same sex. So I didn't identify it particularly as a sin. I went to confession about masturbation, but I didn't develop a Catholic guilt over the attraction to other men. Given how Catholic I was, it's kind of amazing. It was kind of a social guilt, because I thought anything less than one hundred percent heterosexual was not acceptable. I never identified it as being sinful until I was well into my twenties, and I had to confess having sex with another man."

Paul distinguished between sexual play with peer-aged boys and adult sexual activity. Before college, he participated in "sexual experimentation in the Boy Scouts and also before that with a friend of mine. I just called them sexual experimentation, because I was usually not the one who initiated it. I went along with it. I never felt guilty about it." Nevertheless, homosexual acts were proscribed by the Catholic Church, and Paul's actions put him in direct conflict to his beliefs. "In the guidelines for confession you have to swear that you will never do it again, and I knew that I was going to do it again. So, I stopped going to confession."

Sex for Paul happened only once during college, and then off campus. "I had my first sex with a man when I was in college. It was the best sex I ever had in my entire life—the most exciting, or whatever. He was a lot older than I was. I had been getting more and more attracted to men, specifically [more to] black men. I had heard on campus that some guys would go down to Central Park West and they would get propositioned. It got to be known that Greenwich Village was a place where the gay men—we called them fags at the time—would be, or along Central Park West. I thought maybe I'd go down to Central Park West. I did, and I was nervous. My heart was pounding. I was walking along, and I saw this guy sort of start to come up behind me. He got almost up to me, and I came to a little entrance to the park. I went into the entrance, thinking he was going to follow me. But he didn't follow me; he walked along the sidewalk, and I walked along the path that was parallel to the sidewalk, until the next entrance. I was laughing at myself, thinking, *You take the high road, and I'll take the low road.* . . . I finally came out [of the park], and we finally met. We walked a ways, and he said, *Would you like to have some fun?* I said, *Sure.*

"I didn't know what it was going to be. He was a minister. We went to his apartment on 99th Street, just off Central Park West. It was a walk-up. We had a drink, then he said, *Let's get these things off.* We took our clothes off, and it was beautiful. He asked if I wanted to fuck him, and I said, *Sure.* I didn't know that was possible, but I did. He wanted to do me, and that kind of scared me, because I had heard all about disease and I didn't want disease there. . . . But it was fabulous. He gave me his phone number and his name. I went back [to campus]. I went to confession the next morning, and I tore up the address. But within a matter of a week I wanted to go back, but I never saw him again. I thought of him many, many times. Remember, he was a minister, and he didn't have any hang-ups about it. I thought that was kind of a blessing, for me. I went back to being super-Catholic. I said I was never going to do that again," although Paul stopped confessing his sins.

"I was struggling with my attraction to men, and it was getting stronger and stronger. In my junior year, I roomed with a guy whom I was close to in love with. I didn't feel a sexual attraction to him. He was a premed student. He was also the only black on campus at the time."

In addition to his attraction to the roommate, and despite his wanting to keep his feelings and attractions hidden from others, by the end of his college years Paul associated with other students who shared his attractions. "There were another couple of students that I hung out with, one of whom was certain I was gay, and he was trying to find out by introducing me on campus to different friends of his who were gay. The funny thing, [those] he introduced to me, to whom I really felt attracted to, [my friend] whisked me away from. Had he left me with that one, I probably would have succumbed, but he didn't pick up that I had any interest in that particular guy. I look back on it with humor, because he was trying so desperately to look for clues and I was not going to let on at all that I had any interest in that regard. But with this guy, I could do it with this one. We only stayed at that guy's apartment for a half-hour or an hour; we had to stop off for some reason. This seems like a century ago now, but that memory comes back. Bryce never knew for a fact that I was gay during my college years. [But] He had a conviction, and he was bound and determined that I was going to reveal it to him."

Later College. Paul's attempts to hide his actions while simultaneously exploring them also affected the life of one faculty member. "One of the professors that a number of the other students hung around with was a closet gay who [felt] really guilty. He got interested in me, and I was in a kind of love-hate relationship [with him]. He was trying to seduce me, and I was trying to seduce him." When Paul succeeded in his seduction, he went to the campus administration, claiming that the professor had attempted the action improperly; in part this action was to show, to himself and to others on campus, that Paul was not homosexual. "But they [the administration] turned me over to a psychology professor who wisely wondered aloud with me if there was anything that would point me in that direction. I denied it at the time. The teacher resigned and went to another college. . . . I denied [being sexually attracted to men] to myself, and really tried to punish anybody that would try to bring it out."

Paul, too, felt the ascendency of heterosexuality as a powerful influence upon his self-identity. "There was nothing to remotely suggest at the time I was in school that homosexuality would be accepted. Everybody was in the closet, although there were a few guys that you knew probably were [homosexual]. But the atmosphere was so repressive that one would only reveal himself to someone whom he thought was fairly safe."

Bob

Adolescence. Bob's family were upper-middle class residents, first in suburban Boston and then later urban Chicago. "My home life was pretty typical: Professional father, homemaker mother, two siblings, a dog. . . . Higher education was not an option; you knew you were going to college."

While Bob sensed he was different from his peers, those feelings had not manifested into a sensibility that included not being heterosexual. "I did not really define my sexual orientation when I started college, although I knew that I had interesting/affectional feelings toward men. It was expressed in ways that, if I were to see a magazine with a man on it, it would do something to me. It would excite me, both [physiologically and emotionally]. There were visual images that came into my life that told me that was what I was interested in. I was drawn to it."

Early College. In 1956, Bob matriculated to Hanover College, a private, Presbyterian-affiliated institution in southern Indiana. "I went to a church-related, residential, isolated campus, so we never left the grounds of the campus." Although he majored in psychology and sociology, fields in which he might have encountered such concepts to describe those feelings in his own life, Bob had "[n]o terminology whatsoever. The terminology when I was growing up for gay men was *homo*. And you wanted to avoid that terminology like the plague, 'cause that was very negative. I knew that it meant *homosexuality*; I didn't fully understand what homosexuality was. I didn't connect it to me. It was something else, out there, that was weird and different."

Bob joined a fraternity, which allowed him an outlet for homo-expressiveness and homo-socialization. His was a "[v]ery homoerotic fraternity experience. You have a house full of late adolescents with raging hormones, and you have bonding going on. The fraternities then, and today, are actually real strong places where gay men are able to express their feelings about their homosexuality. I think that they do a great deal of service, on the one hand, to people like me, in order to understand that those feelings are real. On the other hand, the negative part is they judge them. But I've found that the fraternity world still today is a breeding ground for gay men to express themselves.

"I was on a campus where, socially, [pledging] was the correct thing to do. My father had been a leader in the fraternity. It was a family history thing; it was a no-brainer. Once I was there and enjoying the company of these hunky guys, it was great," although it was non-sexual, at least in terms of physical contact.

Many of his fraternity experiences demonstrate clearly homo-expressions very close to the surface of what was going on yet never mentioned outright. Such homoerotic overtones, however, were obvious to Bob in retrospect. "There's no question to me that some of the experiences in the fraternity, some of the rituals, some of the silly adolescent games that are played, have lots of sexual symbolism to them. I think that's because it's the late adolescent who's planning it all and has been planning it over the years. Even the leaders of the fraternity, in their sixties and seventies, are late adolescents. We had to wear eggs in our underwear and dowel rods down our pants. You can make sexual symbolism out of all that. I didn't at the time, but as I look back on it, there was an undercurrent of sexuality." For Bob, and as we will see in later narratives, other non-heterosexuals male collegians, fraternities were a form of safe space to engage in homo-social and homo-expressive activities yet not necessarily "be" homosexual.

In addition to his fraternity service, Bob became a campus leader; the non-heterosexual attractions he felt in the fraternity he kept hidden. "I was active on campus. I was involved in a young Christian group, [in] residence hall management and leadership, [as an] officer in the fraternity, [and] on the campus social recreation committee. [My experience] was very traditional. I did date women and thought I was—and tried to perform as—a heterosexual male in that environment. I pictured myself finding my mate on the college campus; we would be married, and live in happiness. I was very traditional. All the women I dated were sorority women, [or have] a connection to the greek community somehow."

Despite his cover of normality, Bob began to sense his homoerotic attractions were not experienced by everyone. "I wasn't out or open with anyone except starting to be with myself, and trying to do deal with that. When I was a junior I made an appointment with a school psychiatrist, through the health service, on a Wednesday afternoon, to go and talk about these feelings. I went in and started talking about them. And he threw me out of his office. He said to me, *That's the dirtiest, most awful thing I've ever heard. You're going to hell. Get out of here. I don't want to talk about it.* It made me feel terrible, but a peer of mine saved my life, because I went back to my residence and he [the friend] was there.

"I was obviously disturbed, so I had to tell him the story. He was just wonderful. He called me a year or so ago and reminded me of that incident. I had forgotten all about it, I had repressed it so much. He knew more about the incident than I did. He told me what I told him [then]; he remembered in great detail what the psychiatrist said, what he was wearing, because he found it to be so abhorrent [for] a professional person. But that was in the late '50s."

The friend's response was "very accepting, very supportive. He was furious [at the psychiatrist] and extremely supportive. He said, *This is not a problem. You don't worry about it. That's who you are or what you are, or whatever.* It didn't affect our relationship. He was a fraternity brother, but I had known him before we had joined the fraternity. I must have known him since I was a freshman. He was a very queer person himself: he was physically tall, gangly, homely, from rural Ohio. We had absolutely nothing in common. I think I latched onto him because we were both very different . . . a little bit outcast, in a sense. But he was a very secure human being, emotionally. He was right there for me."

Later College. Bob's feelings for other men were also "right there," which he continued to recognize more fully and to hide as well. "When I was a senior, I became very close to the dean of men. In fact, I was in love with the man. I knew something was going on. I had very strong feelings, like the mentor/mentee [relationship] and I was his mentee. I never felt sexual toward him, except he was a big guy. Well, I guess I did; I must have had some sexual feelings toward him. [But] there was no way to act on them, no. How could I act on them without getting my head blown off or something? I didn't know; I wouldn't know how to do that."

Bob built upon his undergraduate campus service by deciding to pursue a master's degree in student affairs administration in higher education at Indiana University. He still continued to hide his sexuality. His perspectives as both a student and a campus administrator illuminated what could have happened had he been found out. "I was at Indiana University between 1960 and 1962. If a student were found to be having a sexual act with another student, there would be disciplinary hearings. The sanctions would probably be what we called *social probation* at the time. It probably would be part of the permanent record. There's the transcript; [and then] there are other records that had been kept over the years, about social behavior. They're not governed by law as much as the transcript is." Those documents were just as influential upon student lives, though. "If students wanted a letter of recommendation, they usually asked someone in student affairs administration for it. You'd look in the file and if there were these problems, you'd write it one way. That's changed today; the laws have come to cover that, too. You have to be real careful about that [now], fortunately."

Bob's deception was successful and extended to his participation in a clandestine sting operation against IU students and faculty. "When I was in graduate school, in the early 60s, there was rumored [to be] a gay male group that was forming, underground. I was on the residence hall staff, and we were ordered [to] go out one night, in our cars, trying to find these people, to turn them in to the administration. I was with some fairly high[-ranking] administrators at Indiana University, at midnight, in Bloomington, following cars here and these people there. We heard this group was meeting somewhere in Bloomington; we weren't sure if it were on or off the campus, [but] we thought it was off the campus.

"We had a couple of key suspects. We'd watch for them. The phone would ring, and you'd get in your car and follow. *I'm here, we're going there, we'll meet you over there; come here and pick me up. . . .* It was like a movie. This lasted for about a month, off and on. The key suspects were students. We thought there might be some faculty involved. The stereotype was that there would be some faculty who may be involved in this or getting these guys into this sexual ring. What was the term they were called then? One of the terms was *daisy chains*, where men get together to have sex with men." The undercover attempts at raids and stings made quite an impact upon Bob's graduate education. "It was frightening. It was the most bizarre experience I've ever had. We didn't find a thing; [it] didn't lead anywhere."

None of his colleagues at Indiana University knew that Bob himself could have been listed as one to watch, although he had still not had sex with a man. While he later publicly came out, long after his college days and after establishing himself professionally, Bob felt he was closeted as a student "partly because of denial. All because of denial. I knew when I was [not heterosexual] in late high school and in college, and in graduate school, that I had affectionate feelings toward men, but I didn't connect the word, the community, the ideology [to me] until after graduate school."

Sam

Adolescence. Sam was raised in a Woodville, Ohio, a small town about 260 miles from Toledo. He firmly understood his sexuality as homosexual prior to enrolling in college; indeed he stated his first memories were of homosexual desire. "When I was three years old—that was before World War II, in 1940—my mother put me in bed with my uncle. We had a house that probably should have had about four people in it, and [occasionally] we'd have, like, seventeen. She put me in bed with my uncle because he was up from the hills of Ohio and was staying over with us. This was before he was even drafted in World War II. She put me in bed with him, and I attacked him in the night. I wanted sex with him. I was three years old, and I knew.

"The moment she put me down in that bed, lowering my body with her hands, one on my back and one on my rump, and lowering me into that bed, I knew that I was gay. I didn't know the word gay, didn't know the word *homosexual*, but I knew that's where I belonged. He stopped me. I was in there, going for it. I can remember it as if it were today, and I was three years old. . . . It's my earliest memory: being in bed with my uncle and trying to get in his clothes. Well, my uncle told my mother the next day what had happened. My mother was one of these Nazarene ministers' daughters, and she started in on me. She preached this being wrong, that our family didn't do this, that was not what we did, not what we were supposed to do, and that we were not going to live like dogs. And on and on and on."

Sam learned from this experience, and from others, two important social lessons: sex was not to be talked about, and sex between men was not normal. "We were also told you might have this . . . *feeling* . . . for other men, but when you got married, it would go away. You would outgrow it. But I never outgrew it. It got worse for me." Later, Sam realized that, at least in his family, homosexuality was not so abnormal: "There were nine of us kids, and I'm not the only homosexual in the family."

His homosexual feelings increased, and Sam finally had his opportunity to express them. Unfortunately, the experience lead to further reprobation of his sense and sensibility that would affect his identity through his college years.

"Later on, there was a man in the community who seduced me. Five years later; I was eight. It lasted three years, from eight to eleven. And I loved it. There was no sexual abuse; there was no abuse whatsoever. I knew what I wanted; I knew how to get it; I knew where to go. I knew that I wanted this. Then, after about three years of this going on, I tried to convince another boy to join in. He went home and told his family. And it went all over town, this tiny little town, you know? The man was run out of town, the man that I had the sexual experience with. I stayed, because my parents wouldn't leave. So, after my mother found out I had another homosexual experience, I just stayed in. She just really bore down. It was bad before, but then it was even worse. I had to promise I wouldn't be involved, and I had to listen to her preach. . . . After my mother made me promise not to be a homosexual, I had no contact with any man until two days before I [turned] fifty-eight."

Sam's social life suffered due to the stigma regarding his sexuality. "I went through all those years of [grade and high] school with everybody hating me. They wouldn't invite me to parties. No one wanted to be with me. I was the gay guy that shouldn't be given a chance to be part of anything." But Sam did participate in some school and community activities, including cheerleading in high school. "I still had talent. Do you think I didn't have talent because I was a homosexual? Most homosexuals have talent. I had talent galore!

Early College. In 1955, he enrolled at the University of Indianapolis, majoring in math and chemistry. He lived on campus: "It was [a requirement] at that time, but by the time I graduated it was no longer required." The dorms were where Sam and his friends socialized. "During the week, we met in the dorm rooms. On the weekends, everybody went home. It was a suitcase college. No one stayed there on weekends; it just cleared out. I lived 260 miles from home, and I went every weekend, until the last semester of my junior year, [when] I said, *I'm tired of this*, and I'd stay in town.

"During the week, everybody was there [on campus]. We were not rich; it was not a rich college. Almost everybody there was working their way through college. We helped each other a lot with our problems: lots of jam sessions. Very few people studied together, only when it came to finals. Every night we had dress up night, Monday through Friday. We had family meals where you went to the dining hall (not the cafeteria). That's what promoted the jam sessions; you saw people at dinner, talked to them, and the topics [of conversation, continued later] started then.

"Once in a while, somebody would tell you, *Well, you know Walt Whitman was homosexual*, or would say with disgust, *Well, Leonardo Da Vinci was homo, so was Michelangelo, so was Walt Whitman.* And about the only time you ever heard one of those things was when you were in college. High school students didn't know those things. You got those things sort of fed to you on a personal basis, not on classroom information."

Although Sam still recognized his desires, he did not act upon them. "A lot of men tried me. When I was in college, there were a lot of guys who wanted me. They told me, and they would try things with me. I was kind of popular, especially around exam time; everyone would cram in my room. This one time, I was in my room in my undershorts, and this guy just reached into my pants. He said, *Let's go.* I was very shy; I acted like it didn't happen. Two greek [fraternity] guys invited me out several times in their car, told me they would teach me things. I told them no. I had another who would come to my room, just as often as he could, for three months. I knew what he wanted, but I wasn't going to talk to him about it. He was very familiar, in his touching me, looking at me, longing. He was an older guy. He was always willing to talk to me about sex, wanted to talk to me about sex, and brought the subject up often. He invited me several times to go with him in his car. A car was a very common [come on], back in those days. *Go for a ride.*

"When I was in college, I was an evangelical United Brethren at the time. There were a lot of pre-theology students, pre-ministerial. One of the things I noted about pre-the students is that they are quite active [homosexually]. Lots of gay men in pre-theology. While I was in college at the University of Indianapolis, the come-ons were often for me, not because I had a big dick, but because I had a big chest. My chest was big, and I had big pecs. And the men liked that. They'd see me in the shower, and I'd get lots of proposals. But I never participated, because I was afraid someone would find out. Back when I was eleven, Mom and the whole town found out; that was the fear that was instilled in me from that experience. The man I was with was forced out of town; I was forced into a horrible life, like I was a leper. When I went to college, I could have had a whole bunch of wonderful experiences, a lot of loving, wonderful people. I could have had it all. But I was too afraid to come out. The fear of being found out was overwhelming."

Later College. Despite the fear and the inhibition, Sam continued to experience affections and desires toward men. His homo-affections led him to live with one of his classmates for three years. "When I was a senior, I got a new roommate. I fell in love with him, big time. The thing is, I didn't know he was in love with me. He was a minister's son and definitely was not going to have sex with a man. And here I was, a confirmed person who was not going to have sex. And we were madly in love with one another, beyond mention. Anyway, it became a codependent situation, and we just battled, fought like banshees, all though our senior year and two more years after that, teaching together. Finally, we just had to call it quits. We broke up in '64, on Memorial Day."

During those years, "We never touched each other. I didn't know he was in love with me until years later. I didn't hear from him, and he didn't hear from me. Then, September 30, 1981, his brother called me and told me he had died. He had died of AIDS. That's when I figured out what happened back there: we were madly in love with one another, but neither one of us could do anything about it. Our minds wouldn't let us. And we lived together! We slept in the same bed! We were just so wanting one another so badly, and not partaking.

"So I hid, in my early years until the time I got out of college, I hid behind religion. Then I got married, and I hid behind that. But I was always homosexual. I couldn't walk up to a mirror and say, *You're homosexual*. But I knew in my mind—every sexual experience I had with my wife, I could not perform without having some kind of fantasy about a man.

"I had a terrible marriage, a horrible marriage. The reason I came out was that I needed some love and affection. I hadn't had any for years. I went to a porno shop where they had a theater. I watched the men on the screen, and I watched the men in the room. I had to convince myself that this stuff was really going on. Two days before my fifty-eighth birthday, it was smorgasbord time. It was a wild party for me. And it was fun."

Looking back upon his college experiences, Sam wishes he had not been closeted during college and the ensuing years until he came out. "When my group came along in high school, in the early '50s, things were starting [to change]. After World War II, things were starting to loosen up. Most of the country started feeling relief. You felt a little happier in your life. You didn't feel so contained and restricted on your options. When I graduated from high school, there were no options. There were three things you could do: You could get married, you go to college, or you could get drafted. If you got a job, you were going to be drafted; it didn't make any difference. In 1955, what I should have done was not go to college. I would not have gone to college if I knew then what I know today. If I had to do it all over again, I'd go right to that draft board on September 6, 1955, and I would say to question 18, *Do you have any latent homosexual tendencies?* I would say, *Yes! They're blatant!*"

Rick

Early College. Rick left his parents' home in South Pasadena, California, in September of 1958, to enroll in Pomona College. His parents had met while at Pomona, and moved to South Pasadena in 1948. "I had come from an upper-middle class family. I was reasonably sheltered. I certainly did not come from a deeply religious or morally straight family. On the contrary, my family were casual churchgoers, if that. They raised us to be pretty independent. I would say I was a pretty serious kid.

"My recollection of [myself] is someone who was withdrawn, not real frightened but not sure of himself. But the feedback I've gotten . . . is that's not how I came off at all. [Others] remember me as someone who was much more socially aggressive than I ever thought I was. For example, when I was in college, a freshman, I sort of had the mistaken understanding that if you got into college, you didn't have to do anything else. So I played a lot of bridge my first year in college, had a lot of fun. I loved being a freshman in college and got terrible grades as a consequence. I didn't almost flunk out, but I had to have a real serious talk with myself and kind of reorient myself as to where I was and what I was going to do. The problem, for me, was that I was an immature eighteen-year-old."

Rick's year's at Pomona conformed to the "standard" college study experience of the 1950s. "I lived on campus, in standard housing, all four years. Mostly [I spent time] in small eateries in Claremont. We spent a good deal of time on campus. There were the standard beer-bust places, which I didn't go to a lot, but there were those places as well. When I was in school, I was reasonably social inside the dorm, but I didn't do a lot of outside socializing. I didn't do a lot of 'hanging around' with friends."

This continued a pattern from Rick's high school experience. "My years in high school, I didn't do a lot of socializing. I wouldn't say I was a loner, but I never had a lot of self-confidence. Therefore, I did not put myself in the way of other people. I wouldn't say I was shy and withdrawn, but I would say I was careful. I suspect that comes from [my] orientation and other things. I've always had a sense that I was different. I went to college as kind of a callow, inexperienced, not very worldly fellow. I was the kind of kid that never did what the crowd did. It's funny. I always had a sense of right and wrong for [myself]. I don't really think that has anything to be with being gay; it's just the sort of person I am. . . . [But] I felt limited by who I was."

That self-perceived limitation caused Rick both to hide his sexuality and to retreat socially from others. "Did my sexual orientation affect [my self-confidence and college performance]? I suppose so, looking back. I didn't think so at the time, but I think in all candor, I was always so afraid that someone would find out, that I never really wanted to reveal my whole persona, sit down and chat with somebody about it. I was just having to learn to deal with that as well. Probably the worst thing you could be, when I was in college, was gay. It was frowned upon. It was barely talked about, if it were talked about at all. The gay man of that time was a Clifton Webb-type—a fussy interior decorator or hair dresser. We didn't have a benchmark by which to go from."

Rick had felt the stifling effects of normative social values before he entered college. "I had experienced some teasing and hazing in high school, but it was very hurtful and you had no where to go. . . . Kids and children were just as cruel in the 1950s as they were in the '60s, '70s, '80s, and '90s. If they find you are different, they go after you mercilessly; you're made to feel different, and you hurt inside. So my defense was, I just didn't reveal a whole lot."

Like many other closeted students, Rick had sexual contact with other males prior to college. "I had a couple of gay experiences when I was in high school, with friends who were also in high school. Not a serious thing, but just a physical kind of thing, just an exchange of physical-ness. I had that, but when I went to college, I put that away in a locked chest. I never looked, I never did anything. Now, if the opportunity had come up, I might have, but I was very careful."

Later College. That care extended to denial of his feelings as well as further sexual encounters. "I did not go looking for it. The way it came up in high school was, I was not the aggressor; someone else was. I was the reactor, and that was fine. Since then, the roles have become reversed, and I have become more socially aggressive than they have. [But] It never presented itself in college."

Rick viewed his sexuality—and consequently, his identity—as a "problem" that "normal" students did not have. "This sounds so naive, but when you're young and you have this mystery wrapped up inside of you, you think you're the only one who has this problem. But . . . there were others who had it, too. They all kept it quite under wraps. At least where I went to school. I've found out since there were a whole lot of gay people at Pomona College that I didn't know were gay. When I was growing up, being gay was *sub rosa*. I think I knew I was gay, I suspect, at nine or ten years old. I always knew what I was, but I put this away in a closet. I am a typical closeted gay man. What I *didn't* do is important. I never married because of that. I did not want to hurt someone else because I couldn't face up to who I was. Definitely, I had an identity." But that identity was of a person divorced from his senses of emotion and desire.

"What [this repression] led to was a period of time of 20 years when I was closeted, doing the things that closeted men do. That's probably the reason I'm still alive today. In the 1970s, when this all came out, I was in my thirties. It was what I call *the dark decade*: I did nothing, nothing! I did not come out—

well, I was out to myself; I knew what I was. But I did not act upon it until 1983."

Juan

Early College. Juan attended the University of the Pacific, in Stockton, California, between 1984 and 1988. "My school was so conservative. I was a closeted Democrat at my school, because my school was so Republican, so white, and so wealthy. There were no gay students that I was aware of on campus. [But] it was a comfortable setting: my parents were immigrants, and I was raised in a northern white suburb of Sacramento, so it wasn't far off from what I was used to dealing with in high school."

Juan perceived his sexual difference prior to moving to Stockton. "I knew I was attracted to men. [Nevertheless,] I considered myself straight, or heterosexual, but I knew those feelings were there. I had never acted on the feelings in high school, but I knew subconsciously that they were there."

Like other former students I spoke with, Juan found another, more accepted climate on campus to enjoy being with men. "I joined a fraternity. I think I joined because I wanted the social outlets of it. It was a small private school; there wasn't a lot to do in Stockton; a lot of my friends had gone greek. So I joined for the social aspects of it. Feeling different, as a man of color on a predominantly white campus, it was a way to fit in. I felt odd anyway, being Mexican: socioeconomically and ethnically, I wasn't a part of the campus. To be greek kind of allowed me to fit in. The irony of it, though, is how I really am as an individual. I'm not greek, in that I don't like to be told what to do. I consider myself a leader, but when it comes to someone putting me through an initiation and hell week, I'm not one to put up with that kind of stuff."

Being in the fraternity was both an emotional outlet for, and an effective cover of, his homosexual senses. "Over the years I've come to realize that I joined the greek system to prove to myself I wasn't gay. My being a fraternity member would alleviate anyone's doubts, if they thought I was gay. I think it helped me in the quest to find the perfect woman, because I could date sorority women. I just kept thinking I hadn't met the right woman. Maybe I knew I had attractions to men, but in my mind I thought I just hadn't met the right woman. I also had not had any physical encounters with any men, at that point, so I didn't have that to say, *Well, I like that, that's great.* I was making that conclusion not based on experience with men, but based on my desire to want to fit in and be with a woman."

Though he dated women, Juan's striving for a perfect union precluded serious relations with them. "When I look at relationships with any of my girlfriends I had in college, it just never worked out. I remember breaking up with one of my girlfriends because of my fraternity. She said, *They're more important to you than I am.* I replied, *Yeah, they are.* I think that was where I was getting my relationship needs; I was getting that camaraderie. The fraternity was the first place where, because I wasn't sexually active, I could have the closest thing to male companionship, the camaraderie. But not dealing with those issues of, say, where two men are going together to the theater and have to have a sit across [a seat between them]. There have been a number of men who've come out since we've graduated, of the men I knew when I was active."

Later College. The fraternity proved a source of conjugal companionship as well as friendship. "My first gay encounter was with one of my fraternity brothers. It happened my senior year in college, New Year's Eve. A bunch of us had come back to the fraternity house to spend New Year's. There was another guy in the house who was my year. We were adversaries in that we had different views on how the house should be run, on how the fraternity should do different things. We never agreed on things. He was very staunchly 'Mr. Republican.' He and I didn't run in the same circles in the house.

"We were having a party. It was New Year's [Eve], probably 1:30 or 2:00 in the morning. There were six of us in a room, just talking and drinking. Slowly, people started leaving. [Finally] Ned and I were just hanging out, talking, lamenting about our senior year, our graduating. You know, the stuff you do when you're drinking. It got to the point—I don't know, it was just very dreamlike. I remember us talking and kind of getting very somber and melancholy about the fact that we were graduating and it was our last semester. It was all going to be over. I don't know if it's that we inched closer to each other, but we just kind of knew that there was this attraction. We started kissing. I still remember. It was great; it was like, *Oh, my gosh.* I wasn't scared; we weren't nervous. We stayed together that night. I got up early the next morning, because it was his room. We were in his roommate's bed, which is kind of funny. I snuck out and went back to my room. It's one of those [experiences] where you wake up and you think, *Okay, what just happened?* And we never talked about it. It was this awkwardness between us.

"Two weeks after New Year's, a bunch of us had planned to go skiing. We went up to Oregon, to the house of one of our fraternity brothers. There were probably six or eight of us. Ned and I had not talked about it and had gone our separate ways. He and I ended up together, sharing a sofa bed in the living room. We were intimate that night again. No talking about it; it just happened. I think it happened a couple of more times, during the remainder of that year. It was always late at night, at a party. It was almost like we would search each other out. We had to find someplace to go, someplace we wouldn't get caught. We had to actively make it work."

These furtive encounters were "[a]ll related to alcohol; alcohol was always involved. We never really talked about it. It just happened, then we moved on and continued our distance as we always did, because we didn't hang out in the same circles. If I had wanted to spend more time with him or make it more, I had a fear, because we didn't hang out in the house together, so why would we suddenly be hanging out together? In some ways I did [want to spend more time with him], because I wanted to explore this more, but I also didn't want to, because I didn't want other people in the house to think something was weird. It was a purely physical relationship; he was a fuck buddy. He drove me crazy from day to day.

"I ran into him, years later. He became a lawyer and was working in Sacramento. We got together for dinner and were catching up. He asked me how I was doing; I said I was dating somebody and things were going well. I asked how he was doing, and he said he wasn't dating anyone. I said, *You know, Ned, everyone has to deal with it in their own way, in their own time frame, so maybe someday you can be open about who you really are.* He didn't comment on it."

The advent of sex with men, during his senior year, placed new meanings upon Juan's previous feelings, fostering the beginnings of a non-heterosexual sensibility. "I think [the experience with Ned] was an awakening for me. It opened up something inside of me that I had been trying to suppress for so long. I think, for me, there were so many self-esteem issues related to my ethnicity. I was struggling so hard to be accepted, because I always felt different. It's funny, when I look at my grade school pictures: all blond kids, and then there's me. And then to throw the sexuality on top of that, to feel doubly ugly, doubly unattractive. For me to fit in with society, my thought was I had to find that right woman. Even though that fire had been lit, the flood gates opened" at the end of Juan's senior year.

That insight, followed by immediate repudiation, mirrored prior advice from another non-heterosexual man. "My older brother had a good friend in college who was gay. I knew that, for some reason. I don't know why I knew that, but every time he came over to visit, I thought he was gay. It was subconscious. This was in high school. He came over one time, and my brother went outside. He said, *Can I talk to you? Do you think you're gay?* I said I didn't know. He told me, *You don't want to be gay. It's, like, the worst thing. You don't want to do it.* It was really hard for him to be gay, horrible. I think that pushed me back, so even when I had met Ned and that thing happened, I still didn't have a positive role model who was comfortably out. [Later] when I was home from college, he encouraged me to be straight. One time I was wearing my Greek letters, and he said, *You joined a fraternity. Good, I'm so proud of you, I'm so happy for you. I don't want you to go through what I had to go through.*"

Post College. By the end of college, Juan "had tasted the fruit, and it was like, *Okay!* But there was just no way I could do it. I didn't come out until graduate school, until 1991. After college I moved to the Bay area with three of my fraternity brothers. Four of us were sharing a two-bedroom apartment, and trying to make ends meet, because we were all working entry-level jobs, working in the city for the first time. So many people from my college just go to the Bay area after college; that's where everyone moves. All of our friends were there. We would go out on the weekends. Two of my roommates were dating women we went to school with, so they were over all the time. There is a U of P alumni network in the Bay area, and I just went right into that network and all that entailed. That year after college just kind of continued college life, only we were adults and we were working. I wanted to explore, because by that time I had had [more] encounters with other men.

"People have said to me, *You lived in San Francisco and you never explored?* I didn't even know where the Castro was. I didn't even know where to begin looking. I just knew it was there, somewhere. But I would never have the opportunity to say to someone, *I think I'm gay; let's go check out these bars.* I would have loved to been able to figure it out, but . . . [I] was still lamenting over college life and how much fun it was. Now I wasn't in college, but we were still replicating our [collegiate] lives. My life in college didn't include that, and so it didn't include it afterwards. I think if I had moved to a city where I didn't know a lot of people, and I had a different roommate or was living on my own, maybe I would have had [been able] to take the risk and go find it, but no, I didn't do anything."

Juan felt unable to escape the constraints of his identity—as a collegiate student, as a man of Mexican descent, as someone who should find the right woman—until he was able to leave both his friends and the state. "I came out in graduate school. It was good. I think I knew I wanted to come out, I think I knew I needed to. All the grad schools I looked at were out of state. I had to leave California. I was tired of having U of P all around me, my friends all around me. I knew I had to go elsewhere. I enjoyed it because no one knew me. I didn't have to be something that I [wasn't]. No one had these expectations of me. I got to introduce myself, and people got to get to know me as a brand-new person. I knew I needed to deal with my sexuality [in graduate school]. I came out in a very supportive program, a program for higher ed. I didn't come out until my second year; the first year I had to test the waters, to figure out how comfortable [I could be] with me."

Changes in the larger culture also empowered Juan to stop perpetuating a false identity. Those changes were most noticeable in the late 1980s and early 1990s, when he was working on his master's degree, evident by his increased inclusion of, and attention to, non-heterosexual experiences. "I was struggling and striving for the identity. I would watch the [television] talk shows, and they were always dealing with the drag queens, the male prostitutes, and all that. I remember watching *Oprah*, and they just had everyday individuals who were teachers, lawyers, couples. None of them were drug-addicted. They were the role models I was looking for. And I thought, *Finally, there is someone I can identify with."*

For Juan, his undergraduate years were "a wonderful experience; [I] loved college. For the time that I was there, it was a good place for me and who I was at that time. [It] didn't help me with my sexuality, didn't help me with my identity development—if anything, I think it pushed me further back. I didn't expect [college would help me with my personal identity]. I don't see the '80s as a time of identity development. It was the *me* generation, and I just remember wanting to make money, to have money, to drive fancy cars. I didn't see it as a way to deal with my identity."

Reflections on Homosexuals and the Closet

Although locale and era affected non-heterosexual collegians' experiences and senses (cf., Chauncey, 1994; Fellows, 1996; Howard, 1999; Sears, 1997), the narratives of the men in this chapter show that the non-heterosexual identity types of homosexual and closeted were prevalent across time and geographic region during the last half of the twentieth century in the United States. While variations might exist between the details of individual students' experiences (expulsion, or fear of it, for instance, was neither universal nor unusual among these students; some, but not all, homosexual students had other friends who so identified), the sensibilities of these students—how they comprehended and ascribed meaning to their experiences and senses—were consistent. The students realized that their sexual feelings and activities set them apart from heterosexuals. They knew they were different and felt that the social prohibitions against that particular form of difference required discreet, or secretive, behavior and deployment of their identity.

The distinction of the homosexual and closeted types is that both were formed in direct relation to heterosexuality as well as the contexts of individual sexuality—both the physical and the emotional attachments for other males. They did not so much identify with other non-heterosexuals as much as in opposition to the (physical) sexual aspects of heterosexuality. These desires were contextualized within medical or religious models that subjugated the actions and actors as abhorrent and inferior to heterosexuality. Whereas a heterosexual might define himself in terms of the dominant, binary master category (heterosexual or homosexual), because of the objects and aims of his sexual attraction, that definition was not formed in opposition to the norm; it was the norm. For non-heterosexuals, though, new meanings were created to understand their experiences that did not fit into the normative category. Those who identified as homosexual sometimes tried to find others whose attachments were also evident, if quietly so; those who chose to live within the relative safety of the closet did their best to leave their attachments there whenever they ventured into public spheres, although closet collegians felt not quite "themselves" as they did so.

If closeted men could compartmentalize their lives, keep their sexuality separate from their social milieus, homosexual men integrated the two just a bit more. While their peers in the closet were afraid someone would discover their personal secret, homosexual collegians feared the revelation of both their private (sexual) and public (social) lives. Guilt by association was just as damning and damaging as actual discovery of breaking social or judicial norms, as the experiences relayed by both Walter and Bob show.

The existing models of identity development represent the sensibilities of the students. Gay identity theories would posit the identities as un- or underdeveloped: integration of identity into a publicly acknowledged and deployed identity, capable of being so despite public approbation, is the proposed end result of those models. Neither the homosexual nor closeted students could achieve those ends, given their understandings of their collegiate cultures, and in light of their sensibilities about being non-heterosexual. These students, particularly the closeted types, probably would not be considered as advanced along the stages of student identity development, for their sexual identities were compartmentalized and separate from their public identities as students (more so even than were those of homosexual-type students). In this sense, these students were deviants from yet another norm, one of theoretical analysis.

To understand these students' lives and self concepts only in terms of deviance, however, ignores the paradox of *men* and *de* in their lives. While homosexual and closeted students often considered themselves deviant—as the tropes of conceptualizing sexuality at the time promoted—these students also identified with others. They found other individuals with whom to have sex, with whom to socialize (either in bars in large urban areas or in private homes in smaller towns), even with whom to live. But, how individual men in these types displayed or deployed aspects of their sexual identity—and their senses of what and why they were doing so—differentiated them from the other types of non-heterosexuals within the typology.

The litmus test of "homosexual," whether closeted or open, was not the sexual activity, but how and what the man thought of the activity (before and after the deed), the sensibilities of opposition to heterosexuality. The social meaning ascribed to that clinical definition was clear in the image of what such a person would be, or be like; as Rick noted, the homosexual "of that time was a Clifton Webb-type—a fussy interior decorator or hair dresser." When revealed, either by others in the case of Walter or the self-realization experienced by Duchess, one's being homosexual caused one to be removed from the social settings of those considered "normal."

This exodus from campus and/or community, from either expulsion or choice, was a very real threat to homosexual students' participation in and development during college. As the narratives of the next chapter demonstrate, however, those students considered apart from the heterosexual norm did not always accept the expulsion; particularly as societal mores changed, so too the self-definitions and sensibilities of non-heterosexual males transformed, and non-heterosexual students found new ways to voice and to deploy their different identities on U.S. campuses.

CHAPTER 4

From the Margins to the Ivory Tower: Gay and Queer Students

Although some students continued to understand their identities as closeted or homosexual, by the 1960s, non-heterosexual collegians identified themselves in opposition to those identities; these collegians chaffed at what they viewed as religious and medical models of pathology and/or abnormality. During the late 1960s and early 1970s, countercultural movements in the United States led non-heterosexual students to reexamine concepts of gender, sexuality, and the norms of the dominant society. Such changes fostered opportunities and contexts to position themselves alongside others who questioned the norms, as well as against the norm of heterosexuality; no longer was the marker of identification based solely upon an individual's sexuality (almost exclusively furtive and nonsanctioned) but also by social interaction and political goals.

These *gay* collegians argued for inclusion and participation within campuses across the country. Unlike homosexual and closeted students who often isolated themselves from campus connections with other non-heterosexuals, gay students created structures and opportunities for campus activities to match—or, at least, to emulate—the sanctioned enterprises of their heterosexual peers. Indeed, gay students perceived and promoted their identities more publicly than the homosexual type of student. If homosexuality were, in the words of Oscar Wilde, the "love that dare not speak its name," then gay was the identity that spoke up. While the homosexual and (to an even greater extent) closeted students hid on campus, one motto of this era of social change was "Gay is good" (Jay, 1999; Thompson, 1994; Witt, Thomas, and Marcus, 1995)—or certainly at least equitable to *straight* in concept, if not in public opinion.

By (at least) the late 1980s, another type of student began to conceive of his identity differently still. "Queer" students juxtaposed their feelings and experiences against not only the heterosexual norm but also the gay (and/or homosexual) norms. Queer collegians were not content with duplicating institutional values and components, nor with mere inclusion in what they often viewed as a flawed and suppressive system of controls of sexuality and identity. If gay students wished for the freedom to participate in social and campus activities (whether as representatives, or within separate but equal spaces and places), queer students sought to disrupt the operations of those functions as (usually unquestioned) components of a self-replicating and subjugating dominant, heterosexual society. While closeted students could not handle being seen with other non-heterosexuals, queer students organized public "kiss-ins" on campuses. While gay students found a voice within society, queer students shouted chants indicating their difference: instead of asking for validation ("gay is good") and equal rights, queer students converged upon malls and proclaimed "We're here, we're queer, and we're not going shopping" (cf. Browning, 1993; Duggan, 1992, 1995c), despite—and to spite—the crowd.

Such extensive changes in identification, both individual and collective, are demonstrated within the narratives of collegians classified as gay and queer. In the previous chapter, I discussed homosexual and closeted students, for whom sexuality was on the one hand a defining force upon their identity, and on the other, a "private, personal" matter. In this chapter, I depict students whose sexual identity was as much a public and collective affair as were the social elements of identity construction. I first present respondents who fall within the gay identity type: four representative narratives of students whose experiences and/or ideations of their sexual orientation place them squarely within that classification. Next, I offer three narratives of queer students, whose deployment of their identity was a disrupting factor of institutional functions and precepts and additionally formed directly in opposition to the identities that represented new normative values and identities (gay and homosexual), as well in opposition to the traditional normative presumption (heterosexual).

"Gay Is Good": Visible Students on Campus

By the late 1960s and early 1970s, a new identity for non-heterosexual men began to emerge, both on campus and in the broader society: "gay." Gay students understood their identity as a social one, not one constructed in medical models of pathology (cf., Greenberg, 1988; Katz, 1995). Consequently, their interactions with peers and institutions differed from those of homosexual or closeted collegians. Gay students' ideology was two-fold: first, sexuality—in all of its permeations, including those not considered "normal"—was viewed as a more central (and visible) part of social life and thus far more "normal" than previously understood. Second, just as "other" sexualities were to be included in the spectrum of everyday life, so too should gays be a part of regular social functions, whether as a part of the existing system—university governance, the curriculum, campus statements and missions—or separate (yet equal) functions that mirrored heterosexual (or "straight") functions—student organizations and gay dances being the two most obvious.

These ideas brought larger numbers of non-heterosexual men to participate in public life on campus. Four respondents fitting into the gay type attended colleges from the 1960s through the 1990s; their stories display ways such gay students believed in their equality and how their differences from heterosexual students were viewed primarily as with whom they socialized and had sex.

James

Adolescence. As a teen, James was a Quaker attending a predominantly Jewish school in a different neighborhood from his own. "I didn't feel I fit in in junior high school, because I wasn't good at sports. I went to an all-male public high school in Baltimore, which was very unusual. It was a [academic] tracked environment, and I was on the highest level track. It was a very rigorous academic program. And even though I wasn't in a very macho environment, because we didn't even have gym or sports in high school, it was a very insular environment, with a lot of late adolescent male teasing." Consequently, he felt isolated because of his religion, his place of residence, and his masculinity. "In an all-male environment, I did not have interaction with girls, which was important in terms of developing certain kinds of friendships and ways to interact positively. I felt very isolated because most of the kids in my class were Jewish, lived in a different neighborhood, and had networks of friends I didn't have."

James perceived another distinction from his classmates: his sexual feelings. "I also knew I had these [non-heterosexual] desires I didn't know what to do with. I had a girlfriend, but I wasn't sexually desirous. It wasn't special. I always felt I was trying to be something I wasn't. And because I was at an all-male high school, my best friend (who still is my best friend) was my date to the junior and senior proms."

James cultivated a life apart from school that was more important to him than his academic life. "The young Quaker youth group was very important. Also, I did theater, from age eight to fifteen, in Baltimore. That was very important to me, because I knew subconsciously that I had homoerotic desires and that I was different. I didn't know how to deal with that. The theater group was a community or a family or a connection that made me feel very loved." But by his high school years, James felt compelled to quit performing with the group, "because I didn't want to become a homosexual. All of the older people in the group seemed to be homosexuals. At the time, [my] logic was, if I didn't become an actor, I wouldn't become a homosexual. Therefore, I stopped being an actor. I thought all male actors were homosexuals."

The fear of being associated with, or becoming, a homosexual "was not something I ever articulated, but I knew at the time, and can see clearly back there, that was what I was thinking. I couldn't name it, because naming it would associate me with it. But it was a fear. I felt that I was effeminate, and it seemed to me that that was what homosexuals were, or the older men [in the theater group were], to a certain extent. But the fear was more that this would be this horrible, terrible life that I would live. The image was older men in public bathrooms. The fear was dirty old men who were alone, isolated, and whom everyone hates."

This emotion was coupled with James's understanding of his attraction to other males. "*Life* magazine had a very important article, and I remember reading that when I was in junior high school. I don't know if I've reconstructed this memory from the past; I have to check to see when it came out, to see if my dates are even right. But what I remember is, I saw that, and they talked about men in tight white pants and cashmere sweaters. And I went, *This is me, and I don't want to be that.* I just did not want to be that, but I knew that I was. I knew very young that I was [not heterosexual]. I have a journal in which I talked about the secret that I had, but I wouldn't talk more about that. In fact, I was afraid that even if I wrote that down, it would be revelatory. But I knew I was attracted to guys, in some way. . . . I thought it was something I could somehow overcome."

Early College. Part of James's plan to conquer his attraction to men revolved around attending a coeducational college that he felt could both support his faith and suppress his desires. "I went to Earlham College, which was a small, Quaker, liberal arts college in Richmond, Indiana. I went there from 1968 to 1972, [and] majored in political science. I really wanted to go to a small liberal arts college. I was raised a Quaker, and this was a Quaker school; that was important to me. I think there were about 1,000 students in the college, perhaps 1,200. It was very intimate, family- and community-oriented. I went to school early; I was sixteen, and finished when I was twenty."

Despite his intent to overcome his sexuality, James was clear of his sexual identity when he arrived on campus. "I thought of myself as homosexual. This was my first year. I was attracted to my roommate. I was attracted to a lot of guys, and I just didn't know how to deal with it. I would masturbate, think of them, and then feel very guilty and very bad. And I had a girlfriend. That was a way of maybe affirming that I wasn't [homosexual]. My girlfriend was very good to me. She was Catholic, and she presented to me this notion that we couldn't go all the way. She used to stay over in my room. So we would not have direct intercourse; I don't remember that I really came that much with her. But really, I let that situation be that way; that was just fine.

"Finally, a woman on campus seduced me. She just took me up to her room on a Sunday afternoon and had sex with me. I came quickly. She actually was a good lover. And then, my girlfriend went off to Africa on a foreign exchange program and got back together with her old boyfriend. I was devastated. So I preceded to have another girlfriend, who was my most important friend/girlfriend for several years after that. But by that time I had already had sex with guys."

Sexual activity with other males was not entirely new to James. "I had sex with my best friend when I was a kid, and my brother, but I was twelve or thirteen. That was very clandestine. And then nothing. The first [adult] time was in January of 1970, where I ended up in the same bed with some guy at a Quaker conference. I got very excited, initiated something with him, then came and totally freaked out. I wouldn't talk to him the next day. He had been the boyfriend of the woman whom I became the boyfriend of. He was in the process of coming out; I freaked out, and then soon thereafter I had sex with her and told her that I had had sex with him. She knew he was bisexual, so that was okay. I was having sex with her, through college, but really was attracted to men."

Those attractions did not quickly become physical actions. "I did a lot of fantasizing. My college had an opinion board, where people would put up statements about anything, and then [others] would respond to it. I fantasized about declaring that I was gay on the opinion board, and then immediately decided this was not a good idea. That was a[n imagined] vehicle of coming out. But in college, the second year, 1969-70, I tried to organize a men's group. I put an ad on the opinion board, saying *This is not necessarily to deal with homosexuality but to deal with us as men.* It was subconsciously a way of my wanting to come out. It didn't gel; there weren't that many people interested in doing it. I was also terrified, too. At the women and men's conference, where I had sex, I remember being in a men's group saying I had a secret that I wanted to tell people about. Which, was like, come on, give me a break! And at the end, at an encounter group, this one guy who was coming out or had come out, said, *This is disgusting; you're just being a cock-teaser.* He obviously was attracted to me, and he thought I was playing this game. But basically it was just terror in my mind."

Later College. The cultural and social changes evident and increasing on college campuses in the late 1960s informed James's actions, senses, and sensibilities. "These were anti-war days, counterculture days. There was a Quaker counterculture movement I was a part of, and there was a commune I would visit while I was in school. It was at this commune, at a conference, where I met this guy who I just totally fell in love with. We had sex, in the fields in the meadow, in the sunny afternoon. It was really good, but he was essentially a heterosexual who was dealing with his openness and bisexuality by having sex with men. But he was essentially heterosexual. So that didn't work."

The openness of the period continued to produce some intimate relationships for James, but ultimately they "didn't work" either. "That summer I went to Mexico with a friend, while I was still in college, whom I had the biggest crush on. To this very day I think I must have a crush on him. He, too, would let me kind of have sex with him a little bit, but it was because he was being politically correct—bisexual—at the time. I think that's why a generation of people doesn't trust bisexuality, because of the way bisexuality at the time was constructed as something that people did," rather than as a separate identity, than as actions rather than sensibilities.

The notions of contesting sexuality were (literally) engendered by other contemporaneous social movements. "The women's movement sort of had a huge impact on the counterculture movement and the anti-war movement in '69: immediately, all of a sudden in this Quaker anti-war countercultural youth movement, there was a women's conference, a separate women's group, and a discussion of people's sexuality and sexism. And one of the responses was a discourse that everyone's basically just sexual, and people insisted on their bisexuality. Part of that was pushed by people who later came out; others were pushed by this guy who I had sex with a few times. I think [he] was trying to be very open in the counterculture hippie days by saying, *Yeah, we're all just sexual.* Even my girlfriend was very tolerant at this time. She had other boyfriends.

"It was a time in which people had a lot of sex with a lot of people. . . . The counterculture and hippie movement really deconstructed the notion of gender in a big way. Long hair, beads, flowery dress, meant that gender could be much more fluid. The sexual revolution, with the notion of multiple partners and people were basically bisexual or pansexual, was very important. That was the ideology in which I was embedded at that time. I was a student, but within this I was an activist in the anti-war movement and going to demonstrations. It was that whole period. And then the women's movement, and a real critique of machismo and male sexism, which I just embraced. The minute I understood feminist theory, I became a feminist, because it was articulating all the critiques of the male dominated society and machismo which I suffered from since I was a kid. Those were cultural backdrops that cushioned my coming out and made it less painful than it could have been."

College for James was dominated by his questions about his sexual identity. "The whole time I was in college, the leitmotif under everything was, *I don't know how to deal with my sexuality; what is going on here?* The homoerotic desires were just strong, strong, strong. This discussion about sexuality and counterculture was on campus as well as off campus, but it was very much a part of being a student at that time.

"In '68, when I started going [to Earlham], women had curfews. In those four years, [the college] went from women having curfews to eliminating the curfew for women, to the fourth year when there were men and women in the same dorms. It's just phenomenal, if you think of the change of those four years. All these things were happening which were questioning profound values. So because I was very political and very much linked to these social movements, it gave me some broader comfort zone in which to come out [first as bisexual, and soon after college as gay]. I had very little contact with the [gay] culture, and yet I was already very politically involved in it. The politicized movement which emerged gave me an incredibly important way of coping. So when I came out [as gay, just after graduating from college], I became an activist and a revolutionary. Within six months, it somehow resolved within the context of how I was viewing the world as a whole, this gulf of a contradiction. And I started feeling good about myself. . . . [and] three months out of college I came out; *gay* would be the word [I used], because I was connected to the movement.

"My whole college experience was struggling with homosexuality. College was horrible; it was really bad. For example, I teach now, and I'm always surprised that more students don't come in and come out to me. But then I realize, I wouldn't have come out to one of my professors. Even the psychologist that they had at the school, I think that would have been very hard to go to him, because then he would have known my secret. I think that small, insular environment was very hard."

Cliff

Adolescence. Like James, Cliff felt he did not fit the image and experiences of his peers. He, too, found a social outlet in the theater. During high school, in suburban Pittsburgh, he "had a very small group of very close friends, but was not into any crowd. I was suspicious of the 'in' crowd, because they seemed vacuous. I think of my high school days as defined by my family life [more] than my school life, because I came from a family that does lots of things together: always had dinner together at the dinner table, tended to go on vacation every summer, car trips. Those suburbs were more rural than I think of Los Angeles suburbs being, so it was far enough out that there weren't close friends in the area there that wouldn't involve a drive to be with. My sister and I both did more reading and things on our own."

Cliff was also involved in a nonscholastic religious youth group. Two friends from high school took Cliff to join one group, in downtown Pittsburgh. "In that group there was one fellow with whom I got really aroused. But I didn't act on it. He tried to kiss me; that was so frightening to me that I rejected him, in that sort of *stop/don't stop* way. Certainly, I was looking at the possibility I was gay then. This was 1970 or 1971; would I have used the word 'gay' or would I have used 'homosexual'? I remember looking at a few men in high school and thinking *They're really attractive*, but I remember that, still in my high school years, as not [thinking], *Oh, I must be gay*, but *Oh, that's interesting, that he's so cute*. I didn't have a label for it at that point."

Early College. After graduating from high school, Cliff severed all ties to his high school relations. "I pretty much cut myself off from them [high school friends] when I left high school and went to college. I think partly it was a subconscious move, because I really wanted to find a new life. I had not realized that I was gay at that point, but I wonder if maybe I knew I wanted a new beginning. I certainly didn't acknowledge it to myself." In 1971, he enrolled in "Allegheny College, in Meadville, Pennsylvania. It's a small, liberal arts school, a four-year college.

"I had a great, great college experience. Because the school was so small, everybody there got to pursue their interests really fully. So I was doing lots of art classes, lots of drama classes, doing anything that I wanted to. The doing, for me, had to do with the subjects I was studying: that was where my real interests were. And many platonic relationships with true friends; I felt like I established a community there. It was very, very fulfilling. That's partly why I stayed right through the summers, and did college in three years instead of four, because I was having such a good time."

After two years, Cliff's subconscious, or semiconscious, desires came to the surface. The related emotions and experiences changed his self-concept. "By 1973, I had my first and only sexual experience with a woman, and then my first consummated sexual experience with a man. It's got to be about that point that I realized I must be gay, and probably gay was the word I would use at that point."

Certainly, Cliff's collegiate experience affected his sexuality and identity— but in quite unique ways. "There was a teacher, a technical director, whose house we'd all go over on a regular basis, and play poker and drink and smoke cigarettes and have great times doing this with a bunch of people from the drama department. [One night] the wife of the technical director sat me down in her kitchen, while everyone was in the dining room next door playing poker. She said, *What's the story, Cliff?* She knew I was gay before I knew. I think I probably lied to her. She said—and of course, this is way pre-AIDS— *What you need to do, Cliff, is screw around. You're never going to become a good designer*—which was my goal at that point—*if you don't know what love is. You'll never know what a sunset really looks like; you'll never really be able to put fabulous color and lighting on stage, until you know love. You have to go screw around.*

"I think what she was saying was, you've got to become whole. You've got to fall in love, and you have to fall in love with the person, man or woman, who's really right for you. She gave me fabulous, fabulous advice, and totally appropriate to me! And probably to others she gave it to, too. It's a very '70s framework.

"College life didn't get sexual for me until '73, I think. I became whole; all of a sudden, there was definitely a sense of completion: *This is who I am.* Also, there were concerns, the coming out concerns that so many people seem to experience: who's going to know, who do I let know, how do I tell my parents, is it true? Even with the happiness, there was denial, probably, too."

Sexuality had not been a visible or discussed concept in Cliff's younger experience. "When I was growing up, sexuality in all forms—not affection, but sexuality—was something my family didn't talk about. It was—I don't want to say dirty, but not to be spoken of, which is a pretty fine line in my book. So while I know my sex with Tony [Cliff's first male sexual partner] was exciting, incredibly exciting, and felt right, and in that sense complete, it also, maybe because it felt so great, entered the world of the stuff you don't talk about. *This is sex.*"

Cliff identified other aspects of the higher educational experience that helped him to form his sexual identity. "Part of it was [that] I left home to go to school. So I was out on my own, and that gave me more sense of stability and safety from my parents' knowing, so I could explore on my own without having to be concerned about parents' judgement. I think of my parents as very supportive, but I also know that they had apprehensions about homosexuality. We never discussed homosexuality openly in my family, but I remember one moment when I was sporting a new shirt my mom had made me—this was maybe junior high or something—and I was modeling the shirt for my dad. Doing runway poses, voguing decades before it was popular. My dad said, *Don't do that; you look like a girl.* So there's that sort of thing going on, but it was never labeled homosexual. It was clear that there were gender roles I was expected to fulfill."

Cliff's release of those concepts about sexuality and his self-identification as both non-heterosexual and gay developed during his undergraduate and early graduate years. "It was a slow progression. At that point there's acceptance within, but not enough to proclaim it. There must have been stages in this, where I became more aware of the fact that there are other people who are gay and that this is a possibility. This is '73; we're still in the hippie era. Free love and sexual revolution is in the air. I must be hearing about homosexuality as a component of the sexual revolution. My college activities were very much focused on drama, art classes, smoking dope, hanging out with friends. There must have been gay talk through that."

Later College. The cultural changes James identified as important for contextual understandings of sexuality continued to play out for Cliff, particularly after he left Pennsylvania. Cliff spent two years in graduate school at California State University at Long Beach immediately following his undergraduate years. "The journey across those two years is a journey of experimenting with more men, and because I had great role models at that point, coming out—acknowledging these relationships, flings, one-night adventures—until I could finally say I was gay. I know I took that attitude of *You mean you can't tell?* before I said it. I had two teachers who were gay. One of them taught stage makeup; I was his teaching assistant. He was out and proud and loud and audacious. The very first time I started to get to know him, that was slightly scary and tantalizing at the same time. From him, [becoming] able to go on and acknowledge it to others, too. There was another teacher in the drama department who was gay but much more reserved than [the first]. Both were in long-term relationships, one which was monogamous and one which was not, making it very clear that you can be gay, happy, and out, all at the same time. I think [the former instructor] served as a model for me to be able to acknowledge, probably first to him, that I was having these adventures, that I was having sex with other men."

Cliff's "adventures" consisted primarily of meeting other men in private gatherings of students or university-related people. Cliff would see these men again, in social or scholastic contexts, but not in sexual situations. "We were all going to school together. Did I have sex with them repeatedly? Hmm . . . I think only with my partner, whom I'm [still] with now. We met there. I think I was really experimenting with lots of different guys. To my understanding, the folks I was doing this with were doing the same thing elsewhere, too. The perception was that was the milieu. Because it was still the spirit of sexual revolution and peace-love hippie free love. There may be shred of truth to the stereotype; there may have been more sexual freedom among some groups of artists than other groups. I don't know."

The Los Angeles area also offered other forms of institutionalized socialization for non-heterosexuals. "One of [my] mentors took me to a gay bar, probably my first year. It was kind of creepy, because it was foreign territory to me and I didn't know what the rules were. I didn't know how far I could go. This was 1973 or 1974; it was totally *Tales of the City*: the whistles blowing, the tambourines, the smell of dope in the air. It was exciting, but I didn't know how to pick somebody up to dance with him.

"The visibility of gay culture, both at school and in the urban area, made it so much easier, I believe, for people in that environment to come out, to say who they are, then it would be in places where there isn't other visibility established. I don't think it had to be the West Coast, but I think it had to be an urban center with a gay culture."

While he began coming out socially while at CSU—Long Beach, Cliff remained cautious about how he deployed his identity in mixed (heterosexual and non-) settings and contexts. "Certainly, among my friends, while I was in the process of revealing who I was, I was not identifying as straight in my mind, and I think it's fair to say I never lied by saying *I'm straight*, but I think I was very careful about how much information I would give to whom."

Tim

Adolescence. Similar to Cliff's and James's experiences, Tim recognized feeling different from his peers because of something internally felt (as opposed to an external characteristic or action). "My father was in the navy. I mostly grew up in San Diego, but we lived in some other places, including out of the country for three years. But mainly San Diego, from fourth grade on. I was teased in elementary school. It feels like I always kind of knew [about being non-heterosexual]. Once puberty hit, the sexual feelings I had were pretty obvious to me. I had the terminology; I think I used [gay]. I felt that I was probably gay, and was trying to be open about it. But trying to be accepting of that if that were the case, but if it were going to be a phase, to be open to that."

Tim felt alienated from his high school peers. "The high school I went to I felt was very backward. It's very redneck and conservative. [The community was] not gay friendly; it's not progressive at all. I think I wasn't a very social person; I did all of these very solitary kinds of things. I think I was stubborn; I felt like I didn't fit in, but I didn't make any real effort to [fit in], either. By the end of high school, I was in this punk rock crowd, but I was also in this college prep crowd. But I wasn't really in either in them; I was moving around the periphery of them. Even though I really connected to the punk rock thing, I would refuse to wear my hair like that, dress like that, or do that stuff. I think I was just trying to hold to something of my own. I wrote a couple of essays where I came out to my English teacher; in the psychology class journal assignment, I wrote stuff in there. I was trying to be open about it, I think, or explore it or discuss it in some kind of way, that now seems really, really forward. I wasn't out sharing stuff and was still quiet, but I was still doing these other things that now surprise me."

Whereas James and Cliff found outside activities in which to engage, Tim's activities were internal. "I would read a lot, and I would read stuff about gay people or homosexuality. I can remember reading in junior high about David Kopay [a professional football player who declared he was gay, whose autobiography was published in 1977]. I think that maybe stuff like that, which seemed to be saying it was all right or not entirely negative. . . . I listened to a lot of David Bowie and Lou Reed, that glitter-rock stuff, and that kind of lead me to Jean Genet and different writers like that. I think part of it might be knowing that there were people out there, whether it was David Bowie or Andy Warhol or Jean Genet, that there was something bigger. I guess maybe in combination with having some sort of idea in my head that it was okay and there was this prejudice to overcome. . . . Maybe those two things together. It seems some other people have sex and then it doesn't really alter any of their [ideas about their sexuality]."

Tim attributed his alienation from others to his sexuality. "I felt like I didn't fit in [in high school], I guess, because I had already figured out I was gay. Plus, I wasn't real skilled at making new friends or getting into a new situation." Despite this, Tim accepted and displayed a public non-heterosexual, "gay" identity. "My senior year, there was a guy that would have been my boyfriend, I guess; I don't think we used that terminology. Or maybe we did. I thought of it that way, and I think he thought of it that way. It was more like a dating thing, or something, than just fooling around or exploring." Their relationship was social as well as physical. "And the group of people that I was in perceived us as being a couple. So we were a couple. This guy whom I was with—which just seems amazing to me now—would come into my art class from the class next door. He would just kind of hang out, and we would talk. I got his name out of the phone book, and asked him to go see a movie. Now, especially since I teach high school, it just seems like a very forward thing to be doing. My best friend was gay, and I knew a couple of other gay students in high school that I would socialize with. I didn't have that *I'm really isolated with my sexuality* thing, but it seems like a lot of other people in high school did feel that."

Tim's acknowledgment and deployment of a non-heterosexual identity in social settings (even limited settings) was atypical of the precollege experiences of most gay men. But his experience represented a change over time in how gay-type men viewed their self-identity and ability to relate to and with heterosexuals. He had few questions about his definitions of his sexuality, "Which is kind of weird to me. Hearing certain stories, [it] seems like, *why would it take somebody that long or something?* I mean everybody's different, but it just seems like, especially with gay men, to figure out your sexuality doesn't seem like that difficult. It makes sense to me that somebody could be a woman and it would take them a while to figure it out, but it seems like an erection doesn't lie."

Tim suggested one reason for the difference in his experiences: "Maybe because I lost my virginity at a very early age. I had sex with another guy before I was in high school. It happened right before we moved. But I still talked to him on the phone [after the move]. He was a little bit older, and he seemed to want some kind of relationship. I, at fourteen or fifteen, didn't have the— *shouldn't be doing that.*"

Early College. Like Cliff, Tim also attended California State University at Long Beach, as an undergraduate from 1982 to 1987. Tim moved there, to major in art. "I didn't know that Long Beach had a large gay and lesbian community when I chose to go to school there. I can remember driving down Broadway [the street separating the city from the beach] with a friend of mine from high school, and there were just all of these gay men, on the sidewalk and walking places. Unless it's built up more in my memory; I think maybe post-AIDS it isn't as prominent or visible or something. I mean, it still is, but it just seemed this insane amount of guys. I don't know whether that was the point I was in my life and experiences, or lack of experiences, or whether it was really [true]."

Tim attempted to reach out to the gay community, both on and off campus. His experiences were less than successful. "I called the gay and lesbian center, to see where the places to go in Long Beach would be if you were under twenty-one. I started college when I was eighteen. There didn't seem to be any, and he [the person at the center] said something about the parking lot across from Ripples [a long-established gay bar on Broadway]. Finally he asked me to come in or something, but I didn't do that. I felt like I was coming off as some really troubled person or something, [that] they were going to do some kind of psychological assistance with or whatever. I just didn't want to do that."

Tim lived in campus housing for one year. He met—and successfully pursued—a long-term boyfriend on campus, whom he lived with in the residence halls. Despite this, Tim deemed the overall climate in the residence system hostile. "That was not good. I moved up here, and it was still kind of a situation where I didn't really know anybody and had to meet people. So, I met this one guy who was very obviously gay, and then we became friends. He was a little on the effeminate side, which I think is why I chose to approach him or become friends with him. We became boyfriends after that. We ended up sharing a dorm room together. There was a lot of harassment and things like that, by the second semester, because we were always together. I know that it's not [a typical experience]; sharing a dorm room with my boyfriend in 1982 seems very [atypical]."

Tim's finding personal companionship was both evident and aggravating to his neighbors. "I think I felt it was just common knowledge. There was no way that people couldn't know that we were the dorm fags or homos or whatever. There's no way that the people in charge could not know that, I don't think. We had [insulting] stuff stuck on the door, [and received] harassing phone calls."

In one instance, the harassment turned violent. "We lived on the second floor. This one time I went down to get a screwdriver or hammer from the R.A. [resident assistant] at the desk; there was a pool table and a TV set, and there were people around the pool table. There was one guy who was scary; you look at somebody's eyes and you can just tell. He used to stare us down in the dining hall. He was one of the people [at the pool table]. There were two doors [from the second floor]; one of them was open and one of them was closed and locked. I felt that the easier one to go through was the one that was open; it was a little further away, but I wouldn't have to take out my key. So I [went] through that door, and he just hit me upside my head really hard, to where my ears rang.

"I just went up to the room; I wasn't expecting it. I wasn't the kind of person who felt like I could fight this guy or take that on. So he did that, and I just walked up. I probably should have reported it to—well, I mean, I definitely should have reported it to somebody. But there wasn't any discussion about somebody being gay or gay and lesbian issues [at CSU—Long Beach]. Probably I just figured if something could be done about it, or if somebody was going to step in, or there was that option, then that would have been brought to my attention" by someone on staff at the university.

Later College. That incident was a turning point for Tim: his boyfriend and he moved off campus at the end of the term. "There was no way I was going back. I would have moved back to San Diego or done something else before I went back into the dorms. I don't think I thought that was an option; it never even crossed my mind, as something I would do or that somebody could do. It was really unpleasant on a lot of different levels: the whole harassment thing, feeling unsafe, living there [in] the whole culture of *dorm party, get drunk all the time, vomit in the urinal thing*; rolling beer bottles down the hallway. It wasn't good."

Tim intended to continue living with his boyfriend, sharing an apartment. "That was the original plan, but we got in a fight when we were looking for the apartment. Then we moved separately, but we still ended up back together, but with separate places. I really liked that year. I felt like I was really busy with classes, this part-time job, and this relationship that I was still in, that that was all I did. I think we pretty much spent every night together, alternating from apartment to apartment. I would be hanging out with him, or painting or drawing or doing some work for my classes. There was this straight couple we would hang out with. Weekends, we'd probably go out dancing. I met a lot of people who are still friends of mine now, and it had a feeling of not really like family, but a close group of people. When he moved away to go to another school, that was really difficult for me. Everything was kind of based around him and connected to him. With school and work, and then not being that outgoing of a person, I felt like my whole social life was nonexistent."

Apart from the living conditions, finding companionship fostered better social interaction and college affiliation for Tim. "I guess I felt like the relationship with my boyfriend made me feel connected [to college life] in some way. In the art department, it wasn't a problem or an issue. I think I did a couple of paintings where that [homosexuality] was part of the painting or part of the subject matter, so I didn't feel like that was a big issue there." Campus socializing with other non-heterosexuals was less beneficial. "I did try to [join] the gay and lesbian student union, or whatever it was called. The first year, when I was trying to meet people or figure stuff out, I went to that a couple of times. I found that really cliquish and not welcoming. I think I went maybe twice and didn't go back, because it was very insular. They talked about [only] the business; I think that my intention in going was to meet people and start to be part of some kind of group. I didn't know enough about the politics of the school or what they were trying to do. They weren't very welcoming."

Tim's experiences and relationship with his boyfriend were important both to his scholastic experience and his interpersonal development. "[Our relationship] didn't feel like it was anything that needed to be named, in some sort of special and different way. We were constantly around each other. Sharing the dorm room, it was like all the mutual free time, we were together. Because of that, it didn't really seem like it needed to be named."

Gene

Adolescence. Gene grew up in Korea, immigrating to the United States in the 1980s. His formative years were spent in Ohio. "I could clearly [understand] I was gay when I was in fifth grade. I was watching a soap opera, and there were two lesbian characters going to commit suicide because of [their] homosexuality. I asked my sister, who was in ninth grade, and she said, *It's same sex loving each other, and it's bad.* That was the first time I learned the term, and learned that the term is associated with something bad. Before then, I didn't know what that term meant; it didn't have any meaning to me. [But then] I automatically thought, *Oh, that's me.* I didn't say it, because she said it was bad.

"The first time I ever used the term to describe myself . . . I was a high school junior. I was described by others with that term many times, but when I finally said that I am [gay] was when I was trying to get [the] Ohio State University [gay] student union group phone number from the operator. I called this youth hotline. I used to live in Westerville, Ohio, which is a small town; when I looked in the Yellow Pages, there was no listing for 'gay hotline' or 'gay community hotline,' just student hotline. So I called all the community services hotlines, and I got stuck with suicidal hotline. They asked me why I called this line, and I said, *I want to know the gay hotline number.* [They asked] *Are you suicidal?* I pretended I was, to get this number: I said, *I feel bad being gay, and I need to talk to somebody who's gay.* And they gave me the number for the Ohio State student gay group."

Gene attended meetings at Ohio State University, but found the cultural climate less than inviting. "I had high hopes that I would make friends [by going to gay student groups], that I could finally sit together in the cafeteria and talk about my issues. But at Ohio State University, I couldn't even say anything, because I couldn't speak English that well. Because of that, I felt like I was rejected." Gene continued to search for a non-heterosexual community within which he could feel comfortable, eventually trying gay and lesbian student organizations at another university. "I had to go to Cleveland—it was only a few hours' driving—to Case Western Reserve. I couldn't fit in [at Case Western], so I went to the Cleveland gay community center. There was one black guy, one Hispanic guy, and all the others were white people. They made fun of my accent. I didn't go there; never again. So I tried to find friends through not so healthy channels: gay bars and sex clubs.

"When I went there, I didn't find anyone my own age. Those friendships didn't become close, except for few people who just wanted a sexual thing going on temporarily. I messed [around] with some strange guy, who looked like a leftover from the '60s. But he suggested I move to a big city, that this [my inability to make gay friends] might have something to do with race. So I went to New York and I realized that there are a lot more people who are not like mainstream, white Protestants, and I felt a lot more accepted there, walking around the street seeing all kinds of races and all kinds of people. And in the gay community, too; they weren't shocked by me walking into a gay community center."

Early College. Gene earned undergraduate and graduate degrees at Columbia University, which he attended from 1990 through 1996, majoring in sociology. "I was semi-closeted the first year [at Columbia], but toward the beginning of second year, I was almost out. The first year, I tried to fit in. When you're a freshman in college, you still have a high school mentality, where there's a clique in your mind. You don't want to be labeled as outcast or nerd or unwanted, versus cheerleaders and football players and popular kids. After freshman year, they get into this stage [of] *Who am I? Why am I living? What am I going to do to change the world for the better?* I think that really brought me to break down these labels from high school."

Gene viewed his sexual orientation as progressing from non-open to open. "Near the end of second year, I was completely out. In my third year, I worked at the health services. My director was working on a Ph.D. dissertation, *Do gay and lesbian students drink more and take more drugs than straight students?* I was his research assistant, trying to get his surveys done, and I had to go to all the gay student groups—there are so many gay student groups at Columbia. That really gave me, involuntarily, a public exposure on my sexual orientation, because I had to put a lot of flyers around campus, saying I'm looking for someone who's willing to fill out this survey and do this interview. This was very difficult, because not many people would come to do the surveys to begin with; at the same time, they have to advertise that they're gay. But it was fun. I had to go to a Columbia dance, which was a major event; we actually let [people] in for free if they filled out the surveys. I had to be the usher, so I couldn't be closeted.

"Once a month, there was a big Columbia dance. Columbia gay dances are major events in New York City. It's not just a little, tiny campus event because it's affiliated with actual night club promoters. So all of the Chelsea and Christopher Street people change their clothes and come all the way up to Columbia, which is quite far away from downtown. It's a big event, and a great place to meet younger—or at the time, around my age—people. You know, clean-cut."

In New York City, Gene finally found non-heterosexual communities with whom he could feel comfortable. "I had a close lesbian friend who worked on the survey at the health center office, and my roommate was also gay. He was working on his graduate program. He became a professor at NYU. He's openly gay, [but] was coming out at the time. I had a straight friend, but somehow I lost touch with straight friends, the straight scene, so to speak. If we'd bump into to each other in the school cafeteria and stuff, we'd sit together and talk, but I don't think we'd be buddy-buddy friends. I had so much work to do, a work-study job, manage my personal things, so my social time was really limited, and I could not separate that between gay friends and straight friends. I had to combine everything into one, so gay friends seemed like the most practical way of utilizing my limited social hours for the maximum capacity. It was not like I did not want to be their friend, or they didn't want to be my friends, but it had a lot to do with the time constraints and the energy level."

Later College. Gene's primary socialization changed from on-campus to off-campus activities, reflecting his changing self-concepts of sexuality, social responsibility, and race. "I think I met a lot of people through community events, [but] not so much on campus. I met most of my friends through political meetings. I was involved in radical groups like Queer Nation and ACT-UP [AIDS Coalition To Unleash Power] Caucus—I didn't get involved in main ACT-UP, but little caucus meetings. I was also involved in Asian groups, gay and non-gay Asian groups. When you go in these meetings, you see so many different people, but after organizing these meetings, usually the same people . . . so you get to know them pretty well. Once you get accepted into the circle, you make friends, like chains of networks, so you don't feel like you have to go out to the campus to make gay friends. I deliberately chose to go to gay Asian-only groups not only to empower myself as a gay man but also to empower myself as a different-race person. I'm using ethnicity and race as kind of interchangeable terms here, so I guess you have to change that if you have to use it in some politically correct term paper."

Gene's association with others who identified as queer did not alter his experiences and sensibilities beyond the gay type; he still wanted to be a part of, rather than apart from, social structures. Indeed, he became, after a brief foray into student governance, involved in local gay community politics. "I was vice president of the class first and second year, so that was the most I got involved in mainstream politics. But I got involved in a lot of [gay-identified] political things. There was a photography student lesbian who wanted to have an exhibit of gay and lesbian people kissing each other, so I participated in organizing that. There were a lot of fund-raising parties and rallies. There were death threat messages left on the [answering machine] of one of the gay groups, and they were trying to have a protest; it never came about, because half of us thought we should have a protest and some people thought we should just hand out roses for the people to be aware that we're not evil. Those were such dumb arguments we had! I just remember how stupid it was.

"I was not a radical. I was more involved in community work, outside of the campus, rather than on campus, because campus was so much like a cookie house, little children's stuff for me. I was really heavily involved in major community groups. Campus was more like an obligated thing for me, because I had to go to those things because of my work-study job. I think that had something to do with the maturity level."

Gene's social life revolved around Asian friends in the New York City night life. "I went to places where I felt more accepted, rather than these $20 or $30 [entrance fees per night] major night clubs, which a few thousand people can go in there and do all kinds of stuff that is sinful, I guess. A lot of these [people at] nightclubs do a lot of drugs, and it's an almost open thing for them to have an ecstasy room and a cocaine room. At the time, it was cool. Not that I did any drugs, but it was cool. I mean, I'm from Westerville, Ohio; this was euphoria or paradise for me. It was sinful and euphoric for me, because I guess I learned, when I was a kid, that that is what Sodom and Gomorrah look like. Yet it's so free that you push the boundary to the limitless point to where it's okay to be the way you want to be."

Again, Gene conceptualized his college experience as a fairly linear progression toward self-acceptance of his non-heterosexual orientation. "At the beginning of my freshman year, being gay was something I had to hide, a disadvantage that I should definitely hide in order to succeed. When I changed my perspective on sexual orientation, it became a not-so-proud identity that I could not hide yet that I had to somehow minimize as much as possible, to be ambitious and to succeed. And then, after I got involved in all these groups, not the campus groups but the community groups, I learned of the injustice and the discriminations, and they make you think about unfair situations and [feel] anger, and then you really feel that you have to do something about it. Then it becomes your major issue.

"In this country, I say race is most visible and easy to be discriminated [by].

But if I go back to Korea, all of a sudden race issues are gone and I become the gay person. So I guess, being a multiple minority in this country, you always wonder *why*. For example, in my high school, sophomore year, Fourth of July, I was driving back from the football field after watching fireworks. Guys came to my window and broke the window. Now: class issue, race issue, or sexual orientation issue? I'm a newcomer immigrant; if I were Irish, British, Australian, would this have happened to me? Maybe, because I was different, new. Or is it race, because I didn't look right; I looked like somebody completely different? Or is it because I act feminine or I was not dating girls? I couldn't figure out. But the more I live here, I feel that if I had to statistically count the numbers of incidents where I felt I was discriminated [against], I would say it was [because of] race."

Post College. In his junior year, Gene chose "to have a non-paying internship at the International Gay and Lesbian Human Rights Commission. I went to my home country, where I was born, Korea, and started a gay movement there. I did that right after college, and that's the most memorable event that I did for a social issue. In 1993, I organized the first Korean gay and lesbian human rights group. At that time, there was only one, but now they have between fifty and seventy all over the nations. I went there and tried to start the first visible gay pride march in Korea. We thought we would be lucky if thirty people showed up; actually, three hundred people showed up." Gene later returned to Columbia, to earn a master's degree in American studies, specializing in gay and lesbian studies.

Queer

Queer collegians, like their homosexual and gay peers, envisioned their lives in opposition to those of heterosexuals. But whereas homosexuals saw themselves as differing from straight people only in terms of their sexual activity (which was viewed as a private matter), queer students positioned their differences publicly; this differentiated their queer identity from both "homosexual" and "gay." Their sexuality was seen less as a variation of the norm and more as an agitator to the notions of normality. Where gay students strove to fit into the accepted campus formats and components of student government, organizations, and politics, queer students were more likely to buck the system, as well as to challenge the acceptance of those norms through actions and appearances. The stories of three queer collegians demonstrate how varied—yet ideologically similar—queer college life could be.

Jimmy

Adolescence. Jimmy's experience conveys the heart of a queer identity: the inversion of what one's society depicts or promotes as normal, with what society conscripts as abnormal, as his written and e-mailed responses to me show. "From 1959 until 1970, I lived in Woodstock, Illinois—what I guess you might consider my 'home town'—an 'All American City' in the mid-'60s. It is sixty-five miles northwest of Chicago, and less than twenty miles from the Wisconsin border—a rural Midwestern town which considered itself a cultured place."

Like many of his gay and homosexual counterparts, Jimmy recognized his sexual desires at an early age. "I knew I was gay at [age] ten—consistently aroused by men for as far back as I can remember. I can remember thinking to myself in a dark attic space I used to hide in as a child, that I wanted to love both men and women, that I felt like I was part of both, and wanted to see the world from both sides. I also dressed in drag a lot (through my early teens, much to my parents' chagrin). At fourteen or fifteen, I began having safe sex with men (at first a few years older than I—old enough to have a car where we could go for long drives and beat each other off), but it wasn't until I was fifteen that I had my first romantic peer encounter (sex) in a Chicago hotel room."

Unlike many of the homosexual and gay students, Jimmy had non-heterosexual role models whom he felt provided a positive—if somewhat physical—influence. "In Woodstock, I was surrounded by wonderful gay role models (though none but two were 'out' politically at the time), including my family doctor (who used to pay me $5 to let him suck my cock, and later—when I refused to take cash—he introduced me to Chicago artists, other gay men, and occasionally by accident, members of the football team that I already knew), my school bus driver (a local cop who lived down the street, but was into S&M, so I steered clear of him), my church choir director (who was scared to death and needed lots of coaxing before consenting to a consummation of our shared pleasures when I was fifteen), my elementary PE teacher (a sixties-something dyke that I later discovered was a lover of another lesbian friend), my high school art teacher (who used to rub his dick into my elbow as I tried to draw during class—he wasn't my type, so we sustained a queer friendship with lots of word play and campy behavior), as well as gay-friendly high school teachers (sociology, drama, English lit) who made a safe space for me to come out to my schoolmates, and who supported my work in war resistance efforts.

"My parents owned the only twenty-four hour/day restaurant (a truck stop) in five counties, and I worked there from age eleven to sixteen. It was also the haunt for both gay and lesbian communities in this sleepy Midwestern town, and they all welcomed me into their rituals of behavior, mannerisms, and dialects. It was definitely a queer childhood."

Early College. Moving to college provided Jimmy with more avenues for non-heterosexual experiences. Like the gay students of the 1960s and '70s, Jimmy's campus experience was influenced by the counterculture movements. "In 1970, I enrolled as an undergraduate fine arts major at Arkansas State University, in Jonesboro, Arkansas. In 1970–72, I lived on campus. My first roommate was the freshman class president, and my second, a black political activist.

"I moved out of the dorms the next year. By this time, the war was waning, and we had successfully dismantled the university's mandatory ROTC [Reserve Officer Training Corps] policies. I'd made my impact on the state, successfully guiding a dozen conscientious objectors, each a first in their counties—including a landmark case, the first nonreligious C.O. in Arkansas. I threw myself into drug counterculture as resident counselor at Huntington House, a drug abuse (but now defunct) social service agency.

"From 1970 to 1976, I very consistently (and usually adamantly) identified as a gay man." That identification, however, did not align Jimmy with other non-heterosexual students on campus. "I watched other gay people fleeing from me! I was so outrageously out as a freshman in college that most of the local gay community actively avoided me for guilt by association. There were a few brave souls who allowed their queerness to me (though there was only one who would be seen with me outside the safety of the art department halls). With my Betty Grable hairdo (though sometimes I did Carmen Miranda, replete with fruit and bobbles inserted in carefully coifed curls), gold lame tank tops, and elephant bells that looked like some prom queen's formal, it was hard to miss me on campus. I didn't have to go out looking—I was a walking billboard for queerness.

"Fortunately, my second cousin was the dean of the liberal arts school, and I managed to get away with a lot of disruptive stuff without getting kicked out. In the South, or at least in my family, blood kin are supported, regardless of their eccentricities. [The cousin] always referred to my outrageousness as *youthful folly* or *youthful indiscretion*, noting, when seeing me on campus for the first time (in drag), *You must be Peggy's boy; you look just like her.*"

"Dressing up" was but one manner in which Jimmy juxtaposed his identity against the heterosexual norms he perceived. Jimmy's flagrant consternation of the ideas of how males—both heterosexual and homosexual—should behave continued off campus as well, but not always to the extent with which he felt comfortable on campus. "At least a third of the weekends I'd go home, catching a ride with one of the eight or so students in my class who lived within fifteen miles or so of my mother. Out of respect, I'd tone down my act somewhat when at home: donning a short-haired wig for family pictures (at my mother's insistence) and removing my nose ring when visiting Grandma."

Sex played an important function in Jimmy's collegiate experiences and the understandings and sensibilities he had of his identity. "After my first year at ASU, I'd well established my reputation, and as fate would have it, I began to receive late-night calls from guys—not with drug problems, but the kind of problems that could be solved lying down (among other positions). One of these was a call from a man who I'd later spend the balance of the next two years with at ASU. Johnny was a bisexual black activist several years older than I was. Actually, his phone call that night began, *I've got a problem* . . . (long pause) . . . *My dick is so big no one can do a thing with it.* My heartbeat quickened. I tittered. And, of course, I said, *Come on down, and we'll see what we can do to help you.* A few weeks later, we began our eighteen months as a couple (though the size of his cock was really uncomfortable for me to handle, no matter what orifice I tried to shove it in—and indeed, I tried all of them repeatedly).

"Anyway, Johnny was a man that all of the white folks were fearful of (he was six-foot four-inches, with a gold star inlaid into a front tooth that had been knocked out in a skirmish during a black student's integration protest during his high school senior year), so not even the football jocks would cross us as we walked hand in hand to the dining hall. Of course, this relationship further distanced me from the few racist faggots that had revealed themselves to me, so that simplified my life greatly—no one would have me but him."

Campus contacts formed Jimmy's social network during his undergraduate years. "As my relationship with Johnny distanced in 1972–73 (I had major hemorrhoid problems by this point, and he had other jaws to dislocate anyway), I found myself falling for one, and then a second and a third, older man. The first two were art department alumni and local residents that I met during their visits with the professors. Each evolved into a series of multi-night stands that didn't go any further than that—though I desperately wanted them to."

By his senior year, Jimmy's social circles extended from campus, into town and beyond. "That summer introduced me to the bar scene in Memphis (which is only an hour or so from Jonesboro), and there I met a couple of hair dressers from Jonesboro. These were the local guys who eventually acknowledged they would have nothing to do with me my first couple of years at ASU because they didn't want to be outed. I eventually started hanging out with the drag queens in Memphis, driving in with the hair dresser clan on most every other weekend."

Later College. After branching out to off-campus communities, Jimmy found his world again curtailed primarily to campus contexts, in graduate school. "I graduated with a B.F.A. in fine arts in May of 1974. In 1974, I enrolled at Southern Illinois University, Carbondale, as an unclassified graduate student in the school of fine arts. After five weeks in an apartment three blocks from campus, I met my future lover (Douglas, who died in 1988). I moved in with him the following week. On occasion, I would go to the local gay bar three blocks from our home, to the disco across the street (where gay, bi, and straight students danced), or to Devil's Kitchen and Little Grassy Lakes (where '70s counterculture and gay students nude sunbathed and played). I also spent time in my garden, which became a space for performance art works and social entertaining for the gay and dance communities."

Sexuality continued to be an influence upon Jimmy's personal and social identity and sensibilities. "Despite our experimentation with 'open' relationships, Douglas and I remained fairly monogamous for almost three years. We were clearly a 'couple' as far as other students and the faculty were concerned. We were always invited to social events as a couple; we were both very active in Gay Rights activities. . . . We made it to all the big marches, conferences, etc.; and we did our best to queer it up wherever we were. Of course there were a few distractions from my monogamy. I'm a real modern dance groupie, so I always felt it a personal responsibility to fuck any visiting performer who came on campus for master classes—that is, if they wanted to reciprocate."

The concepts of *men* and *de* help explain Jimmy's queer sensibility: on the one hand, he publicly challenged prevailing presumptions of sexuality, while on the other, he in many ways accepted the values personally. "There were only three or four interludes outside of our marriage (and I really did consider my life with Douglas to be that—writing all of my siblings and parents to announce our commitment, bringing him home for Christmas and all other holidays, having mother-in-law tensions, kissing in front of our folks (but not at Grandma's). My mom's family all loved him."

Jimmy and Douglas found other non-heterosexuals who also displayed a very public queer non-heterosexual image that challenged the heterosexual norms of the Southern Illinois campus. "At Carbondale, half the dance department and a quarter of the music department must have been gay. The head of the dance department was an outrageously queer S&M body builder, and he loved to socialize, so there was a group of a dozen or so of us who would hang out together nude sunbathing at his farm or at Devil's Kitchen. I had lots of lesbian girlfriends, too, including one whom I consider my closest friend and was at one time married to my best male friend of all times, Teddy, who died of AIDS six years ago. Ted was the first gay man I didn't seek to suck, but just had to have as a friend. He was part of my coming to terms with my objectification of men as fuck objects. While I never dismissed my interest in pleasure, I did learn, with him, that a gay man could be a friend as well."

The queer sensibility that challenged the ideas of gender and sexual conscriptions also infused Jimmy's scholastic and artistic work. "The subject of most of the art works I created in both undergraduate and graduate school had to do with gay issues and/or personal/political identity. My first design project was a sixteen-foot by three-foot by sixteen-inch pink triangle sited between my dorm, the art department, and the post office—a work destroyed after its third day of exhibition, reportedly by members of the football team, at the instruction of their coach. I also organized the first gay artists exhibit at SIU in 1975, and produced a series of site-specific dance works dealing with issues of gender and sexuality. In one piece I danced on 2,000 wet pots in a yellow '40s prom dress with my lover, Douglas (wearing his black leotard) in a busy campus hallway at noon. This got me in a bit of hot water, but the faculty backed me, regardless of my inattentiveness to safety issues and university protocol."

Jimmy's sensibility—the meanings he made from his experiences and feelings—was queer, despite the fact that the term and concept for such a sensibility were not labeled publicly as such until at least a decade later. This identity put Jimmy in conflict with both the heterosexual and the non-heterosexual students and identities. "I believe that my outward queerness during my undergraduate years was a real turnoff to most men and especially those in the closet. Drag queens and I got along famously, but I'd have to travel to Memphis to hang out with them and few wanted to go to some cow-town college environment to play. The bi guys were clearly threatened, for being with me was clearly a confirmation of their own queer tendencies, though a few did banter and camp with me if no one else was around to see (including two of the faculty—neither of whom I was particularly attracted to). There were a few guys that I thought were likely gay, though when confronted with my curiosity, they'd always deny or claim they were deferring any gay commitments at the time."

Pozzo

Adolescence. Pozzo grew up in San Diego and could attribute feelings of difference from others to his sexual orientation; like most of the other respondents, he knew clearly at a very young age of his affectional and physical attractions to other males. "I always knew, since I was maybe four years old, that I was attracted to other boys. But I guess being gay, at the time [entering college], was a big question mark." In high school, however, the attraction to other males did not foster a non-heterosexual identity. "In ninth grade, I was in this really boring world geography class. I had this crush on this boy who was in seventh grade. I'm sure he must have been gay, too. I was in this boring class on a dreary, rainy day, with my head down on my desk, daydreaming and realizing, *God, I'm in love with this boy. I'm gay. It's true.* But I didn't act on that impulse. I wasn't really good friends with that boy."

That relationship played out in "masturbation, masturbatory fantasies. That was all. There wasn't a contradiction [in Pozzo's mind]. As long as I wasn't sexually active, I guess it didn't mean as much. I was still going to try to function heterosexually; at least give it a shot. I tried to date a girl. She was really pretty; she was really nice, really smart. I thought if I could fake it with anybody, it would be with her. I just thought I'd repress it all my life. I was very disciplined. I was a very good student. I thought I'd stick that right under the rug and not deal with that at all. Then I ended up having sex when I was eighteen."

Plans of repression were dispelled then. "I had sex for the first time with a man the summer before leaving [for college]. It was so intense. I was seduced by someone I had known from my youth orchestra, seduced in the sweetest, innocent way. We started kissing, and I didn't even realize what we were doing. Suddenly, I was so overwhelmed with sexual feelings, I was trembling, my whole body was shaking. I had no idea that I would have been capable of such passion. It was an overwhelming experience where I felt I had lost control of everything. Suddenly I was just one big throbbing penis."

Pozzo had considered his sexual orientation prior to matriculating: "Absolutely. This was the first time I had been away from home, and after the first week of school, I remember coming home from orientation feeling overwhelmed by the number of issues I had to deal with all of a sudden: my family's breakup, being away from home for the first time, knowing that I really was gay and probably couldn't deny that much any longer because I had had sex with a man and it was a very passionate experience. It was one of those issues that I had to deal with kind of right away, but didn't know how to deal with."

Early College. Pozzo attended Swarthmore between 1984 and 1988, where he majored in history. He looked forward to the cultural change between the coasts. "It was a culture shock that I wanted. I wanted to be on the East Coast. I had this idea then that southern California is this vapid, vacuous place with no culture, and that the East Coast is where all the sophisticated, intellectual, cultured people are."

Despite his desire to find others with whom he could relate, his first years at Swarthmore were lonely. "When I went to Swarthmore, I thought I'd be making all these great friends. It was kind of disappointing. I didn't really get intimate with anyone until my senior year. I guess I've sort of had this pattern of friendships. My longest lasting, most meaningful friendships have all been with women who are very smart and accomplished in different ways. I had gay acquaintances [as opposed to gay friends]. I had a hard time making friends . . . but I can't ascribe that to being gay."

Being in a postsecondary institution—particularly the academic culture of educated peers—helped, in Pozzo's estimation, his ability to accept his non-heterosexual identity. "Swarthmore was this very intellectual, very well in-formed place, so I had access to the view that sexual orientation is all the things that it is. That it is a normal way of being. There was a very popular class, the in-troductory psychology class, and if you looked up homosexuality in that text-book [they used], there's the question *What makes people gay?* Well, another legitimate question is *What makes people not gay?* There was this very intelligent, informed discussion of sexual orientation, putting it into a historical context, mentioning that there are other cultures that have not rejected homosexuality the way modern European cultures do. I was getting access to the right infor-mation on human sexuality, so I felt more legitimate about being gay."

Information about non-heterosexual issues did not ensure a lack of harass-ment or discrimination, but it did provide a basis of understanding and soli-darity with some heterosexual students, who informed Pozzo's thinking about his sexuality. "Once, apparently there was some incident where a security guard had been insensitive to a gay student. A bunch of people from the stu-dent council took to wearing arm bands, to show their solidarity with gay stu-dents. I thought, *Well, there are straight people doing it, so it must be safe.* That was before I was out."

As did other respondents, Pozzo viewed his identity formation as a process or series of stages of self-identification, apart from sexual action(s) or identifi-cation as non-heterosexual by others. "At Swarthmore, there were people who knew I was gay. Like my mom knew I was gay all along. I sort of knew that she knew, but it wasn't talked about. There were other friends who picked up on it. I was trying to lose my virginity with a woman, so during my freshman year there was a sophomore woman—like all Swarthmore students, very smart, very charming—not terribly pretty, and I thought, *Mmm, I could easily lose my virginity with her.* And I was right. She was eager to have sex with me, too, but I kind of blew her off. We were supposed to get together, but I didn't return her phone calls. I think that was kind of a turning point, in a way. Later on I met her for lunch and I talked to her, told her, *I think I owe you an apology.* Because I'd led her on that we were going to get together, and then I blew her off. I felt bad about it, because I hurt her feelings. I realized at that point that I can't do this, because I hurt other people, too. I can't pretend to be straight. She kind of realized what was going on; she said, *Oh, you'll eventually get together with some other girl . . . or, maybe some other boy.* You know, *wink wink.* I just sort of smiled, and I didn't refute what she said. That was one instance where I acknowledged gayness to someone without coming out in general.

"There were a couple of other female friends I had that picked up on the fact that I was gay. The woman I wanted to sleep with but didn't, the woman I was supposed to date but didn't, and a couple of other people who were out and who were cool and popular. These people, by realizing I was gay and not turning on me, not making an issue out of it, sort of made me realize there are reasonable people. It sort of made it easier for me to come out, these little realizations along the way."

Later College. As mentioned earlier, Pozzo's parents divorced the summer before he entered college, which created difficult relations between Pozzo and his family; in addition to his growing understanding of his sexual feelings and self-identity, other topics of conversation seemed strained or verboten. "Finally, things came to a head the summer between my junior and senior years. I was twenty years old. I was living with my dad, whom I was not getting along with very well. I was feeling more confident about being a gay person, but I just needed to make my parents, especially my father, aware that sexual orientation is all the things that I think it is now: a normal way of being, a normal variation of human sexual orientation. My dad went in to speak with my mother on the phone. He wanted to talk about it with her before I spoke with her, and then I spoke to her some days later. We talked for a little while, and then she said, *Well, you know your dad called me and you probably know what it's about.* I said yes. She said, *You know, Pozzo, I always knew.* I said, *Yeah, I kind of thought you did.*

"So after I came out to my dad that summer—which was not a great experience; it was a rather ugly scene—I was out with a vengeance." The queer identity Pozzo fashioned was almost a complete turnaround from his previous, closeted identity; he proclaimed his non-heterosexuality both verbally and through probing the boundaries of identity representation. "My senior year, everybody knew I was gay. I started wearing eyeliner. I was this pretty boy, and I thought this was a time to experiment with these kind of things." Before he came out to peers and his family, "I guess being gay meant I was just really, really hungry for signs and symbols of legitimacy. Senior year, forget it; I [had] tons of legitimacy. *I'm armed, and anyone tries to tell me that anything's wrong with being gay, they're going to get an earful.* Now, it's the same way."

Giving an earful is a response that differentiates queer-type from gay-type students. While gay students might organize speakers bureaus or other educational outreach efforts, queer activities were often more personal and more confrontational. As Pozzo became more public in telling others his sensibility regarding his identity, he came to deploy his sexual identity as an instrument to disrupt the norms and expectations of his heterosexual peers.

Like many of the men in this study, Pozzo had less than fond memories of his experiences with non-heterosexual student campus organizations. His recollections show a queer sensibility concerning gay- and homosexual-type students, juxtaposing his identity against homo- as well as heterosexual norms. "Until my senior year, the gay/lesbian/bisexual/questioning student union consisted of a group of about five men. They were all very, very queeny and flamboyant. I thought, actually, they weren't so bad. The other gay students who didn't want to come out [disliked the group's members] because they didn't want to be associated with such flamboyance. I also remained in the closet partly because of that, but when they graduated, suddenly a lot of people came out of the closet. A lot of those people were angry with the people who had just graduated, because they thought they had sort of poisoned the environment for us. Which I thought was a little bit unfair. When they graduated, I went to a meeting and suddenly there were twenty students there. That was at the beginning of my senior year; then I got busy with my senior stuff, my honors exams and stuff, and so I didn't keep up with it."

Post-College. Immediately after graduation, Pozzo continued to deploy his identity through queer activism and politics. "When I graduated, I joined ACT-UP. The political atmosphere at Swarthmore was very left of center. So ACT-UP's policies didn't strike me as so terribly radical. This was during the Reagan years; Reagan's response to the AIDS crisis was retarded. It was a really hard thing to get him to understand this was a serious health problem. Things like that really fueled our anger, and so it made sense, when the University of Pennsylvania invited Ronald Reagan to speak as part of their 250th anniversary celebration, to stand outside and block traffic. In fact, we saw a lot of faculty members walking into that event giving us the thumbs up. [Later] we stormed the office of the president of UPenn and pounded on his door. We were told he wasn't there, but we pounded until he gave us audience and listened to us excoriate him for having invited such a person."

Pozzo's final semesters in college were full of change, both in his personal identity and in the identities of those with whom he associated. "There were all these people that came out all of a sudden." Sex became, along with political activity based on identity, more important to Pozzo. "I had sex only twice my entire career at Swarthmore, and both guys [graduated] with highest honors, but neither of them was a very satisfying lover. I love smart men, but, God, I had other opportunities! I just remember this beautiful boy with this shock of light brown curly hair. And it would have been great! Instead, I slept with . . . this other guy who had a crush on me all four years. [He] was sweet and was charming, and turned out to be straight. Or at least he married a woman. I guess there are a few genuine bisexuals. And [sex with this one] wasn't great!" Apparently, identity based on sexuality was more obviously fluid, in Pozzo's estimation, rather than fixedly determined by sexual activity; further, how Pozzo positioned his identity—and undertook activities and actions centered upon disrupting the norms to which he believed his identity to juxtapose—displays a queer sensibility.

Rad

Adolescence. Rad grew up in a small town in central Idaho, population 800, "Very rural, tourist oriented. Very redneck. Very religious; we had about ten churches. It was not openly homophobic, but [non-heterosexuality] just was something that didn't exist to those people. There was no talk of it, no one saw it. So I had nothing to look [to], no strings to grab onto. It was a goal to get to the big city, one of the big reasons why I decided to come to school in Los Angeles."

In 1995, he moved to attend the University of Southern California; by that time, he had acknowledged his non-heterosexuality. "I came out to myself my sophomore year in high school, in 1993. I remember sitting on my bed, crying, saying, *You're gay.* And then telling my stuffed animals.

"I wasn't out to anyone in high school, but I had a boyfriend. Toward the end of my senior year, I met a guy through some friends up at University of Idaho. I saw him maybe once or twice a month, so it was kind of more writing letters or calling. It was far enough away where I was able to have—it was a good relationship. He taught me a lot. He was very caring. We're still in touch."

Unlike most of the respondents in this study, Rad began the process of telling others of his non-heterosexual identity prior to leaving for college. "By the time I left Idaho, I'd come out to maybe four of my friends. And my high school English teacher; she was the first adult I came out to. Somewhere between Idaho and Los Angeles—it was, like, a three-day road trip with my dad—I made the decision that once I was here, by myself, I would be out to everyone. I just refused to let myself go through what I went through there. It was the hardest promise I've ever kept."

Early College. Rad completed his undergraduate course work at USC in 1999, after attending for four years. Deciding not only to accept personally his non-heterosexuality but actively to tell others in public settings was not a major issue for Rad. "It wasn't an issue where it bombarded me all at once; it wasn't really an issue at all until about a week into school. The GLBA [Gay, Lesbian and Bisexual Alliance, a student organization at USC] was throwing a welcome barbecue. It took every ounce of courage that I had to walk over to the barbecue and introduce myself. The people I met that first day are some of my closest friends today. It was the best decision I could have made and the hardest one to execute.

"I remember walking across campus, telling myself, *You can turn around; you don't have to do this.* But for some reason my body just kept going, and before I knew it I had stepped into the auditorium and there was no going back. It was a perfect platform for me to get involved and be active on campus. I guess I had it lucky in the sense that I didn't have to worry about people I [knew] being here and finding out, because I still wasn't out to my parents and family. It was a step for me to be out here on campus first."

While at USC, Rad manifested his queer identity through his visible personal style ("I had really funky colored hair and [body] piercings"), his journalism, and his campus activities. He majored in public relations and minored in sculpture. Early in his college education, soon after he stepped into the auditorium, he decided to declare his sexual identity to his parents. "About a month after I'd moved [to Los Angeles], on my eighteenth birthday, I sent both of my parents letters. (They were divorced.) The letters explained everything. I feel much more articulate when I write, so I explained it.

"My mother called me back within a week and said, 'I did suspect it.' I didn't hear from my dad for over a month. That was the most heart-wrenching month of my life. When he finally called me, he was crying and said he didn't know how to deal with it. Basically, he didn't want to talk about it. [But] I [said] we were going to talk about it. He didn't like that very much. For the few months after I came out to him, it wasn't fighting, it was just arguing. Any time I'd mention anything I was doing—helping out with National Coming Out Week or doing stuff on campus—he would change the subject, just blatantly ignore me. It got frustrating. I went home for Christmas, and that was the first time I'd seen him. They both lived in the same small town, so that's good or bad. We had a huge fight; he called me all sorts of names and basically told me he didn't want a gay son. He'd already remarried and had two stepchildren.

"We haven't really spoken to each other since. That was four years ago, almost. It's funny, because the rest of his family has no problems with it. I tried as much as I knew how. Like, I sent him, the same as my mom, articles and PFLAG [Parents and Friends of Lesbians and Gays] stuff and all that. He would just send it back to me. So, other than that, there's been no contact from them, minimum contact from my stepbrother and stepsister. That's because they don't want their children to be gay, as I've been told. That's the most unpleasant aspect I've had of coming out, losing that part of my life, but it was one of the sacrifices I was ready to make and I had to make, I guess, because I wanted to be out to my parents."

Rad deployed his identity by being open about his sexual identity in classes, both to students and faculty. He viewed his sexuality and sexual identity as central to his learning activities. "Not in the beginning. It wasn't something that I even thought about until someone raised the issue with me. I think it was my composition class, first semester. I had been politically active in high school, but just in main[stream] politics. I was getting more [involved] on the gay activism front, and it just occurred to me that my teaching assistant was talking about marriage or something and it was just completely assumed that we were all straight. It didn't dawn on me right away, either; I guess because in high school you so rarely get on any topics like that in the first place. It really hit me as bizarre. That's when I started raising my hand. I would ask, *Well, what about gay or lesbian relationships?* A few times it was met with resistance, but more so by the other students than by the professors or teaching assistants. But I've always been out in classes after that. Sometimes it's been an issue, but sometimes it hasn't been. All my professors have been supportive. Either I had it lucky, or USC's just good like that . . . or maybe I was in informed, liberal classes."

In addition, Rad was open about his sexuality in on-campus work environments, including as a resident assistant during his sophomore year. "I had great bosses on campus. One of them's a good friend of mine now. They've always been supportive. I'd wear my little pink beads or whatever, and they'd be cool."

The decision to come out to himself and others prompted Rad to become involved in gay activities on campus, which was not easy during his freshman year. "I was very involved in the gay group on campus, the newspaper, the mentoring program through the counseling center, trying to work full-time between two jobs, taking a full load of classes. The first year I was involved, gay life on campus was . . . not visible, I think. There was National Coming Out Week, and that was the week that it was okay for the gay group on campus to be visible and do things. Other than that, I don't remember ever seeing or being a part of anything that was public or offering visibility for the gay community. It was supported, as much as I think it could be, by the administration. It was okay to do National Coming Out Week. They let us hang a big rainbow flag. But other than that . . . we never asked for anything more, but I think we would have run into problems if we had."

Part of Rad's queer sensibility was reflected in his desire for visibility, as well as the aspiration to work with other student constituencies for programming and campus change. "Compared to the way things are now, I think [the gay student organization has] changed, not dramatically, but I think for the better. They plan more non-Coming Out Week events. They get support from places I don't think we ever thought of getting support from, or even asking, like other student groups. Support in terms of financial support, like co-programming, and also support in attending events and stuff. At the things I went to last spring—a Pride Week they decided to have—I was amazed at the amount of support from other student groups. We were always pushing for that. When I was more active, my freshman and sophomore years, we would go to the black student assembly and the Hispanic students' functions. So I guess it's finally coming about, more equality in the student groups."

The activities Rad participated in also changed over the years, reflecting his increasing—and later decreasing—involvement in the queer campus community. "My freshman year I was volunteering, doing whatever they wanted me to do. I'd go hang flyers in the dorms or whatever. My sophomore year, I was on the board [of directors for the student organization]. I don't remember what my position was. You start becoming friends with the people who were in charge. We were all friends, and we were all on the board. It was more about programming; I had more of a hand in National Coming Out Week. I was doing research on what other schools were doing. I guess it was a drawback being in L.A., because I had some other ideas that you just can't pull off in a town like L.A. As a group we thought of doing more all-school stuff, with different universities, which is really a good idea, but I don't think it can be effectively carried out [in Los Angeles]. People would always thank us for inviting them, but then they'd never show up. Maybe that's because, would you rather go to USC or West Hollywood?

"My sophomore year was the first Gen-Q [Generation Queer] retreat, the leadership retreat [sponsored by USC's division of student affairs]. I participated in that, and then my junior year I helped plan it. That got me more able to think of moving off campus, being involved. I was starting to question where does leadership go, where can you take queer activism off campus? We'd go to conferences." Socializing would also be "[p]rimarily through GLBA, going to rap groups. People would have parties."

While Rad displayed queer sensibilities, he also embraced some "traditional" gay notions of campus involvement. "I spent my sophomore year as an resident assistant. I made it a goal of mine to be very visible. My freshman year, I knew at least three or four R.A.s who were out and open to their residents, other R.A.s and on campus, and active in GLBA. Those were the people I looked up to the most. I wanted to emulate them, and that's what I did. I ended up being the only out gay R.A. that year. I had a big rainbow flag hanging from my campus window. It was hard; the dilemma I didn't expect was what to tell my residents. We had our first floor meeting, and I told them, 'I'm gay, and I'm active in these groups on campus.' I made it more of an example of what they could do to be active on campus." Unlike Tim, the gay student whose first-year live-in experience at California State University—Long Beach was degrading, Rad "had no verbal abuse, nothing that I had to put up with my freshman year of living in the dorms. I wanted to set an example of being a positive, out, role model, and I think I did that."

Later College. After two years of living, socializing, and volunteering on campus, Rad began to desire noncampus experiences and relationships. "I think I was just randomly dating people, who ended up being these seventeen- and eighteen-year-olds from campus, whom I was getting really disgusted with. I used to write the gay column in the newspaper, a weekly column in the *DT* [*Daily Trojan*, USC's student newspaper]. I wrote it for a few years. I got these kids just randomly e-mailing me: *Oh my God, can I meet you?* So we'd go out, and I'd just get sucked into these things.

"My junior year was a time I was trying to move my life away from school. I had begun making some friends who were not at USC. Mainly from my job, working off campus [at a music store near West Hollywood]. We'd meet up and go out on the weekends. We'd go to clubs. And some of them were gay and some were straight; we'd go to gay clubs, we'd go to straight clubs in Hollywood. It was fun. I also had a large group of friends who lived way out in the Santa Clarita area [about fifty miles from USC], from my first boyfriend here on campus. After moving here I got involved in GLBA, and then I got involved with him. We were together over a year and a half. I got a car, right before my junior year. That's how I got a job off campus."

The allure of noncampus experiences was a dual-edged sword for Rad:

while he could find more people whose experiences matched his own, conversely, the values and attitudes of many of those whom he met were incompatible with Rad's ideology. "You just get such a rush. I remember the first time I went to West Hollywood, the first time they took me to a club. I was just in awe, and I wanted to go out at least five times a week. It was just amazing that such a culture existed; I had no clue. All I had seen was being active" in queer activities, not gay people socializing.

Rad found many of Los Angeles' preeminent non-heterosexual social settings intimidating. The predominately gay L.A. community of West Hollywood "was scary. There was some sense of relief, in the sense that there were plenty of other gay people out there, which I think had mellowed because I had met everyone here before I was taken over to West Hollywood and exposed to that. I had a group of gay people I had been around with, so I knew there were other gay people out there. It was hard because—I don't want to say I didn't fit in, but I didn't see myself represented there at all. I was always the one with funky-colored hair; I was always the one with piercings. Those were extreme things at the time." The gay lifestyle of West Hollywood in the 1990s "seemed so based on drugs, alcohol, sex, what you look like; it was almost scary. I remember for a while that's what I thought I had to look forward to. I thought growing up and graduating college meant I moved to West Hollywood and go to Micky's [a gay dance bar on Santa Monica Boulevard] every night.

"And we did [go out frequently], because it was comfortable. There was still that sense of being around [gay] people in such a big atmosphere. It turned into a love/hate relationship. I realized I loved going there to feel safe and comfortable because I was around so many other gay people, but then you start to realize how everyone bases everything on what you look like and how separated it is. I don't think I realized at the time; I was dancing with my friends, and you don't realize you're being judged so much at the time. Then it comes to a point when you're able to stand back and say, *My God, I never want to be like that.*"

This sense of difference inspired Rad to adopt more unconventional approaches to self-representation, more queer deployments of identity. "I think it was just fuel for being more extreme: more piercings, more colored hair. I guess, in a sick way, to make myself stand out more when I would go out. It was also that I was never able to do that back home; no one was here to tell me *no*. We weren't drinking or anything; we'd go dancing, sit at the Abbey [a West Hollywood coffee house], hang out. I grew to hate it. There was a whole year when, unless I just had to, I wouldn't go to West Hollywood."

It was in West Hollywood that Rad met his initial collegiate partner. "I met my first boyfriend [at USC] about two months after I moved here. Randomly, I was out with a friend of mine, at a club. She's like, *Oh, this is my friend Michael; he goes to USC, too.* We just started talking, and we really hit it off. We were together for a year and a half. It was amazing, [but] it came to a really bad end. We were living together in the dorm. We broke up when I was an R.A. He wouldn't leave, and I had to get my supervisor to kick him out. I look back on him, and my boyfriend in high school, and I learned more about myself in those two relationships than anything.

"In my first relationship, in high school, [sex] was important, because it was the first sexual relationship I'd had with a man. (I never have had sexual relationships with women.) It was there, in both of them; it was a part of the relationships. It wasn't a main factor in either of those relationships. It was like an added bonus."

Rad's recent college experiences provide him with a more immediate sense of what being queer in college means. "I think more than anything, it meant being active. That's the only exposure I had before I came to college. I had gone my senior year in high school to the Gay Pride Parade in Boise. I had stayed far away on a corner to watch it. I don't remember what everyone else sees on the news; I don't remember the leather daddies. I remember seeing all the active groups: the Stonewall Democrats, the AIDS Foundation. That's what I had in my mind, coming here, and that's what I set out to do, to be active. I think that included being visible. Once I got more active in GLBA, I had a very *I don't care, in your face* type attitude. I could care less whether anyone knew I was gay or not. I still have that, but it's calmed down a bit. It was less identity forming and more just trying to be out there."

Reflections on Gay and Queer Collegians

Men who can best be understood as gay during their collegiate years displayed a number of similarities. Some of their stories echo those of closeted and homosexual students, particularly the importance of sex and sexuality in assessing their understandings of their senses and experiences. Another familiar theme throughout the gay narratives is the relationship(s) of their identities to the concepts of "normal" and heterosexuality. Key differences, though, set gay students apart from homosexual students, not the least of which was that gay students perceived that they differed from closeted and homosexual students.

Gay students actively deployed a more visible self-image in social settings; they announced, or admitted, their difference to strangers as well as to friends, either through conversation or confrontation. Whereas homosexual students conceptualized their sexuality as a "private" matter, gay students just as frequently understood their identity as a social one, delimited by the concepts of identity that were undergoing extensive changes during the 1960s and 1970s. Gay students sought roles and activities on campus equitable to those of heterosexual students. Gay collegians discussed their sexuality with others; indeed, they had—and admitted to having—sex with a number of people with whom they had more than simply a sexual relationship.

The *men* and *de* of gay student life also differed, because the concepts converged more for gay students than for homosexual and closeted collegians. On the one hand, gay students wanted inclusion in the aspects of campus life they viewed other students as being active in; on the other, they also wanted acceptance from those others of the differences in their sexuality. In this sense, the two hands seem to be shaking in a sign of peace: the aspirations of the *men* and *de* of these students were not only compatible, they were the same goals.

Queer students did not particularly choose to follow their gay peers in these ambitions, nor into the avenues of institutional governance and programming. Queer sensibilities would deem such activities incompatible with their understanding of a queer identity: apart from both heterosexual and non-heterosexual identities, their very existence challenged and confounded the notions of normality. Not only was heterosexuality seen as a concept that conscripted those who were not heterosexual to subservient and/or deviant roles on the margins of society, any action or deployment of identity (the praxis of one's senses and sensibilities) that did not confront this binary schism was viewed as insufficient.

While gay students struggled for inclusion into heterosexual contexts, queers grappled with maintaining a sense of affiliation with other non-heterosexuals. The *men* and *de* of queer students were much more adversarial. While on the one hand, queer students, too, conceived of their identities in opposition to heterosexuality, on the other hand, queers did not perceive gay or homosexual identities as any less confining (nor less conforming) than heterosexuality. Attempting acceptance of identity through inclusion in traditional, accepted avenues of campus life would be a collusion with the heterosexual norms that foster the view of non-heterosexual identities as abhorrent deviations.

Instead of joining those causes, often queer students flaunted their defiance of the normative rules. Whereas a closeted student understood his identity to be a secret, a homosexual believed his identity to be a private matter, and a gay collegian conceived of his identity in social terms, a queer man found the very notion of his identity to be public in nature and discourse. As Pozzo and Jimmy did, queer collegians questioned the boundaries of gender through cross-dressing and use of makeup to alter their (masculine) physical appearances. More than announce, either calmly or confrontationally, their differences from heterosexuals, queer students often created events (kiss-ins or promenades), or utilized other physical manifestations of distinction (differently colored hair, body piercings) to represent publicly and clearly the differences. In doing so, they disrupted the places, times, and manners of how sexuality (and gender) were considered in public—on campus events, in artistic endeavors, and even in institutional practices and policies. Queer students tended to view their sexuality as fluid: their queer sexuality, while defining them in opposition to heterosexuality, did not relegate them to the other half of the binary construct of sexuality any more than one identity of necessity precluded sexual activities with someone because of their gender.

As with homosexual and closeted types, neither student identity development theories nor gay identity development theories convey the complexities and verisimilitude of gay and queer experiences and senses. Neither do those theories reflect the sensibilities that queer and gay students had of their roles and activities on campus, let alone their identities. Gay identity theories posit gay activism only as a sign of attempted acceptance into a socially stigmatized role, rather than as efforts to redefine that role through full social inclusion; queer activism would be deemed an acting out by lesser developed individuals, but not as a labor to challenge the very precepts that would postulate those actions and individuals as deviant and inverted. Student identity development theories would situate both gay and queer students into lesser-advanced stages of development, due to the students' fixation upon their differences from the norm, rather than, again, accepting their sexuality; in those terms, more developed students acknowledge and accede to the niches that their sexuality confines them to in general society.

The gay and queer identity types complicate the notions of non-heterosexual students far more than the previous two types (homosexual and closeted), in part because gay and queer students view their lives in relation not only to the norms of heterosexuality (as did the previous two types) but also against homosexual and closeted types. As more collegians began identifying in ways we can see as gay or queer, and as they engaged in campus activism, activities, and scholastic endeavors, the notions of what non-heterosexuality was (and was not) changed, as the students and identities considered marginal became more prominent on campus.

By the early 1970s, as the narratives depict, concepts of how to be non-heterosexual on college campuses were no longer conscripted to definitions delimited by comparisons to heterosexuality. The final two identity types of this theory, "normal" and parallel, complicate the distinctions between heterosexual and non-heterosexual students even further. The narratives of students in those classifications comprise the next chapter.

CHAPTER 5

Beyond Textbook Definitions: "Normal" and Parallel Students

In the previous two chapters, I have represented two binary patterns prevalent in existing research on non-heterosexual and student identity (gay and closeted) and two not usually taken into consideration (homosexual and queer). In addition, two more ways non-heterosexual male students identify in college are clear to me from my conversations with the respondents: those who consider themselves "just like everyone else"—"normal"—and those who view their lives as having parallel components. These categories move even further away from the binary master categories of "heterosexual" and "homosexual," blurring the lines of demarcation while conversely corroborating those classifications as well. This paradox is evidence of the diversity in collegiate non-heterosexual identification, which is lacking in the identity development theories currently existing for students and gay men. In this chapter, I present first "normal" and then parallel narrators' educational life stories.

"Normal"

For some students, collegiate life, like their experience within earlier education, was dominated by peer pressure to conform, to be "just like all the other guys." Certainly, an element of this is apparent within many of the stories thus far (James not wanting to be viewed as a theatrical homosexual, the advice to Juan to join a fraternity and not be gay, Bob joining a fraternity to fit into the social setting of his college), but not to the degree to which it influenced the personal meanings, the sensibilities, of their identities. Not to be "normal" conscripted one to a limited role in campus life: an effeminate gay; "catty, backstabbing, bitchiness"; a weak queer. In the words of an undergraduate in the 1970s:

Homosexual did not equal normal—and I wanted more than anything to be normal—regular—one of the guys. Being gay or homosexual back then was still filled with the negative stereotypes of the limp-wristed, effeminate, lisping hairdresser. I wasn't that, so I decided I couldn't be homosexual or gay. . . . My homosexuality back then was just about sex, nothing more.

Sexuality for "normal"-type students, at least in terms of a social identity, was neatly divorced from sexual activity. Homo-expression and homo-socialization were ruled out, but homo-sex was accepted. One could have sexual thoughts about other males, even engage in sexual activity with them (which many "normal" guys did, frequently), but such actions did not necessarily have any bearing upon one's identity. A 1980s undergraduate from the East Coast summarized the experience:

I never really considered [my sexuality]. I mean I remember having sexual thoughts about men as far back as eighth grade. And in high school they were there constantly. But I just never considered being gay. I think the main reason for this (besides my natural inclination to suppress it) was because I literally did not know one gay person. Or, you know what I mean, anyone identifying himself as gay. I mean growing up I thought maybe, just maybe, Liberace and Jim Nabors (as so many said) were gay. And I didn't identify with them AT ALL. Nor did I want to. . . . It was just an insult really.

These young men could not fathom an identity as anything other than that of their friends and peers, who, despite actions and expressions, were deemed to be heterosexual. To return to identity's Greek roots, to be the "same as," their self-concepts were easily more like those they discerned around them, rather than images of gay, homosexual, or queer men they saw portrayed in media (if they found any images at all). The experiences of three men depicted how this concept of self-identity framed the collegiate activities and sensibilities for "normal" guys. Instead of finding (or creating) a meaning of their homo-sexual behavior based upon difference from heterosexual-identifying peers, "normal" students viewed their sexual actions as having no bearing upon how they self-identified, nor upon their social, academic, or extracurricular activities.

Ralph

Adolescence. Ralph grew up in Waco, Texas, during the Depression of the 1930s. Although he and his friends might engage in "playful fooling around," he did not seriously think about what his activities meant beyond the immediate enjoyment he felt. "We never discussed sex. Walking home from school when I was in the ninth grade, there were four of us walking along. Two of the boys in the group had older brothers who had become 4-F and were not allowed to go into the service. One guy said, *Well, you know why my brother and Joe's brother didn't get into the service, don't you?* I said, *No, I don't know.*
"*It's just a little three-letter word.*"
"*'Three-letter word?*'"
"G-A-Y?'"
"And my friend and I said *G-A-Y.* It meant absolutely nothing to me. But then he told us what it was, and we snickered, of course, ninth graders snickering along there on the sidewalk. But that was something I had never even heard of, but I had been involved with some people, here and there, but I just figured that was something I'd outgrow. That was what we were told. I never outgrew it. It got worse!"

The labels did not appear to Ralph to focus on sexual activity as much as it did social behaviors. "We didn't know the word 'gay,' and the word 'queer' was bandied around a little bit. But 'sissy'. . . well, nobody wanted to be a sissy. But I masturbated constantly, with the neighborhood kids. We all did it. But I didn't do it with my friends in school. I didn't feel that [term] matched [my activity]. The only time I could do it with somebody I knew was when we were in the bed, at night, after the lights were out. I wanted to be the perfect [Christian] example, and I felt [homo sex] took me away from that. Yet some of the people that I really respected and liked, I knew that they were doing that, but not with me.

"I didn't think that [gay, or homosexual] was a definition of me, but it was just all the boys were doing it. All the boys weren't doing it, but all the boys were doing it in my mind. And the guys that I ran around with primarily, we never had any sexual contact. I would sleep over at their houses, and [only] two of them, we fooled around when we slept together. But I go back home now, and all my friends I was with from junior high school, high school, and college are all gay. And I didn't know it then. We never talked about it."

Early College. Ralph enrolled at Baylor University in 1944, but was soon called to military service in World War II. "I had to fill out [draft forms, with questions of 'homosexual tendencies']; everyone did. I put 'none.' I wasn't lying. I didn't think I was a homosexual. My sexual understanding was so infantile. All I knew was that I loved to masturbate, I loved to look at guys, I loved to touch guys, and I did not want to touch a girl. Period. Even when I was dating them.

"My definitions about sex at that time were so meager that, to me, sex was a man and a woman. I did not relate that—I knew that what I was doing was fun, but I just figured that it would all change . . . I have known, and I knew all my life, that I was different all of my life. I never even tried to make love to a girl, even when I was becoming engaged. This was after I was a junior in college. I would kiss and hug my girlfriend. I had lots of girlfriends. I would hug them and kiss them, but to think of trying to touch their breasts, oh! Or to try to touch their private parts! I was married thirty-four years, and I never looked at [my wife's private parts], not one time! I dated my wife for over two years, and I never considered trying to have sex with her. . . . [After we were married] we had lots of sex, but I was never interested in having sex with any other girl. I didn't always [think about men while having sex with my wife], but I sometimes did. I never had a dream about having sex with a girl. Any time I dreamed of sex, I was having sex with men."

After his stint in the service, Ralph returned in 1946 to Waco, and went on to complete his degree in history and education in 1949. "I lived on campus. It was never a requirement that we live on campus. When I first started, I was living with my parents. When I was in the service, they moved out, so when I came back I moved into the dorms." Later, as we will see, he moved to a residence close to, yet off campus. "There were lots of houses in the radius of the campus, so [later] I lived one block south of the campus, in a house where fourteen of us guys lived in one house. I went to school before the war, and almost no one had a car.

"Baylor was a rich person's school; I was a GI living on the GI Bill. All of the guys living in the house where I lived were ex-GIs. We didn't do much . . . [because] we had a limited amount of money. We would sit around and talk, or hop in the car and go out to the Circle, to the Elite Cafe, and have the smallest thing we could afford, because they had this delicious house dressing that they kept on the table. They would give us crackers, and we'd eat that house dressing and crackers, and buy ourselves coffee or hot chocolate or whatever, and maybe a grilled cheese sandwich. We must have eaten a thousand dollars worth of that house dressing. They stopped putting it on the table.

"Most of us didn't have cars. I finished in 1949, and in 1949 there were still not a lot of people who owned their own cars. We usually had one or two people, out of that fourteen [housemates] who had access to a car. We'd get in the car and drive out to the big lake outside of Waco, or out to the rivers in the warm weather to go swimming at night. But we never went swimming nude; the only time you went swimming nude was in swimming class!

"I can remember, when I was a freshman in college. At Baylor, you [swam] nude. And there was this guy in my class who kept going down and grabbing my dick. I was afraid for him to do that, because I knew I would get an erection. He didn't care; he had a great big old cock, and he let his get firm. But nobody [else] did that, and I didn't want to do that. I had to distance myself from that guy, because he constantly bothered me. I stayed away from him as much as I could. I was very active in the church. So was he, but he was willing to do these things. So I took swimming when I was a freshman. I took it again when I was a senior, because I just liked to go swimming with all those naked guys. You had to line up along this wall. All those nude guys, I did a lot of checking, visual checking. Loved every minute of it."

Later College. Although Ralph recognized the social disapprobation of homo-affection and -sexuality, he did not internalize that sense into his sensibility about who he was. At the same time, neither did he externalize his sense of sexuality into a public identity. "I never had any feelings like that [guilt over sexual activity] at all. My feelings were, anything that was beautiful, I loved it, and I didn't give a damn what anyone thought about it. [But] I didn't want to get caught at all, because it would just be too much. What I would do was to sneak around and do things. I would sneak in the bathroom and play around under the stalls, you know. In the library, [there were] those big study tables. We'd sit and put our feet in the other person's crotch, under the table. I had several different guys that we would always sit across from each other, so we could play footsie under the table. They were guys in my classes. Some of them were in the religious groups I was in. But we never talked about it.

"I had a roommate, later on. Before we became roommates, he told me, 'I had to move out of that room, with that guy that I was with, because he kept bothering me in the night. He just kept bothering me and bothering me in the night.' So we rented a room in this house a block off campus. We had a double bed, and we slept together. The first night, he started playing around. And we played around every night, but he and I never said one word to each other in the daylight or when we were talking. We never, ever mentioned that we had touched each other. It was so secret. We were [pretending to be] asleep. We were two people, both gullible enough to convince ourselves that we were asleep and the other person was asleep. But I knew he wasn't asleep, and he knew I wasn't asleep. I don't remember just how far we progressed, but it was often that we did the playing around. I was always a little ashamed of it, to the point that I started making the bed to where there was a definite fold in the quilts and things, for my side of the bed. But I learned how to just push that fold away at night. . . . I was convicted in my heart as a Christian that I shouldn't be doing this, and we had had several boys kicked out of Baylor when it was found out that they were gay. My French teacher had been in class one day, and the next day, [he] wasn't there. Most of us just didn't know what happened, except for this group of snickerers who knew he'd been caught and just let go immediately."

But the draconian responses of the Baptist school did not completely deter the sex or queer transgressions upon heterosexual normative cultural institutions. "They had a womanless wedding. A lot of the Baylor students got involved; this was [after graduation,] when I was teaching, 1952 probably. They were having a wedding: two guys, all men. Some were dressed like women, some were dressed like men. They were having a lark. This is before cross-dressing was popular. . . . And the police caught them. They caught all of these guys—some of them were students, and some of them were ministerial students from Fort Worth who had come down. The Waco *News Tribune* reported all of this."

Still, Ralph believed he, like everyone else he knew, should marry a woman. "My college experiences definitely lead me into the idea that I was going to have a family and that I was going to stay married all of my life and all that, and have children (which I did; I had five). But the thing of sex, although it was very prominent in my life, never figured in my plans. I never planned for the sexual part of my life; I just figured that would come naturally. We were never informed of the great homosexual figures of the past; that could have meant so much to us.

"I wish that I had known enough to know how to have gone into a gay relationship and stay there. I do not want to say I should have done it, because I have five wonderful kids and six wonderful grandkids. But I would not have had those if I had had the freedom and the encouragement by some role models to put myself into a gay relationship."

Chris

Adolescence. Chris grew up in the suburbs surrounding Chicago during the 1970s and '80s. Throughout those years he felt a difference from his peers, but did not term it as a fundamental incongruity. Neither did he view his homosexual activity as deviant; his first sexual encounter was at age thirteen. "Summer after my eighth grade year. Totally consensual. It was with an older man, too; it wasn't kid stuff. Totally consensual." But this activity, in his mind, did not correspond to the label of "queer" that his school peers called him; that labeling, he believed, corresponded to gender-related qualitites, like disinterest in sports and small body size, rather than to sexual activities. In terms of his sexuality, and its concurrent effect upon his identity, however, he was just like everyone else.

Early College. In 1987, Chris enrolled at the University of Illinois, which he attended for four years, majoring in the teaching of French. At U of I, he became a member of two campus communities: the formal greek-letter system and an informal cadre of men who have sex with men. "I came from an all-boy Catholic high school. There's a certain camaraderie, in going to a 30,000-person university, [made by] joining a fraternity." In pledging, Chris attempted "to make it [the university] smaller, and get the group of friends I'd always lacked. Originally my intent was to be part of the 'beautiful' crowd. I had come into my own after high school. Other people had told me I was very attractive, and I noticed that the attractive men on campus were involved in fraternities.

"At U of I, [greek life] is a major, big thing: it's the largest fraternity [system] in the country. I was going to join the Pikes, which was the looks house; I had gotten a bid from them, except I was scared for a couple of reasons to join them. One, the financial situation: they were a very expensive house to join. You were going to have buy a lot of clothes, and to keep up the role of Pike was going to be very expensive. Two, I had heard that they had done some pretty hefty things during hazing. I really wasn't sure I was able to keep up my end of the bargain, to be a part of this good-looking house. At the same time, I was looking at Psi Upsilon, which, since everyone has their labels for houses, was a rich, preppy boy house for boys who could not get into Pikes. There I could be a very good looking guy, as opposed to an average guy. So which was one better for me? Psi Upsilon wanted me, so I knew that their hazing was not going to be as difficult." As it turned out, "Hazing involved a lot of homo-erotic things, and I was not sure how I was going to react to that stuff. . . . And nothing was really expected of me, except for being a good-looking, well-dressed guy on campus."

Chris viewed both attending college and pledging the fraternity as opportunities to recreate his self-image. "I very much liked the sense of community [in the greek system]. I was leaving a lot of bad stuff from high school behind; this was my chance to get that group-of-guys friendship that I never had. Within the fraternity, my closest five or six friends were also gay but had not called themselves that yet. There we were able to enjoy our gay friendship in a straight atmosphere, as long as we played the part correctly. Here were a bunch of guys who were very friendly with me, yet at the same time they were almost forced to be friendly with me because of the brotherhood thing.

"There was still a camaraderie there which I had never had on a male level in high school. That sense of community was very important to me, but at the same time I would walk around campus with my letters on and knew that the other people were looking at me as 'hot fraternity guy.' I had never had that before, so I was able to milk that for all it was worth. In high school I was the school queer; the other guys were very astute at figuring out what I liked, even though I had a girlfriend and things like that. I didn't have to deal with a lot of that in college, because I had a safety net of my gay friends who did not know they were gay, either."

Despite not talking about homosexuality, he did experience it. "I first started off, in college, [finding sex] in bookstores, because that was my experience in high school. There were two bookstores [for gay rendevous] in Champaign, two very good ones. And then learning the bathroom system; the undergrad bathroom was the meeting point for all of that. I just kind of happened upon that one time at the library. And then reading the bathroom walls, figuring out where everyone else went. There was a whole system and a mechanic to the whole thing: where to go to meet someone, where to then go to have sex with that person, where the hot guys hung out, where the non-hot guys hung out. So you knew which bathroom to go to; you would just follow the notes. There was a place in the [Student] Union that was only busy at certain times; there was a place in the master's library. But pretty much bookstores and bathrooms."

Chris applied the same standards to both greek life and tearoom sex. "[The bathrooms] were the whole system; that's where we [fraternity men] all went. The funny thing is, it was a title thing as well. Just like a girl dating a Beta at school was considered really cool, if you were able to do a Beta in the bathrooms you were a very cool bathroom guy. There was a pattern to this. You'd start off in the undergrad and see who was in the undergrad bathroom. There were eight stalls. And you'd figure out who was down there, who was good, who wasn't. Then you'd meet clandestinely in the master's bathroom and have sex with people there. There were people that I'd have sex with more than once; there was never a schedule to it, but more than once. There were some guys that I only saw once and never saw [there] again. But I would see them later on [elsewhere on campus] with their fraternity letters on.

"I was bragging to myself. You have to remember, I grew up with a lack of self-esteem. Here was my first chance. Instead of going to bookstores, like I did in high school, seeing what I termed perhaps the physically grossest people—

not necessarily doing them, but seeing them—here was my first chance to see very good-looking guys with very good-looking bodies, who I would think were straight, dropping their pants for me to suck them off. So it was bragging rights to me, and made me feel better about myself, because even though I was only a Psi U, as one of the hottest Psi U's I was able to get a Pike or a Beta.

"A lot of times it was a game. I enjoyed the bathroom scene; I enjoyed the bookstores. There was a game, there was a chase, and it was intellectually interesting to me as well as being sexually fun. There was a sense of excitement when I left the fraternity to go to the library: *Who's going to be out that night? Who's going to be in there tonight? Who am I going to be able to nab? Who's going to show up there that I don't expect?* There was definitely excitement in the whole thing."

Continuing his approach to these two components of his life as normal and not mutually exclusive, Chris applied the same standards of interest, appeal, and status to both his dating of women and his sex with men. "It was important for people to know I was greek. At U of I, there was a definite pecking order, and to be greek there. . . . My goal was to get other fraternity guys. That was my element of fun. And really, that game and that community of bathroom people became my group. I mean, we never spoke, of course, but I at least knew that there were other people out there who were young, attractive, and hot, who also liked doing the same things I did."

Chris made a distinction between sexual behavior and self-identity. He had a private life from his greek peers but engaged in very public homo-sex. The only time he was homo-expressive was behind the closed doors of the tearoom system, yet that homo-sex empowered Chris. "Did I get my self-esteem from the wrong places? I don't know, but I definitely got something there. And it made me feel very good about myself when I was able to nail a hottie there. Sex in college finally made me understand I was an attractive person.

"I get kind of bothered nowadays when I hear about bathroom raids. For a lot of people, that's their first chance feeling comfortable. As sick and as backwards as that sounds, for some people that's their way to express themselves and to find out what this whole thing is about. And that the phase they think they're going through is not a phase. It was definitely a transition [for me]. There I learned the rules, how to pick up someone, what to say and what not to say, how to act and how not to act in order to get sex or to get someone interested in me. It made it all that much easier when I started doing the whole gay bar scene in Chicago, to learn how to hit on men in Chicago."

Later College. Chris's social life had these two distinct components, but he found neither really at odds with the other. "I was greek, so I spent a lot of time at the fraternity, a lot of time at the greek bars. I turned myself straight [in those contexts]. But at the same time, [he continued] the sexual activity which had gone on all through high school and college. I was able to live two separate lives. I did not term the second life anything; I was not gay, but I did gay things. So the behavior was gay, [but] not necessarily the essence. How did I manage it internally? I in some ways disassociated. I had my regular life and my sex life, which was all gay at the time, because my girlfriend lived two hours north, in Chicago."

Despite this statement, Chris's interpretation of his sexuality was far from the compartmentalization evident in parallel lives (discussed later in this chapter). "There was no conflict within me at all. I knew where to go to have sex, I knew where to get it, it was very easy. And then I went back living my regular life: go back to do homework, live in the house, or whatnot. Plus, all my friends in the fraternity, I didn't know it at the time, [but] were gay as well. So there was really no stigma associated with being gay, because we were all gay inside. That subject was never talked about, but at the same time, it was an underlying theme.

"A typical weeknight would be doing school stuff all day, then having dinner together with the fraternity. We always had dinner together. And then it was off to the library, to do homework. I rarely stayed in the fraternity, because it was too loud there to study. So I went to the library, and the library was also the main place where I would go to have sex. So, I'd get some homework done, see who was around to play with, and then come home about 10:30 or 11:00. That was on a homework night. On a non-homework night, sitting at home, watching TV with the guys. Pretty normal."

Another aspect of his life that was "pretty normal" was his romantic involvement and engagement to a young woman in Chicago. He considered the relationship serious. "As far as I know, [it had] everything that a straight relationship would have. A true and honest one. We were. . . . You're going to kind of get into some Clinton-esque definitions of sex. Did I have sexual intercourse with her? No. Did we do everything up to that point? Yes. She was two years older then me, so she lived on her own. I slept over at her place a lot, and we slept together. She'd come visit the fraternity, we'd sleep together. We had a common group of friends that we did not meet at college. As far as I knew, it was normal. I just knew where I could go to find gay sex when I needed it, in Chicago. I got pretty good finding out where to go to get it."

Chris's sensibilities did not change to incorporate meanings of his sexual experiences. He did not self-identify as anything other than "straight" or "normal" for many years. "It wasn't until after college. I didn't think that an emotional relationship with a man was possible; I figured that it was all sexual. So if I was going to go for an emotional relationship, I was going to have to do that with a woman. For me, the age that I started having sex and the amount of sex that I had, caused me to believe that [for] men it was only a sexual thing." His understandings did not change "until after I had graduated, the first year [after, when], my best friend came out. And that caused a rift between my girlfriend and me, and got me out of that relationship" [with her].

"I think the college experience was the first time [circumstances] were set up perfectly for me, to live my gay life as I wanted to live it then. Again, 'gay' was purely sexual to me. And it set up the perfect place, where there were 30,000 people gathered in one spot, with high stress levels, right out of high school, with a lot of drives going on in them that they haven't figured out (although we all tried to come across as undergrads who knew what's up), mixed in with grad students who knew how to—some would say exploit, some would say enjoy—and it was just a perfect situation for me to find the type of sex I enjoyed at the time, without feeling any guilt."

Post College. In 1999, Chris was teaching at Arizona State University, working to complete a doctoral degree in French. "When I have gay students come out to me, I often tell them that it would probably be a good idea to go to a college and not live at home; there's just so much independence and freedom to enjoy, you can take the time to discover what is going on with you, both in your head and sexually. . . . It helps you break down your own barriers and your own constructs of what it means to be gay."

Reflecting back to his own undergraduate experience, Chris valued it highly. "College was a lot of fun. There's a lot of people who are jealous of my college experiences, because I had so much sex in college, and the type of sex and the type of guy I had sex with. U of I definitely enabled that, definitely allowed that to happen. "

Greg

Early College. The late 1980s were also the years that Greg was an undergraduate. Like Chris, Greg grew up outside of Chicago. He first enrolled in a community college in the metro suburbs, earning an associate degree before transferring to Eastern Illinois University in 1988. Unlike Chris, Greg did not engage in homo-sex on campus.

"I would hang out with my friends, in the residence halls, which is where I primarily lived. A lot of my friends were involved with residence hall governance. We also hung out primarily at one bar. That was all at Eastern. When I was at community college, it was basically just an extension of my friends from high school, the ones who didn't go away to college. At the same time, I was working full-time and going to school. So, there wasn't a lot of time for socializing."

Neither Greg's senses nor his experiences were non-heterosexual when he arrived at Eastern; consequently, his sensibilities were heterosexual as well. "When you're straight, you normally don't have terminology about your sexual identity; you just kind of associate that you're just like everyone else. I thought of myself exactly like everybody else. I hadn't had sex with anybody. I was still a virgin, all the way through college."

On-campus living provided Greg both new opportunities for relating to others and changes in how he viewed himself. "In my residence hall, I held vice president and president offices. And then in the entire university residence system, I held the treasurer position. I made some of the best friends of my life there [in residence hall governance]. People were not there because they necessarily wanted to be, but because somebody came by and said, *We really need somebody to go to this meeting; will you go?* And you say, *Who else is going?* And you drag a friend with you, to go with you to this. And it's only within that group of people, these people that just went because they were dragged there, that they elect and bring to the top amongst themselves—not amongst the entire student body, but just amongst themselves—that they make the leaders. There are people who were involved in high school politics—the popular, the pretty people—who went on to the student body governance things in college. Residence hall governance and student governance at my university were opposite ends of the spectrum. We didn't like them, and they thought we were a bunch of geeks. Which we were, but we had a great time.

"The best part of college were the two semesters I was treasurer of the entire residence hall system of Eastern Illinois University. I was not the president of the organization, but I believe that I was probably the most highly regarded member of the executive board. I made more money for the organization than it had ever made. I organized their finances probably better than they ever had. It was a position that I absolutely loved. And I had the greatest time in the world. I was busier than I ever was."

Later College. By the end of him time at Eastern Illinois, Greg's conceptions about his sexuality, and his normality, had changed. "I knew. . . . I was gay in my head. I knew what my fantasies were. I mean, I had purchased, through the mail, gay pornography. I knew that I was attracted to men. The [men] I was in college with I was very attracted to. It was difficult being in a situation where there were people around you whom you were attracted to, [when] you definitely had these feelings. And being too afraid to do anything about it. Or to be around others who might do something about 'it.' I had a gay roommate at one time, whom I disassociated myself from, extremely."

Unlike Chris, Greg did not clue into the clandestine homo-sex culture; further, he was too frightened to pursue gay campus activities. "I didn't know where to go to find anything gay in college. I had contacted the social worker on campus, to find out if there were any gay and lesbian support groups, but it scared me out of my mind to go. So, it was mostly fear of what others would think: parents, friends. But at the same time, I did try. It was very difficult for me, but I would come home, at my parents' house, and talk to gay people online.

"I did start [cruising and having homosexual encounters in] the park and the forest preserves stuff, like, the summer before my last year. I look at it as kind of a rite of passage and as something kind of something transitionary. The few times I've gone back to see what it's like now, after I've been in a relationship and stuff like that, it's been like, *Oh, this was so stupid.* But what I would consider my first sexual experience was after college. I consider the first time I had sex to be the first time I was in bed with a man. [The prior activity was] jerking off. I mean, it was all—I was so scared. It was just kind of situations I found myself in. The first time I feel that I had sex with somebody was the first time there was kissing, and there was actual passion, and I was really enjoying it. The other times were just kind of circumstances I found myself in; there wasn't much else there besides just orgasm.

"For me, once I found the sex part, it all made sense. Finding the sex part and finding that there actually were gay bars and places that I could go to and stuff like that all happened at the same time. So it was like, *Oh, my God!* Making associations with other people who were gay and realizing how much that we were alike. And not just the fact that we liked sex with other men, but so many other things as well. Once I made all those realizations, it was like, *Okay, this is it for me.* But it was all the people who had known me at that point, that it was very, very difficult for me to come out to."

Greg viewed his time at Eastern Illinois as important and beneficial. "I loved my college experience. But I'm still jealous about the sexual part of it [of others who had sex during college]. Because I had no sex in college."

Reflections on "Normal" Collegians

Ralph, Chris, and Greg, although they attended different institutions at different times, each recalled experiences and senses of being "just like everyone else"; during their college years their homosexual activity did not change their sensibilities of how their sexuality related to their concepts of self. Clearly, although they have since identified as non-heterosexual, during those times these men would not have responded to an self-concept as anything but "normal." "Normal," as Greg pointed out, is an unconsidered position, a concept so self-evident that to even question its qualities is to call into question one's own normality. Each of these men made it clear that the terminology, the concepts, of non-heterosexuality were available; but in each case, the markers of identification were not necessarily sexual activity, but social roles ascribed and decried by heterosexual peers. Despite the homo-affections, even in disregard of the sexuality they exhibited, these collegians considered themselves (as well as their experiences and emotions) "normal," "just like everybody else."

Indeed, in some respects, they were anything but abnormal: Ralph dated women and eventually married while in college; Chris applied the same standards to his heterosexual dating as he did his homosexual tricking; and Greg reveled in and developed in traditional campus student development activities. None of them had friends or acquaintances who openly identified as non-heterosexual while in college, but neither did they join gay or queer student organizations or causes.

The concepts of *men* and *de* were not evident in the sensibilities or experiences of these students, for "normal" collegians integrated their non-heterosexual *de* experiences into a sensibility that included such actions without an identification of difference from the *men* of their cultures. None of the "normal" students were particularly troubled by feelings of duplicity or hypocrisy, reflecting no conflict between *men* and *de*; they found no dissonance between homo-expressive and -sexual behavior and holding fast to a non-homosexual identity (as unexamined a position as that might appear). Their actions were woven into the daily (or nightly) patterns of their lives, often integrating homo-situations (checking out nude swimmers, having sex with other students in the library bathrooms) alongside non-homo-situations (attending swim class, studying in the library). In the cultural contexts of their campuses, they were not considered (openly considered, at least) as anything but "normal," because they neither incorporated their sexual activities and senses into a non-heterosexual sense of self nor deployed their sexual or affectional activities publicly. Nevertheless, the experiences of these "normal" students would probably not be classified as such by student development theorists or practioners; neither would their experiences fit within the existing models of homosexual development. The existing theories of development do not reflect the senses these students had of their lives, nor the sensibilities they formed about their identity.

Parallelism

In contrast to the integration of homosexual activities into their sensibilities and concurrent lack of consideration of meaning of those acts to one's self-concept experienced by the "normal" students, other male collegians keenly felt the disjuncture of the homo- and the hetero-experiences. These men did feel conflict between their identity and their actions. For such students, who exemplify the "parallel" type, the undergraduate years were a combination of distinctly different sets of cultures, acquaintances, and behaviors. By day (usually, but not always so, though), these collegians attended class, worked on or off campus, spent time with friends from school, or participated in home or family life. But by night (usually, but not always confined to those hours), they engaged in different behaviors: they lived a "shadow existence," cruising bars, parks, or other sexualized spaces, looking for male sexual partners; they took great pains to ensure their anonymity (at least as far as beyond those sexualized settings). Unlike Chris, parallel men did not think of their lives as normal nor see their behavior mirrored in their peers; unlike Greg, they considered their sexual activity as sex, and not simply fooling around or reaching an orgasm; unlike Ralph, these men did not cohabit with the other men with whom they have sex. These parallel collegians ensured that the two social milieus they are maneuvering in never converge. In the words on one student from the late 1940s, "I felt I was leading two lives."

Dennis

Early College. Dennis attended two undergraduate institutions in Pennsylvania in the late 1960s and early 1970s: first Westchester State College outside of Philadelphia and later Duquesne University, a Catholic institution in Pittsburgh. He found the transition to postsecondary life quite liberating. "I never dated girls after high school. I didn't have to play that game anymore. I was gay. Of course, the word when I was there was 'queer,' and I knew I was queer. I knew I was different. I knew I wanted to be with men. But I didn't think I could tell anyone. I hid it. I didn't act out on it on campus. Not until I sort of accidentally ran into someone else like me did another person know."

Dennis had perceived for several years that his sexual desires differed from those of his peers. "I was twelve the first time [I made connection between myself and the word 'queer']. I was twelve the first time I has sex with a man. I liked it, but it was a 'bad' thing. I was told it was a bad thing, but I knew that I liked it. I had bad feelings about it as well, when I wasn't acting on it. I liked the acting out on it. But when I was alone in my own head, in my own room,

I would look in the mirror and think, *Well, queers are dirty old men. You're not old, and.* . . . So I had very confused feelings about it, which don't do a lot for your self-esteem, but I did like the acting out of it, and I did seek it, in spite of my feelings that it was *bad.*"

Dennis's search was not on campus, however. "Socially [in college], I would hang out with a crowd, so I wouldn't be attached with any particular person. During the week, I would study my head off. I was a music major; not only did you have to take all the subjects everybody else was taking, you had a major instrument to practice, a minor instrument to practice, and an elective instrument to practice. So there were three hours a day of practicing. Unless you're a music major, people don't understand; they're really quite busy. I didn't have time during the week to do anything socially.

"But predominately on weekends I had my own little private life. When I went to school in Philly, on Friday after class I would get on the bus, go into 69th Street Station, get on the el [elevated train], and go into the city. And [I] would cruise the train station to find some old man to spend the weekend with. Now, when I say *old man*, I was seventeen, he was probably thirty, you know? I'd find some older business guy on the way home from work, [who would] pick me up in the men's room in the train station. And I'd spend the weekend with him.

"That was sort of my weekend routine. When I was back home in Pittsburgh, I was real secure, and I would go to the gay bars. I was underage, but the weekend would come and I'd be in the gay bars, dancing my fool little head off.

"Thank God I was dedicated during the week, because I didn't get any [homework] done. There were basically at least two and a half days a week that I wasn't putting in the practice time other music majors were. And they're probably now playing in a symphony somewhere, because they were putting in the time. I did [want to practice more], but that got in the way of my personal life. Lots of things, through my life in my younger years, lots of achievements that I may have made or would have liked to have made, I didn't [do], because they took time away from what I saw as my personal life, or my sexual life. And it came first."

Dennis did not share his knowledge of his weekends with his friends or peers. "No one [in classes] *knew* I was a gay man. I think everyone suspected. I don't think I was fooling a lot of people. I was quite thin, quite cute, and quite effeminate. My saving grace in high school was that I played football quite well, so I didn't get teased like the other ones did. [In] college, I think people were really past the teasing stuff about that. They just thought that I was a music major; it was okay to be effeminate. Not that all music majors were, but it was okay, if you were a music major. If I had been a PE major, they might have killed me. I think a lot of people suspected, but I was not out, and no one knew. I did not share these feelings with anyone except the strangers I would meet and get to know, off campus and in the city."

Dennis never kept in touch with the men with whom he would spend his weekends. "Oh no, that was off-limits. There's a man I think about to this day. I would love to be able to find him. He was just the nicest person, and I would have no idea of where to start. But no, I kept in touch with none of them, but I got to know them very well. I would seek them repeatedly. I remember this guy who worked for Scott Paper Company. He was just this big, beautiful man. He used to take me to this wonderful place that overlooked the Delaware River. We'd put a blanket out and fuck in the daylight. It was a secluded place, this place he had found for us. He was just really romantic with me, this young kid. I was frightened of commitment; I just knew I liked the sex. Yet I wanted the continuation of seeing someone. I was frightened of the commitment, because commitment meant people would know, because we'd be together. But there were lots of people I wish today that I would have kept in touch with, because they were wonderful people. And then there were some weirdos along the way.

"The men I would meet or be attracted to or would have these 'non-relationship relationships' with were always older, because I thought I could learn from them. There was some bit of father figure in that. It was never people my own age, never. Even once I met other people on campus who were gay, there was nothing sexual about that. Sexuality was expressed with older men. Older men were outside of my way of life. Even if I ran into a younger man outside of that, that was too close to my real life."

Later College. By the time Dennis moved back to Pittsburgh and transferred to Duquesne, he began to "be gay" on campus. But, as before, his idea of being gay was exclusively sexual and not social. "I actively pursued a professor. He was my music theory teacher. I would start by putting a star next to his name on every one of my papers. He would ask me what this meant, and I told him I thought he was the most handsome man I'd ever seen. He actually took me out for a drink and explained to me why nothing could happen, because I was a student of his. He might have been queer, but he was ethical. It was obvious to me he was a gay man. . . . He never denied he was gay; he never admitted he was gay; the word gay never came up. It wasn't used toward me, either. It was just two people."

Like Chris, Dennis was aware of the subcultural tearoom activities of non-heterosexual men on campus. "The first chair flute for the Pittsburgh Symphony taught flute. It was nothing to be in the men's room and have [him] looking through the cracks between the johns, to see who was in the toilets, cruising. So you knew that was going on; it was just never talked about. That's where gay people met other gay people. Straight men aren't meeting women in the bathroom; that's where gay men met other gay men. Especially when they weren't out enough to know where the bars were. That's why they meet in bathrooms, parks, bus stations, train stations.

"I think another reason that leads to that underground behavior is because you view your sexuality, your gay-ness, as just your sexuality. You'll still hear a gay man today say, *It's no one's business what I do in my bedroom.* Being gay is so much more than my sexuality, just like being straight is so much more than your sexuality. But I think in those days, at that age, I thought being gay was about sucking dick. That was what being gay was, with another man. And it wasn't about being a whole person who happens to be gay. So of course, the activity only revolved around sex."

Evaluating his college years after thirty years, Dennis makes a distinction between his identity now and his identity then. "I would say I was gay, but differently than I use that word today. 'Gay,' meaning my sexuality, ruled my every movement, thought, and interaction with people. I was either trying to flaunt it to those I wanted to know, or to hide it from those I didn't. But not like I would say today gay, meaning a whole complete person who is gay. Most academic situations I would try to hide it. That was a conscious effort. But the minute I got away from that, in my own time, I was using it to my best ability to get what I wanted: sex. I was very preoccupied with sex. For a gay man I was cute; in the straight world, I wasn't. Girls weren't falling all over me. I wasn't real manly; I wasn't masculine. I didn't fit in there at all; I never fit in there. I was thin, effeminate; but I was cute in the gay world.

"When I think back on my college years, I would just like to relive them all, all those years, because there was so much that was so wonderful, yet I didn't appreciate it because I was so caught up with my sexuality. It clouded and ruled so much that I missed out on so much else. If I could have been open and free about who I was, I could have enjoyed other things more. I feel like I really missed a lot because I was so preoccupied with that and had to hide that, as opposed to just be who I was, to walk through campus and enjoy campus the way other people did."

Alec

Adolescence. Alec's separation of his sexuality, his sexual identity, from his "everyday" life started well before he left home for college in the 1970s. "I thought about my sexuality from early on. When I was a freshman in high school, we moved from the city into the suburbs. I did high school . . . about twenty-five miles from Chicago. I had an awareness of being attracted to men from the time I was very young, about eight or nine years old, I guess. When I was ten years old, I started taking the bus and going [to] downtown Chicago by myself. I can't imagine ever letting my kids do that at age ten, and I certainly know my parents didn't let my sisters do that. I'm the oldest of seven. But . . . I had freedom to get on the bus at age ten and go downtown Chicago and spend the day or spend the afternoon or the evening.

"On one of those several trips I would take downtown, I discovered pornography. It was male pornography I was interested in. That was back in the mid-'60s, and physique magazines were all the rage. There were kiosks on the corners, where they would sell newspapers and magazines, and there was a particular one where I noticed on the very, very top shelf there were these physique magazines for a dollar. It took me probably weeks or months—I don't have a good recollection—to get up the nerve to ask to buy one of those. I'll never forget the response. The man did sell it to me; then he yelled at me to get away.

"I knew that was probably something I couldn't take home. I thought that a place probably where I could take it and have privacy would be in a public restroom. As Jo Anne Worley used to say, WRONG! And so, it was probably age ten or eleven or so that I discovered that public bathrooms are not all that private. It would take many years for me to explore that in a more physical, personal way, but I had knowledge very early on that stuff was going on in those bathrooms."

Such comprehension influenced what Alec did and how he behaved. "My life in high school, and for a good chunk of my life, became separated into sort of parallel lives. I had a life where I was the honor student, the valedictorian, earning all A's, the 'good boy,' the kid that never got into trouble, the kid that all the aunts and uncles loved and adored. And I had another life, where I was being a bad boy. Where I was masturbating in bathrooms, where I was buying pornography, where I was discovering a way to be sexual that was outside of the expectations of the family I grew up in.

"The messages back in the '60s were still very anti-gay, they were very pro-family. That's not the right language; that's language of the '90s that I'm putting back to that. There wasn't even an awareness that I could live a healthy life as a gay person. Gay meant just sick, perverted . . . *those people.*"

Alec did not think that the duality he felt in his life would change when he went to college. "The parallelism continued. When I got to college, I had, since

I was older, I had access to more ways of discovering what homosexuality was—and I'm using that word because that's the word that would have operated in my mind at the time. Prior to that time, when I was in high school, I couldn't go to the bars, I couldn't go to the movie houses, I couldn't go to the bookstores. I didn't know that a lot of that even existed, at the time. So my only way to understand homosexuality was through the medical language (I was deviant, I was a freak) or the language around hermaphroditism. I didn't have a way of knowing at that time that that was not all one big solid clump of stuff that got thrown into me. I just assumed it was all part of one package; being a hermaphrodite meant being a homosexual, meant hating your body, meant sex in the bathrooms. It was all together."

Early College. Alec attended public universities in the Midwest for undergraduate and graduate work. He viewed his matriculation as an occasion to redefine and redeploy his concept of self-identity; however, he rarely availed himself of the possibilities. "When I got to college, the opportunities to explore homosexuality in a different way came available. I could go to a gay bar. Now, that wasn't something that I was doing on the up and up; it was still a very closeted activity. But I did. I had, when I was a sophomore in college, a friend who was openly gay. I was playing around the edges. I was having all of this kind of bathroom sex, but it was not coming into the rest of my life. Here I had this friend who is gay, who is making no small attempt to put the make on me, and I'm this coy little seventeen-, eighteen-year-old boy who is not ready to declare, but really excited about dancing around the edges.

"It was about that time also that I started throwing out the possibility of using the word homosexuality to identify myself. I remember that it was when I was seventeen or eighteen, I was really angry and frustrated, and I wrote a vengeful letter to my mother and father."

Despite Alec's increasingly diverse understanding of his sexuality and identity, he still viewed his as juxtaposed to normal experiences and identities. "I did not think that toilet sex was normal. Today, I don't think of toilet sex as *not* normal, but I also don't engage in it very often. There are lots of ways for me to experience today what it is to be gay, that I didn't have a clue existed before. I never back then in college or high school thought that my sexual activities in public restrooms was normal. I classified myself . . . as just sick. I don't want to leave the impression that I was very, very sexually active at that time; I was not. I was frequenting public bathrooms often and masturbating, sometimes knowing I was being watched, sometimes not being watched, and having a magazine of male models. In high school, it was probably a handful of occasions when I let somebody give me a blow job. I did not have the courage or the inclination to correspond. Plus, I was chicken [very young]; that's what people wanted. In college, it was much the same. The first two years of my undergraduate degree, I only went home with somebody from a bar one time. And that somebody turned out to be a close friend of the friend that I told you about earlier.

"Then, in my little parallel life, where I was out whoring in bars (except not being very successful about it), I met this guy and wound up going to his dorm room. Now that was an unusual experience for me: there was no urinal in that room. It was the first time that I experienced body to body . . . instead of a hole in the wall. While it was titillating, while it was exciting, while it was a step in a different direction, I was really, really scared. I was scared that somebody would have seen me, either walking out of the bar, walking down the street with him, or coming out of his room. I was just terrified. Then, the next day, my friend said, *So, you went home with so-and-so.* I had no clue [that they were friends]. I was horrified. I retreated into my shame. I simply didn't have at my disposal a way of thinking positively about that."

Later College. Alec's experience in a study abroad program was pivotal to his understanding of his identity, and how his identity was subject to quite literal social punishment for deviating from the norm. "It wasn't probably until I was nineteen and living in Madrid when I really started to experience a gay identity. Still with a very small group, with very select individuals who knew that was going on; there were a handful, and I trusted them. I don't think at nineteen and twenty there was much distinction [between the concepts of 'gay' and 'homosexual']. The word ['gay'] was out, was being used; that was probably four or five years after Stonewall. It was certainly there, but the words were synonymous; I wouldn't have been able to tell you the difference. That might not have been true for other people who were using the word, but for me that was true."

In Madrid, Alec began to feel differently about his sexuality. "What I felt was that I was a long way from home, and they weren't watching me as closely, whoever they were: my family, my friends. . . . *They* were everybody. I felt the pressure to conform was so strong; it was coming from everywhere. I felt that in Spain, I could play with finding out more about this male-male sex thing. I learned for the first time about street cruising, and boy, did I like it. I think there was simply a moment when I allowed myself to look back at somebody. I can't remember how I knew, that first time somebody cruised me on the street. I had more [sex] in Spain, deliciously more. I was having public bathroom sex; I was going home with people; some of the people I met in bathrooms I went home with. It just seemed so much more available. I remember also there being a sudden romance in sex. I don't mean like romance in the typical way. My associations with sex had been dirty, dark, poorly lit, bad smells. I didn't have good associations with sex. [But in Madrid] the bathrooms were not scuzzy. When I would go home with people, it was sex in a house. There was color; there were three dimensions; there was light. It was really very different, and I remember all of sudden kind of enlightened by what sex could be. I liked it.

"I started getting excited about creating this identity, and then I got arrested in a gay bar in Madrid, for being there. Franco was still alive. Spain was ruled by a fascist dictator. I had been to that bar several times. The bartender (Rafael was his name) was, oh, so tasty. That was the year of *Cabaret*, Liza's *Cabaret*. *Maybe this time, I'll be lucky.* It had just come out, and I had seen it already probably two or three times, dubbed in Spanish. I identified with that movie like no other movie. Well, the *Wizard of Oz*. I know that's really facile, but it's true: Judy and Liza for me have been serious icons. So, I'm in this little gay bar, somebody turns on the jukebox, and it starts playing 'Cabaret.' I think, *It's my moment.* So I go into this lip-sync thing in the middle of the bar."

When he was acting out in the bar in Madrid, Alec was not on stage but was in an open space in the bar, with men circling him; the area was fairly well lit. "It was not a spotlight, but it was definitely my moment. It was an odd sort of moment, because [before] I didn't ever feel sexually like I could be the center of attention. I was wearing yellow, tight hiphuggers, bell-bottom hiphuggers, with this really tight little t-shirt, doing Liza. And doing her rather dramatically. Minutes after that was over, I thought it was time for me to go home, and I went to get my coat. I was stopped at the door, and that's when we were all taken to the commissary downtown. Spent the whole night there. The rumors that were going on were anything from imprisonment to being deported. I really thought I was up the creek.

"Sometime during that evening I was called before a panel of five, six people, [in] a rather large room with one long table. They're all sitting there, and I'm standing in front of them. They're going through this inquiry. My Spanish at that time was already quite good; I had studied about seven years by that time. I pretended not to understand quite as much as I actually did, and my accent got a whole lot worse than it was. I thought it would be better for me. I was aware that there was a game going on. The line of question was to elicit did I know what was going on in that bar. I said I was there for a drink, I was having a good time, and it seemed like people were having a good time; I didn't know why they were asking me these questions, I didn't know why I was there. At one point, someone referred to me as *the good boy*, and I said, *Yes, I am a good boy.*

"By morning I was let go and I was free to be on my way. But it was one of those critical moments that was a very strong message: it would not be good to live that way; it would not be good for me to choose a life where I was going to be arrested or I was going to be shamed. So I was sort of scared away from this incipient revelation of what it might be to be proud as a gay person. I went back to my underground kinds of feelings. I stopped going to the bars, I stopped cruising, I stopped doing the bathroom things for a couple of weeks. But you can't keep a good queen down; I was back on the streets in a very short time. But my spirit was broken. If you could look at the parallel lines of the two lives I had created, they were kind of converging, and then all of sudden, nope, that didn't work.

"The year after I got back from Spain, I met the woman who was going to be my wife, and we got married. I did what everybody expected I would do. The first six years I was married, gayness was something that existed only in my head; my fantasies were all gay. The tensions in my life were gay. I might be riding the el in Chicago, and be conscious of attempting to sit next to an attractive man. Sex for me in those years—sex that was not with my wife—would be feeling the pressure of a man's leg, pushing up against mine in the el. Now, that stuff can make you crazy. Finally, one day, I walked into an adult bookstore, and I got a blow job. Sex for the next eight or nine years was back to this parallel stuff of husband/father/provider/sex partner on the one hand, and then on the other hand, adult bookstores/rest areas. They had to be places that were dark because I was really afraid of being identified.

"My personal experience, while not unique, was different from a lot of gay men in that I chose for a very long time—I would not probably have used the word choice during all of that—the decision to live these parallel lives. It wasn't until my mid-thirties when a real change of self-notion started to take effect. I have felt that the ordinary experience . . . for resolution of gay identity happens during undergraduate years, and so I felt like it was necessary for me to move beyond the college years to allow a piece of my story where that got resolved for me, but it didn't happen until fifteen years later. I had a convergence [of the parallel lives] in my thirties; I had an approach in my late teens."

Pete

Early College. Pete first enrolled in a community college in a Mid-Atlantic state in 1978. Two years later, he transferred to the University of Maryland. He found his life at Maryland "very socially active: I wanted to move away from home. I knew someone, a relative of the family's, who was in this fraternity. He would invite me to parties at the fraternity. I looked at all the fraternities in the area, I decided I wanted that one over all the others, so I pledged that fraternity in the spring. I lived in the fraternity house my second semester at the University of Maryland. The fall is when I ran for office in my fraternity: corresponding secretary.

"Once you joined a fraternity—at least, this is how it was at the University of Maryland—you had to participate in everything. You were busy all the time. Every night of the week there was something to do, and there were very few study breaks, very few opportunities to study. You never did that. But there was a minimum grade point average which you had to have to be a pledge, which I think was a 2.0, so I know I did better than that my first semester.

"Things changed as I got older, but initially I did everything in the fraternity house. I slept in the fraternity house; we had parties in the fraternity house; I hung out in other people's rooms in the fraternity house. We would go to sororities that had parties. I didn't hang out in the sororities, but Monday nights were the nights you could have dinner at somebody else's house. I knew some women who were in the sororities, so I would go there and have dinner with them.

"I knew that I was gay long before I joined the fraternity. The fraternity was a vehicle for me to get out of my parents' house, because I was living at home. At the time, there was a movie called *Animal House*. My best friend, a heterosexual friend, saw that movie seven times. He really, really liked that movie. He was one of my straight circle of friends who didn't go to the university; he went to Catholic University. I would hang out with him at CU all the time, and he knew I was gay. He always wanted someone to go to the movie with him, so I saw it with him more than once. That movie piqued my interest in fraternities. I knew this brother-in-law of my brother; he and I were friends, he would invite me to the parties, and I thought it was really neat."

Fraternity living brought a sense of male camaraderie to Pete's collegiate sensibility, as well as a sense of belonging. "You could be around all these guys. It was an immediate social mechanism. There were other fraternities that were sort of 'jock fraternities,' and I didn't think I would fit in that. There were other fraternities that were 'drug fraternities,' and I certainly didn't fit into that. And there were other fraternities that were 'geeky fraternities,' and I didn't fit in there. This one was just extremely average; they were average people. No one was overly masculine. There were other houses that were considered 'looks' houses."

Pete, like Alec, kept his homo-socialization separate from his campus activities. "I definitely knew I was gay, and I was having relationships with other men. But I did not do that my first semester in the fraternity. I was incredibly busy with the pledge masters; you were constantly busy. You had something to do every night, or every other night. You were up so late in the evenings that you would go to class, and if the class were early, you'd spend the afternoon sleeping, to catch up. The first semester I was completely immersed in the fraternity."

Soon, however, Pete scheduled noncampus, homosexual ventures. "It was in the second and third semesters that I was there that I started to go downtown to Washington, D.C., and take more liberties. I would occasionally not spend the night at home, in the fraternity, and people would notice. They would say, 'Where were you last night?' Or 'You didn't come home last night.' Especially my roommate. I would say, 'I was out with some friends.' Since I was a local, from Maryland, I had a lot of friends in the suburbs of Maryland that I went to high school with or that I was in Scouts with. The people in the fraternity knew that, because I would occasionally invite them over, or they would come over. So they were another circle I hung out with. I would say, 'I was out with them; I was in Bethesda; I spent the night at their house, 'cause we were out partying.' Which was a reasonable thing to say, because that was a common practice.

"But in the middle of the week, when it was so obvious, like if it was a Wednesday or a Thursday night [that] you didn't spend the night, that was unlikely. So I would concentrate on doing it only on Friday/Saturday. In that case, I would say I spent the night at my parents' house. And sometimes I really did spend the night at my parents' house, because I would go home on the weekends occasionally. Sometimes some of my friends—my gay friends, when I started making gay friends—would call my parents' house or the fraternity house. And there was a club in Washington, D.C. called The Frat House. And it was one of the very few places I would go to. It was the place to go at the time. So they would call my parents, and my father would say, 'Where do you know Pete from?' And they'd reply, 'From The Frat House.' And that's something I did at the time, to sort of conceal the fact that I was gay [from my parents]."

Pete took more measures to keep his two social identities from converging. "As I started to migrate from being in the fraternity to being more gay and out, I did meet other gay people [from the fraternities] in the bars. And that was very intriguing. You were almost part of a further, secret society amongst the fraternities, because you knew someone in this house who was gay, you knew someone in another. There was this very interesting sort of dynamic that occurred because of that. You almost reveled in it; you relished that experience. It was a further thing that you had that was sort of secret.

"At the time [in the early 1980s], people who were straight did not go to gay bars. If you were in a gay bar, you were gay; and if you were in a fraternity, you had a vested interest in keeping it [being gay] secret. So you maybe recognize them, or you would have a conversation about it, and that was pretty much it. Unless you were attracted to the person, and then you might have a relationship with them. You would [say something to others], especially if you had a University of Maryland shirt on. That was a vehicle for conversation with someone: *Oh, you go to Maryland?* And then it was, *Are you in a fraternity house? Does anybody in your house know you're gay? Who else in your house is gay? Do you know of any other fraternity people who are gay?* You would measure the extent to which people in the house knew, because you didn't know the culture of the houses. You might have an idea about the cultures of the houses, but you would only know your own culture very well. People always had curiosity of another house."

Later College. Such secrets fit nicely into Pete's understanding of—and maneuvering within—both worlds. It was apparent to him, on some levels, that even the straight world of his fraternity had underpinnings of homo-affectional and -sexual elements. "I really loved that attention [in the house]. The whole fraternity system was a great vehicle for having a relationship with another guy that was reciprocal—but not sexually. It was very caring and nurturing without being physical. That was an attractive thing about it. Well, during the initiation period, it was extremely physical. Hell Night was very, very physical: lots of touching and bizarre behavior. But after that was over, it was understood—I don't know how, but it was understood that was not the way it was. It was only that event where the physical-ness took place. It wasn't sexual; it was physical.

"There was no sex, per se, but there was a lot of touching and hugging and even kissing (but not lips kissing; kissing like on the neck or something like that). That occurred at the culmination of Hell Night. But the thing that was attractive to me was that that was always in the back of my mind. When that occurs, it reveals something very significant about the persons engaging in that behavior. That was always in the back of your mind, that these people will do this or engage in this behavior."

Despite Pete's attraction to and enjoyment of fraternity life, within a year he had begun to move away from a social life based on campus and in the greek system, and toward one based in Dupont Circle, a section of D.C. popular with gay men in the 1980s and 1990s. "I used the word *migrating*. I was totally immersed in the fraternity system at Maryland. I participated in everything during Greek Week; I went to all the parties. That was my first and second semesters. I was an officer, and I took that responsibility seriously. We went on retreats. Then I started going downtown and to the bars and stuff, and I decided that was a better life for me, personally. I just think that [gay socialization] was more of who I was. I was having sex, and I decided I was done with the fraternity scene. I didn't want to have that experience my whole undergraduate life. I didn't want to do that anymore; essentially, I saw something I wanted to do more. And that was to be downtown and experience the gay life fully, to be in the clubs, to dance, meeting and making a new network of people, local D.C. people. The two groups, I knew, couldn't mix: I couldn't bring my gay friends I was meeting in the clubs to meet the people in the fraternity house, nor the other way around. On top of that, I needed a place to call my own, physical space. And I was sharing it in the fraternity house. No one had a room of his own, and I certainly couldn't bring another guy there. Although I did once; it was very scary.

"So I moved out of the house into an efficiency-type apartment in Washington, in the basement of somebody's house, with my own private entrance. I loved that. I had ultimate freedom, which I had never had before. I had my own car. I distanced myself physically from the fraternity and moved closer to the gay scene. That was probably my junior year."

As Pete's involvement in D.C.'s gay circles increased, his activity on campus—particularly with his fraternity—decreased. "I would go to the fraternity meetings once a week; you had to go to Monday meeting. I did that faithfully the first semester, and then it was in the second semester I went every other week. The third semester I would go once a month. And then I stopped going completely, without saying anything to anybody, in my senior year. I didn't even say goodbye. I just slowly severed that relationship. At that point I didn't care at all about the relationships I had established there; I had slowly separated. It was a slow and progressive thing, but there was nothing unkind. It was not problematic; there was no disturbance that made that happen. It was just a progressive thing. . . . If you didn't attend the events, people would call you a ghost. The term was designed to make you appear, I think, more often; so it was not derogatory, it was more persuasive, I think. I didn't care that I was a ghost. I just decided that I was going to be a ghost and never came back again."

Post College. After graduation, Pete moved back to College Park, living in a group house with other gays and lesbians. "I moved away, then I decided that being gay and being out on campus was a great experience. Then I got involved [in campus-based non-heterosexual activities] as a graduate student. I felt at the time, as a master's student, I had more freedom to do that. I was older, I knew a little bit more. I didn't know anyone else in the fraternity who was there any longer. Everyone who was a senior to me was graduated and gone, as had the freshmen and sophomores. So I was back to my own institution as a master's student, and I could do what I wanted to. I became a member of the lesbian and gay student [group]. I did the rap groups for a while, but then I realized I didn't have anything to rap about; the rap groups for me were just another way of meeting people. Then I helped to organize some of the parties; the house that I lived in was the house to have a party in, if you were a member of the gay group. The president of the organization lived there, and a lot of gay people lived in that huge house."

But as an undergraduate student, being gay was a distinctly different experience from what Pete would later find in graduate school. As an undergraduate, being non-heterosexual and a college student "meant living a secret life. I thought it was exciting and dangerous. I also thought it was exhilarating, and at the same time disappointing. At the time, there were many people who were not out. It's not like today. Even today, I know people are oppressed, but it's not to the same extent. So if you really liked someone, there was always the threat that they were not going to come fully out or were not going to want to continue the relationship."

Andre

Early College. In 1983, nineteen-year-old Andre enrolled in Bradley University, a small school in Peoria, Illinois, about three hours from his hometown of Chicago. He stayed at Bradley to complete master's work in college student development. "I hung out in the residence halls. Being from Chicago, I didn't know anyone, really, at Bradley. I came there with no family, no friends there. I choose Bradley sight unseen, so I really made a decision to set some roots down in the residence halls, 'cause that's where I lived, that's where my R.A. lived. My resident advisor was very warm and welcoming. And I needed that, for not only was Bradley three hours away, it was predominantly white, it was a private school, and there were very few African-American folk visible. Not to say I had to gravitate to African-American people, but having come from Chicago, and the south side of Chicago, where black folk were everywhere, now I went to an environment that was very different. It wasn't necessarily scary or threatening; it was just very different."

The size of both the institution and the city were comforting to Andre, at least at first. "Bradley was a small enough school that people cared about me. People knew my name. Peoria was about 124,000 people; the school was about 9,000, including the graduate school. It had a small-town feel to it without necessarily being out in the boondocks. I needed that place, at that time of my life."

His freshman year, Andre was "a young gay man who wasn't even conscious of his gayness completely. . . . I knew something was wrong, sinful, though I may not have used those words, particularly that year. I think the term 'sinful' would have come into play more my senior year, because I joined a student group, Inter-varsity Christian Fellowship, a faction of which went to a very heavily Pentecostal church, where that terminology and sentiment was very heavy. But my self-identity was one of *wrong: I have to be a very good boy. I've got to be the best at everything I possibly set my hands onto. My ethics and my morals must be above reproach, because if anyone were to find out I was this different person, this*—I wouldn't even say gay, because I didn't even use the word, I hadn't acknowledged it—*if I were this different, wrong person, then at least I would have all of these good things to fall back on.*

"That sent me into being an extremely codependent, moderately neurotic type of person who got overly involved in everything. After my first year, I joined the residence hall staff, I became an assistant resident advisor. Throughout my college career I got involved in student government, I was on the president's visioning committee working with faculty and staff. I was in good with the campus police because of some of my work. I was a stickler for the rules as a residence hall staff member. I was caring but very demanding of the staff that I eventually started to supervise. I was a benevolent despot, in a lot of ways. And all that was to extol those values that I so desperately wanted to have, to protect myself from anybody ever questioning my sexuality and finding out how wrong I was.

"There were some benefits to that. I tapped into an almost infinite source of energy. That type of fear, that type of cloaking, was like a nuclear furnace, because if I were to try to be that way now, I would be a dried up husk. I don't have those motivations anymore, to be *the best*, so that no one will ever question me. I don't have that energy where I must keep going. I'm not that compulsive anymore."

Despite the increased drive and motivation to achieve, Andre's "secret" caused him discomfort when he interacted with heterosexual peers. "Conversations, particularly when in a group of other men they were talking about dating, about having sex—or wanting to have sex, 'cause most of them never had any sex with these women. But having sex with women, joining the fraternity, going to sorority formals—I wasn't talking like that. That wasn't on my mind; that never crossed my mind. What also helped me realize the difference was that I felt somewhat fearful letting people know that I hadn't had those experiences. You have to realize, I did not date in high school. The only date I had in high school was my senior prom. If I were hearing myself say this and did not know myself, I'd say, *Well, didn't you deal with that in high school?* Well, to some degree, but [in high school] I didn't live with these people twenty-four/seven. . . . Also, I wasn't as athletic as some of the boys there, and though that doesn't necessarily relate to sexual orientation, it let me know I was different."

Andre recognized this difference was due to his sense of sexuality. "If I had to label my identity as a gay identity or a queer identity, [those times were when] I began to touch upon some of those emotions. I became aware, ever so slowly, that I was sexually attracted to some of the men I was hanging out with. Maybe in a cursory way; those were not the words in my mind, but now I'd say, *Oh, he's cute.* But it was a preverbal type of knowing; it was more like a warm feeling of difference around this person I was gravitating towards. Another concern of mine [during these conversations] would be not to say anything. *Don't say anything; just let the conversation happen.*

"There was a sense of quiet panic. I knew those were not my experiences, not my concerns, not my urges; those were not on my agenda. It was a survival thing. *Don't let on to these people that you've not had these experiences, that these are not your concerns. Just let it go. At best, just let it go quietly. If they approach you, just simply laugh it off, blow it off.* If it was something that I could easily say that was immoral or wrong, sometimes I used that as a defensive tactic: *Oh, I don't think that's right; you should wait until you're married.*"

Later College. Andre could not always maintain the separation, however; at one point, his role as a straight campus student administrator came into direct conflict with his burgeoning sensibility of his sexuality. "There was, towards the end [of my time at Bradley], when I was a graduate student, a young man who wanted to start a gay group. This is one of the times I regret the most. He was a really young guy, I think a freshman. He put out a call, you know, real grass roots type of thing, and these students came together, very secretive. They had a fledgling little budding of a group. My response was *Oh, my God.* Part of me was like, *Wow, they did that.* Second part of me was, *Well, what's going to happen to them?* Third thought was *I cannot be associated with this group.*"

The student eventually brought Andre into conflict with an underground lavender railroad for runaway non-heterosexual youth, operating in Peoria. "As life would have it, this young man became a resident in one of my residence halls. He actually was being harassed through some folks either on campus or off campus, and he was housing runaways, gay and lesbian youth from the community who were running away from abusive homes or abusive situations. I had to cooperate with the sheriff and campus police to go in and try to talk with him, try to have him explain who were these people living here, why were they living in our residence halls. Part of me calls it cowardly, part of me calls it my only desperate way, but I met with him with all of these huge honking police officers who were very uncomfortable with the situation. He was an eighteen-year-old with these sixteen-, fifteen-year-olds in his room. I was the one doing the talking. And all I wanted to do was make sure they didn't get hurt, that no one did anything to them, but I could not for the life of me come out and say, *I'm gay,* or *I'll look out for you,* or *I'll help you find resources."* Andre's conflicted impulse was to "take care of them, but you can't let anyone know you're gay. You couldn't give them that extra reassurance of *Hey, I understand.*

"If you could imagine, they're all sitting on the floor, because [the student] had removed his bed. Three of them [the student and two minors] were huddled like little puppies. The scene is very vivid in my mind. [In the end] I helped them not be evicted—not right that moment. I gave them several days; I would come back to double check to make sure they were no longer living there. He had to promise that he would not do this again, and he had to return his furniture. I protected him from any type of criminal charges by telling the police that I would handle it, be the judicial official and pass it on to my bosses. The student stayed for some time, but I don't think he graduated from Bradley. I think, partly, he was out, but in some ways he was not sure, not savvy, not sophisticated yet, and still dealing with regular developmental concerns [in addition] to homophobia and not having a support system. It was bad enough, sometimes, just being a student, and he was dealing with all these other issues."

Most times, however, Andre was able to maintain distance—both personal and psychological—between his campus life and his non-heterosexual feelings and experiences. "I never, for the eight years I was there [Peoria], thought about going to a gay club. I was in that much of a state of panic. That was almost unthinkable, would almost make [me] ill. But, did I ever go to adult bookstores and have anonymous sex? Yes. Was this adult bookstore close to, or at least nearby, these gay clubs? Yes. But that presentation, that disclosure, that I would go into a club and say *Ta-da! I'm gay,*—or that's the way at least I thought it was then—was unthinkable. But it shows you the power of your sexual needs and desires, and finding some type of sexual outlet. That's when I started to visit [the bookstores]. We only got paid once a month. And so, I got my money, the first day, I would go."

Andre recalled his sensibilities concerning his sexuality in those days. *"I'm paid, I got money, I need to do this, this is the only time I'll be able to do it.* I would literally repress and shut off any of that moral talk about it being wrong. I would disconnect it, and I would go. I would sometimes try to defuse it by saying, *I won't do it ever again.* Those stupid promises. *I'm going to do it this time, but I'll stop.* Or I'd simply cut it off and not think about it. But after a night at the club or at the bookstore, having sex or whatever, I would have my walk of shame. There was deep psychic pain and shame: *Oh, my God, I did it. This was so dirty and wrong.* Walking those two miles back up [the hill], I would try to figure out a way how I would never do this again. Or try to do it financially and go, *My God, I can't afford to do this.* When you're at the bookstore you can obviously buy pornographic material and stuff like that, and sometimes I wouldn't have sex but I'd pick up some stuff, pick up some magazines. And that would be my sexual outlet, as opposed to meeting up with a guy or whatever. I'd bring that home, read it, look at it, and then after a few days, rip it all up and throw it away.

"You have to realize the risk I was taking, or at least the way I perceived the risk. I was very well known on campus, very well liked. . . . So I had to leave at night, 10:00 or 11:30. Make sure that when all the partygoers left (because most of the students all left in groups) I would leave, and take an unknown route. I would walk, literally, two miles, all the way from the top of the Bradley hill to downtown Peoria. And afterwards I had to walk back up. Oh, please, the things I did! And late, late, late at night or early in the morning, 'cause you'd just stay there. I'd stay basically all night. I would leave the bookstore—I just remembered the name of it, it was Swingers' World—I would leave there probably about 4:00 or 5:00 [in the morning]. I would try to get back before the sun really got up and before anybody saw me. There were some students who had jobs at supermarkets and stuff like that, who'd be up and around. So you're like, *Oh, my God, I got to get in before people see me come in.*

"I never had sex with anyone from campus. I would have known if they worked on campus. My people were totally non-Bradley people. They were townspeople, several business folk, one of whom supervised one of my staff people who had a co-op job [in town]. I would know regulars by face, who I enjoyed or who to stay away from. . . . You get to know some of those folks; I did, at least. After I became a bit more of a risk taker, I invited one or two back to my apartment. [At the time] I was a hall director; I was on the ground floor of a residence hall, and all the traffic went by [my apartment]. Sometimes I just wouldn't even know why I even did it. They would ask, 'Well, can we go to your place?' I'd say, 'Well, I have a whole apartment; come on back.' I still had to come into the lobby, like everyone else, and then go from there. I would organize it so that I would go into the least visible entrance to the building.

"I remember one situation that happened there; I just ask for an ultimate forgiveness. Here was another young man, also from Chicago, working out there [in Peoria]. He was a tradesman. I invited him back to my apartment. We had sex. It was fun; it was good; it was tender; it was very cool. And then afterwards we dressed, and as he was about to leave he then turned to me in the doorway and said, *Could I come back and see you again?* And without any connection to my heart, I said, *No.* And he got clearly the message: *No.* I never saw that man again. Inside of my heart, my recollection—and I don't think I've sugar-coated this or romanticized this—he was truly another gay soul wanting to reach out, touch, and connect, and stay connected. In my fear and cowardice . . . I said *no.* Having since come out—and I came out in 1991–92—that has plagued me. I just go, *My God, if things had been different.* If I could have just said *yes.* I enjoyed him; it wasn't like I was being condescending or anything. He needed something and I desperately needed something. I needed to have a connection. Even if it was only two weeks, who cares? It would have been nice. To me, that's where homophobia, homo-hatred, that kind of stuff, came out so clearly, so starkly with me. I feel so horrible about that. To this day, I hate that I have ever done that."

Such an example demonstrated the extent to which Andre's parallel lives influenced his behavior and sensibilities in both. Being a visible minority on a small campus in a medium-sized city also impacted his experiences. "Because of the secrecy of that type of place [the bookstores], the anonymity, the very rapidity, the lack of commitments, I did a lot of stuff. I led this secret, shadow life. There's a greater chance that someone will know you, in some of these smaller environments, particularly in these college towns. There's so many chances that you can interact with someone in public."

Despite Andre's growing connection to "regulars" in the Peoria homosexual sites, he still conceptualized his identity as separate (although not entirely equal) parts of "good boy" very connected to his campus community and "dirty" gay person hiding from society. "Did I still feel it was wrong? Yes. It was just these bubbles of time and space where I would suspend all that stuff in experience and enjoy those sexual things. Then the bubble would collapse, and all those moral things would come rushing back on me. Then I would feel very guilty. And then, if I made those promises or tore up those magazines, then I'd go through this time of just being a straight arrow. Realize,

I only got paid once a month so I only got to go once a month. So I had the rest of the month to redeem myself."

Reflections on Parallel Lives

Redemption, atonement for past transgressions, half-hearted promises to one's self not to do *that* again are common themes among the collegians who lead parallel lives. Like their "normal" counterparts, they feel they should be normal—or at least, not be non-heterosexual. Depending upon the individual and his circumstances, this could play a very important part in the daily actions of his life (as it did in Andre's and Alec's), or a less significant part if the man compartmentalizes the cultures and/or aspects of his life (as Dennis and Pete did). For most of these men, being non-heterosexual (be that called "gay," "queer," or "homosexual") was not something that was a part of campus life; it was an aspect of off-campus life. When the two worlds intersected, as it did when Pete or Andre would rarely bring someone back to campus, the student would feel uncomfortable in both student/straight and citizen/sexual roles: as Pete said, "The two worlds, I knew, couldn't mix." This discomfort fostered in these men barriers between not only the two sets of sites of socialization but also their emotions and the people they knew in each set of sites. Pete felt he could not nurture his growing gay friendships while maintaining his fraternity membership, so he in effect deactivated; Alec had a gay friend to whom he could not be open and honest; Dennis did not keep in contact with or become emotionally attached to the men he saw on the weekends (even when he would seek them out again), in part because it would interfere with his collegiate responsibilities; and Andre would not see the young man from Chicago again for similar fears/reasons.

For these collegians, Mendelsohn's (1999) concept is quite evident: the *men* of their lives (the non-heterosexual culture in which they were raised and participated in) was in direct conflict with the *de* of their lives (the homosexual and -social aspects of their identity that were compartmentalized and separate from their "regular" experiences and senses). While Mendelsohn's idea might be pronounced in the experiences of parallel students, student identity and gay identity development theories are not: these students would appear to be developing independently and separately in each theory's stages, with little or no connection to what was going on in the other part of the men's lives. Again, the theories do not reflect the reality of non-heterosexual collegiate experiences and sensibilities.

Non-Textbook Non-Heterosexuality

As in the types of non-heterosexual identities displayed in the previous chapters, the concepts of normality and dominance formed the foundation of how students classified in the parallel and "normal" types made sense of their experiences. The parallel students separated "good" and "bad" social settings, creating a dichotomy between the acceptable (the norm of heterosexuality) and the inadmissible (the deviance of non-heterosexuality). Rather than incorporating one or the other into their self-concepts, parallel collegians respected those definitive boundaries and traveled between both.

"Normal" students, on the other hand, had no concept of themselves as "other" or bad; in some senses, their identity integrated all of their behaviors into a fairly cohesive whole. The importance of being "just like everyone else," however, prevented the "normal" students' sensibilities from incorporating the fact that their senses and experiences did not match the presumed (and promoted) norm of heterosexual identity (which was based upon a lack of homosexual desire and/or activity). These men were not in denial; instead, it would be more accurate to view their collegiate identities as distinct. They clearly acknowledged—and even acted upon—the behavioral aspects of homosexuality, considered those activities in relation to their perceived ideas of non-heterosexual identity, and rejected the notion that they were anything but "just like everybody else." Their sexuality had no bearing upon their social identity (presented to others) or personal identity (as understood by themselves at the time).

For all intents, these students would not be thought by most educators on campus as homosexual, gay, or queer. Parallel and "normal" students would not be found in gay student organizations, at campus dances for non-heterosexual students, or as participants in political or social functions for campus change. To these collegians' sensibilities, the sexual deeds did not equal the terms of non-heterosexual identities, let alone necessitate association with those whom the terms might identify. Like the closeted type, "normal" and parallel students are a hidden population, experiencing circumstances and constructing meanings of their senses in manners that neither student identity development theories or gay identity development theories address.

In the chapters of Section II, I provided narrative accounts of lives of men who attended college between 1945 and 2000. Through examining how and why they comprehended their vicissitudes, I proposed six ways to classify non-heterosexual male college students, in order to better understand their collegiate experiences. The following section concentrates upon the analysis and implications from the data and the typology. In the next chapter, I place the six types (along with one none of the study respondents exemplified) into a chronological, comparative narrative, to provide a historical context for these developments in non-heterosexual identity. This overview of the changes in identity for non-heterosexual male college students over the last half of the twentieth century continues the process of juxtaposing normative centers with abnormal fringes.

MAKING SENSE OF NON-HETEROSEXUAL IDENTITY

CHAPTER 6

Collegiate Non-Heterosexual Identities, 1945–2000

As the previous three chapters describe, non-heterosexual collegiate identity types developed over time, in response to social and campus concepts as well as to other non-heterosexual identity types. To understand how the identities of non-heterosexuals on college campuses were understood by those students, one must place those identities into a historical perspective, for not only the environments of the institutions affected (and in some instances, effected) collegiate non-heterosexual identities, so did the events and public opinions of the times. In this chapter, I present a history of the changes in identity type for non-heterosexual collegians from the 1940s to the end of the twentieth century; such a chronicle contextualizes the life stories of the interviewed men, placing them in a historical framework.

Again I utilize the central tenet of queer theory—the dichotomy between what is considered "normal" and what is considered "not normal"—to emphasize that these identities were not forged out of whole cloth but in relation to prior and concurrent ideations of normative identities. A chronology of non-heterosexual activities on campuses displays how college students and experiences affected the self-identity and -identification of non-heterosexual students. Examining the data (interview as well as archival) through queer theory conveys these revisions of identity as the margin of non-heterosexuality became more central both to the collegians' experiences and to their sensibilities of what those experiences mean. Such changes in the collegiate experiences and senses of these students over the latter half of the last century consequently effected the typologies proposed in this study.

Each man in this study developed a sense of who he is (a traditional goal of collegiate education and college student development theory) not only through his examination of his own life but also in comparison of his experiences and feelings with those of his peers (both heterosexual and non-), of individuals and images he found depicted in the media, and of those members of academe (faculty, administrators, advisors) whose decisions and requirements impacted his life. Examining how non-heterosexual identities operated on a specific campus, the University of Kansas, I offer other forms of data (historical, photographic, and journalistic, primarily) to place the respondents' experiences and sensibilities into a historical context.

I chose Kansas not because the institution or its students were necessarily

FIGURE 6.1: **How Specific Non-Heterosexual Identity Types Viewed Their Relation to Other Sexual Male Identity Types**

RELATIONAL SYMBOLS

≠ Not Equal   ≅ Equitable But Not Identical
// Concurrent   ≈ Self-Perceived as Equitable

HOMOSEXUAL
Heterosexual ≠ Homosexual
Period: 1940s to Late 1960s   Narrators: Walter, Duchess (chapter 3)

GAY
Heterosexual ≠ Gay ≅ Homosexual
Period: Late 1960s to Present   Narrators: James, Cliff, Tim, Gene (chapter 4)

QUEER
Heterosexual ≠ Queer ≅ Gay
≅
Homosexual
Period: Late 1980s to Present   Narrators: Jimmy, Pozzo, Rad (chapter 4)

"NORMAL"
Gay ≠ Normal ≠ Homosexual
≈
Heterosexual
Period: 1940s to Present   Narrators: Ralph, Chris, Greg (chapter 5)

CLOSETED
Heterosexual ≈ Closeted ≠ Homosexual
Period: 1940s to Present   Narrators: Bob, Sam, Rick, Juan (chapter 3)

PARALLEL
(Gay ≈ Heterosexual) // (Non-Heterosexual ≈ Gay)
Period: 1940s to Present   Narrators: Dennis, Alec, Pete, Andre (chapter 5)

special or unique, but because the changes on that campus are indicative of changes on campuses across the country. With one of the oldest student organizations in the United States, the University of Kansas—and its students—experienced and instigated seminal court cases, administrative responses, student programming, and collective identity development. In this regard, Kansas symbolizes the sites of challenge to non-heterosexual identities on college campuses. It is fitting, if not ironic, that a school in the center of the country should serve as a model of how the marginality of non-heterosexuality came into focus.

The concept of "normal," both to those who choose that as nomenclature and others who juxtapose their experiences to those considered "normal," is very important to the identity process for non-heterosexual males. The differences of experience and self-understanding, however, changed over time, and the epistemological understanding of non-heterosexual collegians' identities expanded to include not only relationships to heterosexuals but also to other non-heterosexuals. Figure 6.1 summarizes the juxtapositions of each identity type to the other (perceived) types prevalent in the time period in which each type came to prominence.

To understand the types, one must examine the qualities and experiences that constitute the classifications, as well as how the types formed in relation to other ideations of identity (both heterosexual and non-heterosexual). I present the identity types in a chronological manner, based upon years of prominence of the identities within higher education in the United States. Significant overlap of years occurs between the types, reflecting the fluidity of the identity types and the queer, not entirely linear nature of queer histories (cf., Bravmann, 1997). Examining the types chronologically, as each developed into prominence, adds to one's understanding of how each type influenced the men who exhibited those qualities and sensibilities and those men whose experiences differed.

Putting It Together: A Short History of Non-Heterosexual Identities on Campus

Homosexual: 1940s to 1990s. From the 1940s through the present, men who identified as other than heterosexual formulated and understood their sexuality in relation, first and foremost, to heterosexuality. Walter, one of the homosexual males from chapter 3, believed that most people were not as he felt he was, that they were not homosexual. Duchess (also from chapter 3), growing up in the Tropics, experienced attractions to other males but the concept of homosexuality "wasn't even real. . . . It didn't exist." Heterosexuality was the norm upon which the men within the homosexual type of identity compared their own sexual desires and experiences.

The ramifications of normative heterosexuality did not stop in the bedroom (or, as Arnie Kantrowitz and Malcolm Boyd pointed out, the drive-in or the school dance); the social mores of American collegiate culture extend into nonsexual contexts as well. Dating of women and eventual marriage were the presumed goals for college men. For homosexuals in the 1940s, the notion of being abnormal was not only the promulgated medical model for depicting their feelings and desires (cf., Bailey, 1999; Katz, 1995; Loughery, 1998; Tierney and Dilley, 1998) but also an accurate description of their lives. When not hiding from others who were straight, homosexual male collegians might socialize in small groups of others who identified as homosexual; they might have sexual encounters with men who might or might not so identify, often in public places that concealed from the public the activity within; homosexual students (and faculty) might be expelled if heterosexuals uncovered even their identity or that of their non-straight friends (as evident from the narratives of Ralph, Walter, and Robert, and in the scholarship of Retzloff [1991] and Harbeck [1997]). Homosexual identity, then, was formed in direct relation to the sexual and social norms displayed by heterosexuals: how individuals met, forged relationships with others, displayed their sexuality in public, and also with whom they had sex.

Often, the relationship between homosexual and heterosexual was viewed as opposing (as both Walter and his grandmother revealed in their conversation about his emotional attractions). In the lives of homosexual college students, though, the identity (along with the resultant emotions and activities) was always private, not public; personal, not political. As Duchess's actions as late as the 1980s demonstrate, "behaving" homosexual in public was not desired: "we would still behave very hetero." The acts of homosexuality were viewed as distinct from those of heterosexuality; the actions were social as well as sexual, and both were prohibited.

Relatively few artifacts remain to inform us of how homosexual men experienced campus living. As Bob indicated, some notions of institutional restrictions are extant in conduct materials; Bailey's (1999) examination of student conduct records at the University of Kansas reflects this as well. Walter's narrative in chapter 3 touched upon off-campus socialization, secretive, so not to attract attention; other historians found evidence of off-campus gatherings both more and less publicly known and held (Howard, 1999; Loughery, 1998; Marcus, 1992). Jack Campbell, who eventually founded the Club Baths chain of gay bathhouses, told Loughery that the University of Michigan in the late 1940s and early 1950s was "rampant with gay activity," with the Men's Union swimming pool "almost as wild as a bathhouse" (Loughery, 1999, 172); on the other hand, as Walter (and Bob) also attested, campus crackdowns against non-heterosexuals were not relegated only to those who deployed a queer sexuality (or sensibility) on campus. Mere socialization with other homosexuals—or those suspected of being—was enough to be investigated, reprimanded, charged with crimes of indecency or conduct unbecoming a student, and possibly even expelled (Baily, 1999; Dilley, 2002).

Gay: 1960s to 1990s. By the late 1960s, changes in identity because of a number of social movements (including, but not limited to, the women's movement, the antiwar movement, the hippie movement, the "Sexual Revolution," and the burgeoning gay rights movement) resulted in evolutions in how non-heterosexuals viewed themselves and their collective actions (Allyn, 2000; Baily, 1999). "Homosexual" was no longer the type or term that most non-heterosexual collegians identified or called themselves. Gay identity, as outlined in chapter 4, formed in relation to the dual norms of both heterosexual and homosexual identities. Gay students viewed themselves as different from heterosexuals, but usually only in the details of the gender of one's sexual partner, which was the common denominator with homosexual students. This was a clear distinction to non-heterosexuals of the time: gays viewed social change and action necessary to form a just society. Consider this excerpt from an early 1970s position paper of Lawrence Gay Liberation, Inc., an offshoot of the Lawrence Gay Liberation Front at the University of Kansas:

The "gay community" should not be confused with the stereotyped "homosexual" community which is as repressive and limiting as the "straight, heterosexual" community, since in both of the latter groups the limiting and harmful stereotypes that society has imposed on femininity, masculinity and sexual roles are emphasized. Many straights limit love to heterosexual situations involving aggressive men and submissive women, and, because of societal oppression, "homosexuals" have been forced into one-night stands and impersonal sexual encounters in contrived situations. By contrast, the gay community offers a unique opportunity for Gays to work for a freedom and self-expression based on consideration of others as individuals, without the overtones of exploitative sexuality endemic to the straight community. This encourages personal freedom of expression of affection towards others of either sex. (Lawrence Gay Liberation, Inc., n.d., p. 1)

Paradoxically, many of the methods used to achieve this social change were based upon the notion of changing the system from within. In many respects, as Tim's experiences demonstrate in chapter 4, gay collegians were quite similar to their straight counterparts: working, going to classes, "hanging out" with boyfriends, developing "a close group" of friends, joining campus organizations and governance. Juan's observation in chapter 3 of gays on *Oprah* in the 1980s confirmed this view of similarities over difference:

> they just had everyday individuals who were teachers, lawyers, couples. None of them drug-addicted. They were role models I was looking for. And I thought, *Finally, there is someone I can identify with.*

Despite the growing publicity of non-heterosexual individuals and lives, many gay students often struggled "internally," quietly cautious about sharing too much of their personal lives, particularly with non-heterosexuals.

The similarities, rather than the differences, between heterosexuals and non-heterosexuals were posited by gay students as the basis for equal treatment by higher education institutions and administrators. No longer limiting conversations about non-heterosexuals on campus to regulation and prohibition of non-heterosexual acts, gay students viewed themselves as a class of people, and aligned themselves with other minority students and student groups. The classification was not based on sexual role or activity per se:

> Since members of the gay community pursue same-sex relationships, which may or may not involve active sexual expression, they are usually considered (incorrectly) to be exclusive "homosexuals" by the straight world. The result is that the gay liberation movement is derided by those who have been conditioned into considering same-sex relationships sinful and a threat to society or, at best, evidence of sickness. But, "sin" is a purely subjective concept, non-rationally and arbitrarily applied whenever convenient; and the concept of "sickness" comes from psychiatrists who have dealt with homosexuals professionally, a biased situation since only those with mental problems seek therapy. (Lawrence Gay Liberation, Inc., n.d., p. 1)

Indeed, the differences believed and presented by most of these students as simply a matter of the gender of those for whom one had sexual and affectional desires, coupled with a lack of society's approbation of same-gender relationships.

The role of the gay student on campus was markedly different from that of the homosexual student. Again, from the early 1970s:

> Gays are no longer content to hide in their closets or the few "safe" refuges such as selected bars where they are tolerated as long as they pay and shut-up. They will no longer tolerate being fired from their jobs or denied housing because of their sexual orientation, or being harassed or arrested because they showed affection for someone of the same sex in public. They demand an end to such discrimination. (Lawrence Gay Liberation, Inc., n.d., p. 1)

Just as the social politics of the day influenced students to express themselves as either a part of, or apart from, postsecondary educational institutions, so too the identity politics of the times fostered actions and events surrounding gay students.

> In choosing "gay" the young activists explicitly rejected the word "homosexual." It was too clinical, they concluded, reducing homosexuality only to a physical act, reinforcing the notion that homosexuality was only about "sex." (Clendinen and Nagouring, 1999, p. 31)

"Gay is Good"—adapted from the slogan "Black is Beautiful" by Frank Kameny in 1968—became a rallying cry of the more political of these students (Clendinen and Nagouring, 1993; Jay, 1999; Kameny, 2001; McGarry and Wasserman, 1998; Teal, 1995); others began to incorporate their views as non-heterosexual students into their course work (in essays and artwork), and in their extracurricular activities, including student employment, campus dances, conferences planning political policy and strategy (Sprung, 1973), and gay student organizations.

Gay Student Organizing, Part I: 1967 to 1980. Gay students also demanded equality in access to, participation within, and funding for student organizations and governance, reflecting the gay ideology of equality and inclusion. These students formed gay campus organizations in the months following 1969's Stonewall Riots; while some disagreement and discrepancy persists about the actual dates that specific organizations formed, most researchers (and participants) of the times agree that the Student Homophile League, which formed at Columbia University in 1967, was the first (Dilley, 2000; Duberman, 1993b; Kaiser, 1997; Marcus, 1992; Miller, 1995).

The origins of the Student Homophile League display how the reasons for

forming and joining a gay student organization were on the one hand political and on the other very personal. Bob Martin was a freshman at Columbia
University in 1967. After his roommates at the university forced him to leave
their suite, for hanging "sexy pictures of men on his walls" (Allyn, 2000,
p. 152), Martin decided to study the history of homosexuality in America. His
scholastic work in New York, along with the general social collegiate climate
of change, enabled him, under the pseudonym Stephen Donaldson, to organize other students into a collective designed to reform the institution—and
society. As he wrote in a letter to the editor of the *New York Times* in 1967, "it
must be evident that the contemporary fear of possible implications of close
emotional relationships between persons of the same sex is itself unhealthy
and even paranoid" (Donaldson, 1967).

Although the Student Homophile League was met with letters of outraged
protest to the university and in the local press, "the handful of courageous students [about a dozen, in Kaiser's (1997) estimation] who signed up as members proceeded with their work of education and counseling" (Duberman,
1993b, p. 172). Among their first acts was to issue "a thirteen-point declaration of principles which asserted 'the fundamental human right' of every homosexual 'to develop and achieve his full potential and dignity as a human
being'" (Kaiser, 1997, p. 146). Some of the programming of the Student Homophile League, and the campus organizations that came after them, included coordinating "rap" sessions, organizing general discussion groups,
advocating for courses on homosexuality and gay life, conducting "zaps"
(jamming of phone lines and offices of offensive persons or organizations),
hosting speakers, joining other student activists to protest institutional actions, lobbying local and campus governments to end discriminatory practices
and policies, and sponsoring social events (Bailey, 1999; Duberman, 1993b;
Lichtwardt, 1992a, 1992b; Marcus, 1992). First and foremost, the original student organizations were concerned with protecting the rights of individuals to
engage privately (albeit sometimes privately public) activities.

Other chapters of the Student Homophile League, as well as campus-based
chapters of the Gay Liberation Front political organization, formed on campuses "from Berkeley to Harvard" (Marcus, 1992, p. 172). Among the first
were University of California at Berkeley, the University of Oregon, Yale Uni-
versity, the University of Kansas, the University of Southern California, Pennsylvania State University, and New York University (Dilley, 2000; Kaufman,
1973; Reinhold, 1971; Walters, 1972).

The historical records concerning the formation of the Gay Liberation
Front at the University of Kansas are contradictory. The Lawrence Gay Libera-

tion, Inc., position paper states the organization was formed in the summer of 1970, but it's unclear whether that date represented the founding of the corporation or the Gay Liberation Front, particularly since the GLF was still active as of April 1972, when it sponsored dances in the Kansas Union Ballroom (see below). Further, promotional materials for the 1989 Gay and Lesbian Awareness Week proclaim that year as the twentieth anniversary of the forming a non-heterosexual group at KU, while the materials from the 1995 GALA events proclaim that year as the organization's twenty-fifth anniversary. If the organization had not been comprised primarily of non-heterosexual students, the record might be clearer, as the GLF could have registered as a campus organization.

Litigations for Legitimacy: 1970s to 1980s. After legal decisions in the late 1960s and early 1970s regarding student organization recognition for other types of student activist groups were upheld to guarantee the rights of non-heterosexual student organizations to exist and to assemble on campuses, gay students began to petition for institutional recognition. Many cases were contested or denied, and consequently also ended in litigation.

A clear line of decisions emerged, based upon prior case law concerning the rights of students to assemble and speak freely. The illegality of homosexual acts in individual states was often considered and debated—and frequently rejected by campus administrators—in the establishment of the rights of non-heterosexual student organizations. Kansas offers clear examples of what this meant for gay students and organizations.

On September 5, 1970, the chancellor of the University of Kansas, E. Laurence Chalmers, Jr., stated a position representative of the judgment of most administrators of the day:

> Formal recognition of a proposed student organization confers only one significant advantage. A recognized student group may submit requests for funds to the Student Senate. Since we are not persuaded that student activity funds should be allocated either to support or to oppose the sexual proclivities of students, particularly when they might lead to violation of state law, the University of Kansas declines to formally recognize the Lawrence Gay Liberation Front. (KU News Bureau, 1970)

The GLF hired William M. Kunstler, one of the attorneys who represented the Chicago Seven, to represent them, along with five faculty members, a graduate student assistant, and three other students individually, in a suit against Chalmers and the Kansas Board of Regents. Kunstler, however, was barred from appearing before U.S. District Court Judge George Templar, because of Kunster's notorious reputation. The student leaders of KU disagreed with the chancellor's decision; by September of 1971, the Student Senate had approved allocating $600 to the organization, to aide the organization in its court costs against the university; Chalmers instructed his vice-chancellor to disapprove the expenditure and return the legislation to the senate.

Templar ruled, on February 12, 1972, against GLF and ordered it to pay court costs for the defendants. Two days after the district court ruling in 1972, the leaders of the student government began proceedings to change the University of Kansas's classification of campus and community organizations, to avoid the problems presented by that case by distinguishing between "recognizing" (and thus sanctioning the organization and allowing opportunity for funding) and "registering" any group that met basic requirements (particularly yearly contact information for persons in charge). The Lawrence GLF appealed Templar's ruling, and, in light of other case law established after the decision (particularly *Gay Activists Alliance v. Board of Regents of the University of Oklahoma*, 1981), and the changes in organization recognition at the university, the appeal was upheld.

A number of other legal cases in the 1970s highlight the actions of postsecondary institutions to regulate gay students and gay students' abilities to coalesce around policy issues that affected their rights and identities. Institutions denied non-heterosexual students access to campus resources and privileges granted to other students and student organizations on the basis of religious beliefs of heterosexual students of the institution, issues of moral education, potential illegality of actions of individual members of gay organizations, and reflection of such recognition upon the reputation of the institution (cf., *Gay Student Organization of the University of New Hampshire v. Bonner*, 1974; *Gay Alliance of Students v. Matthews*, 1976; *Student Coalition for Gay Rights v. Austin Peay State University*, 1979). Colleges and universities attempted this line of arguments in their decisions to limit association of non-heterosexual students, despite continuing rulings of the courts that such actions were discriminatory and unconstitutional.

A case from the University of Missouri reflects how the concept of non-heterosexual identity changed, and resulted in reforms to campus environments that affected the experiences and sensibilities of non-heterosexual students. In 1976, the University of Missouri denied recognition to the student organization Gay Lib; the university allowed the students to appeal and to provide evidence that it presented no imminent danger, including a revised mission statement. The institution still decided to deny recognition, utilizing Missouri's law classifying sodomy as a felonious criminal activity. Gay Lib filed a civil suit (*Gay Lib v. University of Missouri*, 1977), claiming infringement upon their rights of free association and equal protection, which was eventually supported by the Eighth Circuit Court of Appeals. As the university would finally be instructed by the appellate court, "denial of recognition impermissibly penalized the group's [Gay Activists Alliance] because of their status rather than their conduct" (Kaplan, 1990, p. 323). In other words, the courts ruled that these students were being discriminated against because of their collective and individual identity, rather than specific illegal activity.

It is easy to forget the context of social change that engulfed U.S. college campuses in the early 1970s, just as it's simpler to outline the facts of these court cases than to examine how the action of stating one's sexuality publicly—as a source of identity and of discrimination by a university like KU—affected the lives of the students involved. David Stout was a founder of KU's Gay Liberation Front and was very much involved in the efforts to gain gay students a place at KU's table. He found himself embroiled in campus and social issues that stretched beyond sexual identity.

These were very exciting times. There was the Vietnam war, race riots, Stonewall, gay liberation. . . . After the Student Union was burned we [the Gay Liberation Front] were investigated by the KBI [Kansas Bureau of Investigation]. It's the only time I've lived under martial law. We couldn't leave our house at night. Everyone remembers those killed at Kent State, but few remember the student who was shot and killed on the KU campus . . .

You have to keep in mind how frightening it was for those of us at the time. As a leader in the GLF, I was in the newspaper, the radio, the TV. That first year of the organization there was a lot of support. I can remember when I lost that support. It was the fall semester of 1970 when the students came back, and we were inundated by this deluge of gay and lesbian students. We started to have different fractions and splintering.

I had come out to my family so that they wouldn't be shocked when they learned about it in the media. I lost their support and the support of people in the gay organizations. It was devastating to me. I made a serious suicide attempt at the time but survived. In the last meeting of the GLF in the fall of 1970, I told them what had happened and that if they wanted to have people standing out in front of the TV cameras and doing what they would not do themselves, then they needed to support what that person was saying. (Nelson, 1992, pp. 5–6)

After winning rights of assembly in courts, gay student organizations then attempted to secure funding for their social and campus activities on a parity with other student organizations. Usually this was met with resistence from institutional leaders and administrators, and also resulted in a number of legal cases brought by gay students. These students affected institutional structures for interacting with non-heterosexuals as well: as early as 1971, postsecondary institutions began to respond by forming administrative units to work with non-heterosexual students, including the Lesbian-Gay Male Programs Office at the University of Michigan in 1971 (Zemsky, 1996, p. 208).

Moreover, gay students challenged the authority of the institutions in many instances, struggling for the recognition of rights of speech and assembly on campus (Harbeck, 1995; Kaplan, 1990; Teal, 1995; Walters, 1973). Whereas homosexual students believed sexuality was a private concern, gay students asserted more visible and political roles on campuses—as non-heterosexuals. Their ability—indeed, their rights to do so—came through a series of legal battles throughout the 1960s and 1970s. Students engaged in sit-ins and other protests to challenge university policies prohibiting their rights to free speech and assembly (i.e., "100 in N.Y.U. Sit-In Charge Bias Against Homosexuals," 1970; "400 In 'Gay' Protest Dispersed By Police," 1970). As early as 1968, the Student Homophile League at Columbia was challenging the institutional (and institutionalizing) practices of members of the psychiatric and medical establishment:

When the medical school staffed a panel discussion on homosexuality with a group of "experts" known (except for the Kinsey Institute's Paul Gebhad) to regard it as a pathological adjustment, SHL representatives invaded the meeting and publicly demanded that in the future the decision of homosexuality be placed "in its proper setting as a sociological problem of deeply entrenched prejudices and discrimination against a minority group." (Duberman, 1993b, p. 172)

Gay students organized more openly, to challenge the institutional oppressions they experienced (Bailey, 1999; Dilley, 2000, forthcoming; Jay, 1999). If gay students came out into public more, so too public were the postsecondary control efforts against them. Institutions responded by attempting to deny or severely delimit social and political activities by non-heterosexuals on campuses. While the expulsions and (most) of the entrapment exercises ended in the late 1960s, the institutional regulation of students because of their sexuality did not.

Gay Student Politics: 1970s to 1990s. While the first openly gay man to run for student body president at Princeton lost the 1977 election ("Princeton Students Vote," 1977), at other times in the decade students elected openly gay candidates to similar positions, first at the University of Minnesota and later at Michigan State University in East Lansing ("Gay Student Body President Elected," 1978). Jack Baker, student body president of the University of Minnesota, was a twenty-nine-year-old law student who had failed in his attempt to marry his partner, UM librarian Mike McConnell. He ran on a gay activist platform (almost queer in its imagery) of "Mom, Apple Pie and Gay Liberation." In 1972, Baker "came to the KU campus [to] encourage GLF" (*Gay Liberation News*, April 26, 1974, p. 1); he returned formally in 1974, sponsored by KU's Student Union Activities.

Baker was perhaps the most visible gay student politician, receiving much publicity for his campaign photos in high heels and being profiled by *Look Magazine* in 1971. Starting in the 1970s, other non-heterosexual individuals who were open about their sexual identity (or in the process of deploying their sexual identity more publicly) also became members of student government bodies. Randy Shilts, who would later rise to prominence reporting on gay life and the AIDS crisis of the 1980s, was a member of the Gay People's Alliance at the University of Oregon and participated in student government there:

. . . I was elected to a five-member student committee that gave out over a million dollars of students' incidental fees to the campus student organizations. Then I was elected chairman of the committee. My slogan was "Come Out For Shilts." It was obviously a gay thing. Straight people didn't get it.

When I was elected committee chairman, I became the number-two person in the student government after the student-body president. Because of my position I was able to give money to the Gay People's Alliance, which was the first time it got money from the student government. Then we did things like have a gay pride program with speakers. We also put on the first gay dance at the University of Oregon, a gay-straight sock hop. It was all sixties music and Motown. We allowed straight people—you know, we were very liberal (Marcus, 1992, p. 230)

Members of the gay student organization at the University of Kansas were also elected to similar positions in the Student Senate (Lichtwardt, 1992b), as were others who were in various stages of openness in deploying their sexual identity. After overcoming the issue of institutional recognition, the KU GLF—and its successor organizations, including Gay Services of Kansas, Gay and Lesbian Services of Kansas, and LesBiGays OK (Lesbian, Bisexual and Gay Services of Kansas)—faced changing sentiments and socially conservative student governance. So they ran—not into the closet, but for senate seats. They faced down challenges to publicize membership lists, to be included in the institution's definition of "minority," annual attempts to defund the organization, bomb threats and automobile sabotage, and the proliferation of "Fagbusters" t-shirts on campus.

By the mid-'80s, non-heterosexual men and women were a vocal presence in campus politics: Ruth Lichtwardt, the director of GLSOK (the longest-serving of any in that position—close to three years) represented off-campus students from 1984 to 1987; David Hardy, who later became associate director of KU's Organizations and Activities Center, represented first graduate students (1984 to 1987) and then architecture (1987–88); Gordon Woods, for whom KU later named an endowed leadership scholarship, served liberal arts and sciences students (1984 to 1986) and then was elected holdover senator (1986–87); Kevin Elliot was a member of the Minority Affairs Committee during the mid-'80s; and Michael Foubert was elected by graduate students (1984 to 1987). The involvement of openly gay students in Student Senate continued into the 1990s, including Arthur Satterfield (graduate school, 1991 to 1993), Michael Sullivan (Social Work, 1991–92), Alan Pierce (off-campus, 1994–1995), and me (graduate school, 1991 to 1993). In 1998, the KU Student Senate passed legislation expanding its constituency base, formally giving to Queers and Allies (the most recent incarnation of the non-heterosexual student organization) one senate seat to appoint annually.

Pressed by circumstances challenging their rights to participate in campus society and activities, non-heterosexual students involved in campus governance—like their heterosexual peers—discovered new aspects of their identities as elected student leaders. The social roles and postsecondary experiences of those students were a far cry from students like Walter and Bob, who were afraid of expulsion and/or denigration if their identities as non-heterosexuals were known (or worse actions if their activities were revealed).

Gay Student Organizing, Part II: 1970s to 1990s. The efforts of gay students to create campus institutions for themselves is impressive: before 1969, there were no official student organizations for non-heterosexual students on U.S.

college campuses, but by 1996, there were more than 2000 (Gose, 1996). Not all non-heterosexuals enjoyed all the aspects of the new visibility: homosexual-type students did not thrive in gay organizations, as Duchess' experience highlighted. This pattern, of the earlier classifications of students not fitting into the social and political goals and efforts of later non-heterosexual students, repeated, as conveyed within the queer narrators' interactions with gay groups (and gay students interaction, or non-interaction, with queer groups).

Still, some campus activities did seem to rally diverse types of non-heterosexual students. Gay dances were focal points of non-heterosexual socialization on college campuses in the 1970s and 1980s, providing opportunities for promotion of the college groups and for challenging heterosexual norms of propriety, dress, and gender. These opportunities to establish a public identity with others who also identified as gay was a major innovation of gay students; the dances of the 1970s and early 1980s were important social events attended by both students and non-students. Not surprisingly, the dances were also sites of contention between administrators and gay students. The Lawrence Gay Liberation Front sponsored dances to help fund its lawsuits against the university; since GLF was not a registered organization, it had to rent space in the Kansas Union, thereby making the dances in the early 1970s cost prohibitive. Harassment and intimidation were also factors in the dances; in April of 1972, GLF held a dance at which "jeering spectators line the balcony of the Ballroom in an attempt to intimate the gay students who were at the dance . . . a student grabbed a dollar from the cashbox and ran . . . [and] finally a group of four to five students grabbed the cashbox containing approximately $75 and beat-up the gay student who tried to stop them" (Gay Liberation Front Emergency Position Paper, 1972, p. 1).

After the change in organization registration policy, such overt discrimination seemed to dissipate. GLF dances became widely publicized and apparently quite popular. GLF and Gay Services of Kansas sponsored "queer balls," a Halloween "Mary Hartman, Mary Hartman" look-alike contest, and even a performance by the Village People. As Lichtwardt (1992a, 1992b) remembered, several hundred people would attend dances at the University of Kansas Union Ballroom,

> including many from Kansas City who would normally have been at the bars. A DJ with a huge light and sound system was at one end of the room, booming out disco music (yes, it was that era). Crowded tables were set up all around the sides, and beer was being sold from a booth. People were dressed in everything from street clothes to gender-fuck.

The hallway outside the Ballroom was jammed with people trying to get some fresh air and other just strutting around, showing themselves off. People we talked to had come in from Manhattan, Wichita, Topeka, and even Omaha for this dance. . . . Going to the Lawrence dances became a regular event after that. I don't remember ever seeing them advertised—somehow the Mall grapevine always knew when they were. . . .

None of us in Kansas City knew much about the gay organization at KU except that it was a student group that held the dances to raise money. Because I knew of GLSOK's existence through the dances, however, one of the first things I did when I became a KU student in the spring of 1981 was try to look them up. (Lichtwardt, 1992a, p. 1)

Such events, and related experiences of students (or would-be students), were common at institutions where gay students had organized (Jay, 1999; Kantrowitz, 1977). Lichtwardt and her peers forty miles away from campus might not have seen the advertising, but KU's gay students did advertise their successful dances (photo 6.1 and photo 6.2). Parades were also organized by

PHOTO 6.1 (above left): **Gay Liberation Dance at the University of Kansas, 1973**

PHOTO 6.2 (above right): **Gay Liberation Dance at the University of Kansas, 1974**

Such advertisements and imagery would not have been conceptualized by closeted or homosexual students of the 1940s, '50s or '60s; further, no campus administrator would have approved the notices prior to the social changes and court rulings of the 1960s and 70s.

gay students, not so much as protests but as appropriations of dominant forms of self-expressions of collective identity; gay students continued to host parades through the end of the twentieth century. At Kansas, students organized and/or participated in celebration parades and demonstration marches on campus as well, in Lawrence (as depicted in photo 6.3) and Kansas City, and in the March on Washington in 1993.

Very much like the "outsiders" in Horowitz's (1987) typology of college students, gay collegians formed media outlets to convey their experiences and identities. A long string of gay-themed and -produced newsletters began to be produced at KU in the early 1970s. I've already quoted from one, *Off-Centre*; others included *Lawrence Gay Liberation Front News, Gay Liberation News, Lavender Luminary*, the *Yellow Brick Road*, the *Vanguard*, and the *KU GALA Update* from the Gay and Lesbian Alumni Association. These publications announced meetings and events, news about gay rights from around the country and campus (long before the Internet provided such information so quickly), and

DAVID DOEMLAND/*LAWRENCE JOURNAL-WORLD*, COURTESY UNIVERSITY ARCHIVES, UNIVERSITY OF KANSAS LIBRARIES

PHOTO 6.3: **Gay and Lesbian Awareness Week Parade**

KU's non-heterosexual student organization, Gay and Lesbian Services of Kansas, began to sponsor parades through downtown Lawrence, Kansas, in the 1980s. Although they started small and students were the primary participants, non-students eventually joined in marching in the parades. The Freedom Coalition was formed by campus and city residents in the early 1990s, to lobby the city to follow the University's lead in enacting antidiscrimination laws in housing and employment. A town-and-gown enterprise, the Coalition worked closely with gay students at KU who had successfully worked throughout the 1980s to add "sexual orientation" to the University's antidiscrimination policies.

PHOTO 6.4: **Producing *The Vanguard***

Beginning in the late 1960s, newsletters became a key source of information dissemination for gay campus organizations. Several were produced at KU over the years, including *Off-Centre* during the early 1970s and the fondly remembered *Yellow Brick Road* in the 1980s. *The Vanguard* began in the late 1980s and continued in various formats and frequencies through 2000. This photo shows the high-tech production process: sitting on the floor in the LesBiGays office in the Kansas Union, folding the xerox copies by hand.

UNIVERSITY ARCHIVES, UNIVERSITY OF KANSAS LIBRARIES

UNIVERSITY ARCHIVES, UNIVERSITY OF KANSAS LIBRARIES

PHOTO 6.5: **The Fourth Estate Notices Gay Students**

In the 1980s, mainstream media outlets became interested in covering gay events and issues, and campus media were no exceptions. At KU, no such issue was more imminent than the University's classification of and funding for the gay student organization, Gay Services of Kansas (later Gay and Lesbian Services of Kansas). From April of 1983 to April 1985, the issue received no less than 50 articles and a score of letters to the editor in the *University Daily Kansan*, KU's student newspaper. The representative during that time was Ruth Lichtwardt, the longest serving director of GLSOK. Lichtwardt is pictured here being interviewed on KJHK-FM, KU's student-controlled radio station.

information on community outreach efforts provided by the student organization (see photo 6.4). Gay students also had to deal with straight media, as David Stout's recollections earlier reflected; in the mid-1980s, Ruth Lichtwardt, the director of GLSOK, was interviewed dozens of times by the local and campus press, particularly in regard to gay student organizing and Student Senate funding (photo 6.5). Such media exposure presented new images of gay senses, experiences, and sensibilities to heterosexual and non-heterosexual students; but while allowing for public representations of non-heterosexual identities, media coverage also provided an opportunity for some to challenge or attempt to curtail gay student efforts to organize and socialize on campuses.

Other services commonly provided by gay student organizations of this time include peer counseling (cf. Gair, Toy and Blair, 1972), confidential support groups, legal referral services, and speakers bureaus. Gay Services of Kansas offered all of these; indeed, by the early 1990s, the speakers bureau provided service to dozens of classes each year, answering questions from hundreds of students. Organizing and participating in such public discussions of personal identity offered a unique form of identity deployment; non-heterosexual students engaging in such programs (such as those shown in the photo of a speakers bureau at KU in spring of 1992, photo 6.6) were analyzing their identity—their personal senses, experiences and sensibilities—and conveying that analysis to heterosexual audiences.

JENNIFER HOEFFNER/*UNIVERSITY DAILY KANSAN*, COURTESY UNIVERSITY ARCHIVES, UNIVERSITY OF KANSAS LIBRARIES

PHOTO 6.6: **Speakers Bureau**

Gay and Lesbian Services of Kansas ran speakers bureaus. Each year the organization trained members to speak to classes in sociology, psychology, religious studies, and social work. Usually four students—two men and two women—would speak from their own experiences and senses of being non-heterosexual, as this photo from a psychology class in October 1991 depicts.

While these activities on the surface might not seem quite as political as civil rights marches or free-speech rallies, one must, as James encouraged in chapter 3, remember the influential motto of the women's movement: "the personal is political." College students in the homosexual type (or viewed as such by other, gay-identified males) might take part of some of these social activities, but such activities alone did not foster a gay identity. By creating public events and organizations for non-heterosexuals to meet and that were also publicly identified as such, gay students changed the paradigm of what was considered "normal" on college campuses, by providing open spaces in which non-heterosexual men socialize and identify. Such institutionalizing of gay identities (particularly as depicted through activities and students on college campuses) helped, by the early 1980s, to foster less marginalized ideas for non-heterosexuals about how to live their lives; the college experience was different for a non-heterosexual student who matriculated in those times, for

CHRISTINE MCFARLAND/*UNIVERSITY DAILY KANSAN*, COURTESY UNIVERSITY ARCHIVES, UNIVERSITY OF KANSAS LIBRARIES

PHOTO 6.7: **Lobbying to Change Policies**

Gay students at Kansas staffed tables to spread news and opinions. In the spring of 1992, these GLSOK members distributed information concerning the Department of Defense's anti-gay policies and procedures. Reserve Officer Training Corps programs, which the DOD ran at KU, followed those policies, rather than the University's, which prohibited discrimination based upon sexual orientation. Their efforts eventually led high-ranking campus administrators to travel to Washington to meet with lawmakers and policymakers about the DOD policy—but not to a change in ROTC practices at KU.

a young man who had grown up with distinct images of a gay culture that would provide him with an identifiable place in America, a place where aberrance was normalcy, where the intimacies of personal life were not at war with the impulse toward public ambition. (Browning, 1993, p. 6)

That said, gay efforts to reform campus policies were somewhat more clearly political. Perhaps the largest of these efforts at KU, mirroring those of the early 1960s and 1970s, were the protests against KU's compliance with Department of Defense ROTC policies. Non-heterosexual students balked at the hypocrisy of the university's inclusion of "sexual orientation" within its non-discrimination clauses yet accepting the DOD policy against allowing non-heterosexuals from enlisting or receiving DOD-funded scholarships or appointments. The gay students at KU in the early 1990s built coalitions with other minority groups, including the Women's Student Union, Native American Student Association, Black Students Union, and Hispanic American Leadership Organization; although the organizations did not always agree upon specifics of how to define or to serve minority students at the university, they all agreed that the institution was not doing so appropriately. Gay and Lesbian Services of Kansas collected signatures against the policy and staffed information tables in the Kansas Memorial Union (photo 6.7) as well as conducted marches and demonstrations against the DOD (photo 6.8).

Queer: 1970s to 1990s. If the personal were political to gay students, then the public was political to those who identified as "queer," as presented in chapter 5. Indeed, for queer students, the personal became not only political but also publicized and problematized. As early as the 1970s, Jimmy's appropriation of public space on campus for his performance and physical art, along with his styling himself his freshman year in drag, most definitely charged common spaces and institutions with the personal (and with personality). Similarly, Rad's 1990s nonconformist dress—including alteration of his physical body, his hair, and piercings—were part of his desire "to be active" and visible in his (sexual) difference, including in his vocally questioning of the noninclusion of gay and lesbian topics in courses; Rad's involvement in campus publications, writing a column that dealt squarely with his sexuality unapologetically and as important to understand his world view, is also indicative of queer students using existing public forums to challenge the presumption of heterosexuality (in this case, "objective" reporting institutionalized through the campus newspaper).

Queer events are fairly easy to identify, as they were often promoted and

Photo 6.8: **Protesting the Military Ban**

In the early 1990s, KU—along with many other institutions in the United States—experienced demonstrations over accepting Department of Defense policies to guide ROTC programs on campus, rather than the institution's non-discrimination policies. At Kansas, a strong coalition of student government, Women's Student Union and the Native American Student Association protested on the national Day of Action, April 10, 1991. In the words of Michael Sullivan, the GLSOK co-director of the time, "It's going to take a war of protest to stop this discrimination."

PHILIP MEIRING/*UNIVERSITY DAILY KANSAN*, COURTESY UNIVERSITY ARCHIVES, UNIVERSITY OF KANSAS LIBRARIES

MIKE TURNER/*UNIVERSITY DAILY KANSAN*, COURTESY UNIVERSITY ARCHIVES, UNIVERSITY OF KANSAS LIBRARIES

Photo 6.9: **Candlelight Vigils**

Perhaps the most widespread form of gay remembrance and complaint in the 1980s and 1990s were candlelight vigils. They were held to demonstrate against anti-gay violence, remember those who died to AIDS, and the struggle for equity on campus. This photograph is of one held on April 16, 1991, in front of the Lawrence City Hall during GLSOK's Gay and Lesbian Awareness Week.

presented as such. Browning (1993), wrote of queer "shop-ins," of young activists traveling to suburban San Francisco to publicly be identified, en masse, as queer, to flaunt their abnormality in a prime site of American cultural and social reproduction—the shopping mall. The queers viewed their actions as "'queer visibility' expeditions, walking hand in hand into stores, shopping a lot, buying a little, and engaging in exaggerated mimicry of the straights who surround them" (Browning, 1993, p. 33). Such actions would invert the normal space or event, by publicizing the abnormal(s) engaging in normative behaviors.

Students at the University of Kansas participated in parades through campus and other public campus events in the 1990s to deploy their queerness on campus. As a graduate student at KU in the early '90s, I participated in such activities. During Gay and Lesbian Awareness Weeks we would have candlelight vigils, perhaps the most prevalent form of campus demonstration in the late 1980s and early 1990s, to protest discrimination and exclusion from campus cultures (photo 6.9). The student organization also publicized and promoted "promenades" across campus, where volunteers would walk while holding hands with friends of the same gender, each couple paced about ten feet behind the previous couple, to invert the gender norms of heterosexual behavior (photo 6.10). In a campus kiss-in held in the spring of 1992, several dozen men and women joined hands in a circle at noon in the center of cam-

PHOTO 6.10: **Queer Promenade**

Civil demonstrations took somewhat new forms in the 1990s, as the influence of queer ideology took root among non-heterosexual students and their organizations. During Gay and Lesbian Awareness Week in the spring of 1992, GLSOK conducted a "promenade" along Jayhawk Boulevard, the main street on the KU campus. Same gender couples held hands and walked from the Kansas Memorial Union to a rally at Wescoe Hall—not in a single line, but at some distance. The act of two men holding hands while walking—an inversion of the typical heterosexual practice—disrupted the expected norms both of homosexuality (not public) and public displays of affection (always heterosexual), and was sufficiently newsworthy to garner a photograph in the campus newspaper the next day.

KRISTEN PETTY/*UNIVERSITY DAILY KANSAN*, COURTESY UNIVERSITY ARCHIVES, UNIVERSITY OF KANSAS LIBRARIES

pus, on the sidewalk expanse in front of Wescoe Hall, where students traditionally ate lunch and passed the time between classes. We held hands, made a large circle, and then kissed the person to the right, then to the left; some kept on kissing for several minutes, with different partners of the same gender (Solon, 1992; photo 6.11).

Queer students utilized many of the same tactics as those of gays in the 1970s, but instead of simply promoting non-heterosexual visibility, queer acts were crafted to invert public and private space and to highlight the power differentials embedded within the norm of heterosexuality. In the 1970s, the Columbia Student Homophile League's demand to view the "proper setting [of homosexuality] as a sociological problem of deeply entrenched prejudice and discrimination against a minority group" (Duberman, 1993b, p. 172) was a

KRISTEN PETTY/*UNIVERSITY DAILY KANSAN*, COURTESY UNIVERSITY ARCHIVES, UNIVERSITY OF KANSAS LIBRARIES

PHOTO 6.11: **University of Kansas Kiss-In**

Public demonstrations such as this one in the spring of 1992 gained in popularity on college campuses in the United States during the 1990s. Such activities allowed non-heterosexuals to deploy queer tactics—and public expressions of non-heterosexual identity—to raise consciousness on campuses about the unquestioned assumptions of heterosexual norms and privileges in American culture. But such exposure came at a price, as one of the men in this photographed discovered when someone anonymously sent the photograph to his father.

gay viewpoint, a gay sensibility; the meaning understood through a queer sensibility would view the sociological problem in terms of power and control, and as resting with straight people (who dominate) rather than the non-straights (who are subjugated by heterosexuals). Rather than blame the victims or appease the perpetrators of the discrimination, queer students would argue for an even great political change, more akin to revolutionary rather than integrational reform.

The dichotomy between reform and refutation mirrored the differences between gay students and queer students. Whereas a gay activist in the 1970s could proclaim, "If we wanted to, we could boycott Bloomingdale's and that store would be closed in two weeks" (quoted in Clendinen and Nagourney, 1999, p. 30), such actions rarely occurred. By the late 1980s and early 1990s, queer activists were not only boycotting stores but shutting down stock exchanges and Catholic masses (Clendinen and Nagourney, 1999; Signorile, 1993). And, instead of protesting the media for presenting unflattering and/or biased representations of gay life, queer students utilized the fourth estate not only to challenge the norms of American society but also to question to the very presumption of "the norm," as Rad attempted to do through his column in the campus newspaper.

A rallying cry of queers was "Queer liberation, not gay assimilation" (Thompson, 1994, p. 369; Witt, Thomas and Marcus, 1995, p. 394). Promenades, kiss-ins, and mall-ins were viewed as tools of liberation, echoing the sentiments of the early gay (primarily non-student) activists of the late 1960s and early 1970s. One particular historical element of the late 1980s and early 1990s is the rise (and subsequent fall) of institutional committees to investigate non-heterosexual concerns on campuses (Gay, Lesbian and Bisexual Concerns Study Committee, 1993; Neiberding, 1989; Study Committee on the Status of Lesbian and Gay Men, 1991; Task Force on Lesbian and Gay Concerns, 1990).

While (most) queer students were challenging the legitimacy of institutional auspices, gay students (primarily, but not exclusively) were working within institutional channels to attempt to effect change on campuses like Rutgers, the University of Kansas, the University of Michigan, and the University of Oregon. Gay students in the 1980s and 1990s worked with schools to better their inclusion in campus environments and services; queer students were political, as Pozzo's queer collegiate (and immediate post-graduation) experience in the '80s depicts, but in a more "traditional" sense of demonstrations and protests, combined with nonconformist notions that sexuality was comprised of more than how or with whom one engaged in sexual activity.

Apparently, from Jimmy's actions and intentions, queer identities were formed—and articulated—before the terminology for the type was prevalent. This new understanding of *queer* is evident even though the term had been used at other times by heterosexuals and non-heterosexuals, to reflect generic non-heterosexuality (Chauncey, 1994); indeed, the terms gay, homosexual, and queer appeared interchangeable both in the respondents' narratives and in the contemporaneous autobiographic accounts of other non-heterosexuals (Hemric, 1973; Marotta, 1983). For instance, although Jim, Pozzo, and Rad each identified as "gay" at the time, in their own analyses, as well as mine, their self-concepts and activities around or involving their sexuality did not match the gay type.

Further differences and similarities are apparent within the other types of identification exhibited by non-heterosexual collegiate males—within their own struggles. "Aside from their obvious differences, gay and queer identities have both emerged out of, and given rise to, collective struggles of identity politics" (Carlson, 1998, p. 110). A gay student would not necessarily feel impelled to "be active," to educate heterosexual students about sexuality, or to serve other non-heterosexual students as a mentor in a peer-mentoring program; a closeted or homosexual student would, in most instances, be unable to conceive of how to go about such activities. Both types might, though, wish for those who could and would be out and active on campus, as Sam and Juan vocalized.

The identities reviewed thus far have been publicized, to some degree: a non-heterosexual presenting a non-heterosexual identity in at least some social contexts. But these were not the only identity types on campuses in the United States in the latter half of the twentieth century; four others were evident, although not usually publicly.

"Normal": 1940s to 1990s. While there is a clear, historical narrative connecting the events and identities of gay (and even queer) college students from the 1940s to the late 1990s, the same can not be said for all of the types. The social changes of the 1960s, 1970s, and even the 1980s did not affect how all non-heterosexual men conceptualized their identities or their sexuality. Four types of identification remained consistent over those times, despite the revolutions.

Some non-heterosexual collegians continued to identify as "normal," a type that is evident in each decade covered in this study. Whereas gay identities were formed in juxtaposition to heterosexual and homosexual identities, "normal" men identified decidedly not as homosexual and, if anything, as just like heterosexuals. They (usually) dated women, but they also (frequently) had sex with other men, (often) in clandestine contexts. As Kirk Read wrote of his first homosexual experiences,

> I didn't think of Rich as being gay—he was just a friend with whom I had sex. I wasn't in denial—I just didn't know that having sex with another guy gave me a special identity as a gay man. I didn't know that was an option. The gay men in Lexington were either closeted or frightening grotesques. (Read, 2001, p. 60)

For these men, their sexual activity with other males had no relationship to their identity, nor did it preclude these men from having sexual experiences with women. In the 1940s, Ralph could have sex with his roommate every night, but it did not mean he was not heterosexual; indeed, he later married and had children. If "normal" collegians' social identity had any impact on their homosexual activity, it was to replicate the social mores (of the desirability of sexual partners, of the notion of non-vaginal intercourse not counting as "sex") of the dominant heterosexual society: in the 1980s, Chris could feel he had earned "bragging rights" for having tearoom sex with men from more prestigious fraternity houses in the way he would if he were dating a sorority girl from a "good" house. "Normal" students fit into no other type nor aspect of non-heterosexual student history; while these men engaged in sexual activity that would preclude their inclusion into a heterosexual identity (for obviously they knew and experienced something about the non-heterosexual subcultures on their campuses), they certainly did not identify as non-heterosexual (be that as gay, queer, or homosexual).

Parallel: 1940s to 1990s. If the "normal" identity type can not be classified as either heterosexual or non-heterosexual, the parallel type can be viewed as corresponding to both classifications. Men who continued to lead two lives, to have concurrent and parallel identities as both straight and non-straight, also appeared consistently across decades. Those collegians who displayed this type of identity had concurrent (although not strictly simultaneous) identity formation in relation to heterosexual and homosexual identities; complicating this schema, though, is the relation that each half of the parallelism had to the other. A split between the collegiate and sexual worlds is evident for parallel men: the individuals in the parallel type each indicated that they avoided having sex on campus, or with someone whom they knew from college; if it did happen and others found out about it, as in Alec's case, the men would feel "horrible" and "ashamed."

Closeted: 1940s to 1990s. Horror of being found out as someone who experienced same-sex desires and actions, and the resulting shame, are closely aligned to the concepts framing another non-heterosexual identity type consistent across all decades. Men who were closeted fostered and presented an identity type that was aligned with neither heterosexuality nor homosexuality. For these collegians, the closet walls, formed by the conceptions of what others would say, think, or do if they found out the closeted collegians were not heterosexual, created a barrier between who the students thought they were and what they felt others would think they were. This barrier created a shallow (sometimes distorted) college experience for closeted students: "My friendships have gotten very deep now. In the past my friendships were, like, through a mask."

Living in the closet, in the words of one respondent, was "Knowing something intellectually but not accepting it emotionally." Closeted men could neither identify fully as heterosexual (since they knew, intellectually, they were not) nor homosexual (since they believed, emotionally, such an identity to be wrong or prohibited). This dichotomy is displayed in Paul's attempted seduction of a faculty member at his school, only to report subsequently to the administration that the professor was not heterosexual; in Bob's attempts to date women while living in a fraternity house that gave some subliminal outlet for his homosexual emotions and desires; and in Sam's obeying his mother's orders "not to be a homosexual," while feeling everyone in town hated him because he "was the gay guy that shouldn't be given a chance to be part of anything."

Denying: 1940s to 1990s. Inevitably (but unintentionally), the narratives in this project do not address a final possible type of identity: denial. Those collegians who consistently denied their non-heterosexual feelings never addressed or expressed a non-normative identity. Such a person (along with closeted identities) was, conceivably, not "a part of anything," either by choice or circumstance. Although Paul believed he was in denial, in fact he was not, for he admitted to himself that he had "homosexual tendencies." Denial did play some part in the decisions of identity deployment of closeted men, as Bob's self-analysis revealed, but he, too, had admitted to himself (and others) that he had homosexual senses and feelings.

To understand the qualitites of the classification denial, one must look beyond the respondents to this study. Andrew Holleran, the prominent novelist and commentator of gay life, wrote eloquently about his undergraduate years at Harvard in the mid-1960s. His depiction of the inability to perceive, let alone process, the experiences and senses into a non-heterosexual sensibility is telling of campus experiences and sensibilities of collegians in denial:

While sitting in the john one day I noticed the partitions between the stalls were sheets of limestone in which the imprints of trilobites could be seen. I also noticed advertisements for nude wrestling scrawled on the doors in Magic Marker. As everyone knows who has gone to school, one can read certain things at a certain age and just not get it: *Moby Dick*. *King Lear*. Ads for nude wrestling on bathroom walls. Such was the force of my denial, I didn't even associate such things with myself. And when a hand reached under the partition between the toilet stalls one day and stroked my left leg, I stood up, horrified, pulled my pants on, and left. The johns in those days sounded like Niagara Falls when flushed, and the sound, I was sure, let the slimeball who had touched my left calf know just what I thought about that sort of activity (Holleran, 1997, p. 9).

Denial might, obviously, be formed by some collegians without relationship to other identity types; again, Holleran was evocative: "Ten years after graduation from Harvard, where I saw nothing in terms of sex, I now saw everything that way" (1997, pp. 16–17). Collegiate men in denial can refute the possibility of being non-heterosexual, and rarely question the presumptive paradigm of heterosexuality, for to do so would bring into question the sexual and affectional impulses they are cognitively denying.

Reflections on Changing, Multiple Non-Heterosexual Identities

Despite their (reflective) desires for role models and opportunities for socialization when they were in college, gay students maintained a more private public life than a public private life, more so than would allow for such activities—whether as a result of repressive campuses and social environments or their own personal predilections. Those gays who were part of queer activities were often viewed by queer students with varying degrees of scorn or avoidance, as displayed in Pozzo's and Gene's accounts of forging queer identities in the late 1980s and early 1990s. Homosexual students rarely felt comfortable commingling with queer students, and vice versa, as Pozzo's story of Swarthmore's gay student organization's changing of the guard conveyed.

To be certain, individuals who identified as gay have conducted queer activities on campuses since the early 1970s; despite their nomenclature for self-identifications (often "gay"), to understand their role on campus and the impact that campus activity had upon their identities in relation to heterosexuals and other non-heterosexuals, queer is the type that best comprises and classifies their experiences. Queer identity, then, was formed in relation to the norms of heterosexual, homosexual, and gay identities. Queer is most definitely oppositional to heterosexual, but it is also juxtaposed sometimes even crossly, as Pozzo's contemporary estimations of the students involved in Swathmore's gay/lesbian/bisexual student organization depicted, with homosexual and gay identities.

Just as particular sexual acts alone did not connote identity, neither did singular (or specific) social activities constrict a non-heterosexual student's self-concept and -identification. By the early 1990s, the movement of non-heterosexual student types into spaces and events of other types reflected the fluidity of sexual identities. Gay students could be involved in queer activities like ACT-UP and Queer Nation, but in a *social* context rather than *political*; instead of joining protests, gay collegians might associate with queer groups to meet other non-heterosexuals who did not fit into the dominant gay paradigm. Instead of arguing, as gay students did at the University of Kansas (among other institutions), for inclusion in Reserve Officer Training Corps (ROTC) programs under institutional anti-discrimination clauses, queer students would argue for dismantling ROTC programs. If gay students were adamant in their belief of the similarities between gays and straights (particularly the image of white, suburban couples), queer students coalesced around issues of difference, both with heterosexuals and within gays; the realities of race (and racism), gender, power, and health were the rallying points of queer students (as the narratives of Jim, Pozzo, and Gene conveyed in chapter 4). These distinctions were important and powerful to gay students who felt they did not fit into gay student organizations.

Apart from denial, all the identity types in all decades and collegiate contexts were formed in relation to presumed straight identity; heterosexuality was perceived as the master category of normality. As one respondent commented,

> I don't think back then that I thought in terms of "gay" and "straight"—those are political terms that gained real currency in the early 1980s, but didn't really exist back then in my lexicon. I thought then in terms of "homosexual" and "normal."

In addition, later non-heterosexual identity types were also formed in relation to (presumed) non-straight identities. In the words of Juan,

> I knew I was attracted to men. [Nevertheless], I considered myself straight, or heterosexual, but I knew those feelings were there. I had

never acted on the feelings in high school, but I knew subconsciously they were there.

The comparison of the margins to center, of the different to the normal—particularly as they pertain to sexual identity—is at the core of queer theory. Classification only by the gender of (preferred) sexual partners is insufficient to understand non-heterosexual students. Figure 6.1 is again helpful: over time, the qualities and aspects of particular, non-heterosexual identities moved from the margins to, if not the center, then at least other sides of what was considered the norm(s).

In the 1940s and 1950s, heterosexuality was the sole standard to which collegiate males who were not heterosexual had to compare their experiences and ideation; this resulted in the dichotomous understanding of identity, heterosexual or homosexual. But as later homosexual students engaged in the processes associated with identity development (as outlined in both gay identity development theories and student development theories), two norms now existed for comparison. For some of these students, neither identity resonated, although homosexual might be a closer match than heterosexual. Consequently, the gay type came to represent changes in social and interpersonal activities and awareness of these non-heterosexual males. By the 1980s, the gay identity type was regarded as another norm with which to compare one's behaviors and emotions; the juxtaposition of those against the existing types offered for contemporary non-heterosexual collegians another, novel type form of self-identification: queer.

The tenets of queer theory were evident, even before the general use of "queer" or the construction of queer theory. Public transgression (semipublic, prior to the 1980s) of accepted cultural norms was evident in the womanless marriage at Baylor in the 1950s; in the 1970s, Jimmy taxed the rules of gender and sexuality by dressing in drag and producing performance art that questioned the normative functions of heterosexuality. In each case of identity development, from closeted and homosexual to queer and "normal," individuals evaluated themselves against what was considered, presented, or observed to be "normal." This relational context was also apparent in the ideations of men who considered themselves and their identities as needing to be hidden because they were not normal (the closet type), who viewed themselves as "just like everyone else" (the "normal" type), and who kept their "straight," normal lives separate from their "gay," clandestine lives (the parallel type).

The distinctions of the types matter, both to the individuals involved and for an true understanding of this far from static student population. The changes in how non-heterosexual collegians identified, and how they deployed those identities publicly and politically, are evident in the student organization at the University of Kansas. In 1970, members of the university community (including students and non-university affiliated citizens of Lawrence, Kansas) formed a local chapter of the Gay Liberation Front. By 1971, the GLF's efforts concentrated upon the university, and the group became a nonsanctioned, officially unrecognized organization. In 1976, after winning limited recognition from the university in part through proving a majority of student members, the GLF changed its name to Gay Services of Kansas. In 1983, women were recognized within the name as separate yet equal, and the organization became Gay and Lesbian Services of Kansas. As the minutes of the organization and the recollections of officers and members collaborate, from 1990 through 1992, the members of the group debated at some length upon the inclusion of bisexuality and/or transexuality within the nomenclature; queer was also considered, but always rejected as too confrontational and too derogatory to the membership. Arguments against the change were overruled by 1993, when the organization became known as Lesbian, Bisexual and Gay Services of Kansas (or, informally, "LesBeGayS"). Reflecting further change in the personal and political self-concepts of the membership and the organization, the group again changed its official name in 1996 to Queers and Allies. This name posits both difference from the norm and acceptance of those who accept that difference; it is paradoxically defiant and embracing at the same time.

The paradox reflects a quality of the identity types in the theory outlined in figure 1.1. The types of non-heterosexual male identity contain an inherent contradiction of identity theories: on the one hand, the classifications convey the essentialism of "being different," while concurrently showing that the difference is understood—and accepted or not—through the social construction of meanings and behaviors associated with (or ascribed to) those identity types. The college experience for the respondents in this study cannot be truly understood without utilizing gay identity development theories; conversely, the non-heterosexual identities and experiences are less meaningful, less contextualized, without examining them through the lens of student identity development theory. Neither set of theories (of the marginal nor the typical identity), by itself, conveys or explains these lives; the theories did not keep pace with non-heterosexual collegians' changing identities—their senses, experiences, and sensibilities.

As the critical lens of understanding identity moved to center upon the margins, so too did the margins come into focus. As those margins were examined and comprehended, they, too, became norms, creating an ongoing, expanding process of identity formation. In the final chapter, I offer final (but formative, rather than summative) conclusions about identity, and potential implications for educators and practitioners who utilize understandings of identity development theory to serve students.

CHAPTER 7

On the Fluidity of Identity

Of Research and Researchers

I heard once, in a graduate class, that those of us who conduct research do so to answer questions about ourselves, to try to solve problems that confront our personal lives as well as confound our professional analysis. Certainly, in my mind, I now see a clear route from the boy who tried to figure out who he was by consulting first an encyclopedia and later scores of research and theory about the lives of those who were not straight, to the sometimes queer, always gay man who conducted this study. The research, too, is closely related to the boy, slightly older, sitting in the winter moonlight of the Florida Keys, asking questions of a stranger, comparing and contrasting emotions, experiences, excitements.

In this project that was, ultimately, about the fluidity of identity, I am uncertain what to make of my own life, my own story. From this vantage point, four years after first proposing this work, I realize I am that same person I was twenty years ago; but college—the experiences and senses that influenced my sensibilities—changed me and how I view myself. I am now a professional questioner; some might say I am a professional queer. I discovered ways to be both in college.

Out as I might feel (and/or be), like the narrators in this study, my identity shifts, depending upon the contexts. As Mendelsohn stated, "Since I grew up gay, I'm used to imposture, to sculpting false identities for myself, when necessary, out of the silences that are other people's assumptions" (1999, 107). I was considered by those who knew me as an undergraduate in Oklahoma as "gay" and social. Friends in graduate school in Kansas, by the end of my time there, would probably say I was "queer" and political. I wonder what colleagues consider me now: some days, despite what I study, I neither feel very gay (a simple response, perhaps, given the hyperconsciousness of imagery in West Hollywood and Los Angeles) nor very queer (particularly since my energy and time now go into scholarship and teaching, not all of which directly relates to things queer). My self-concept always modulates; indeed, my sensibility is somewhat shifty, depending upon the contexts and my sense of the contexts.

The person I am—in the context of the present—is both the same as before and different; the same as (some) others yet different; the opposite of others, yet the same. To utilize the theoretical constructs from chapter 2, on the one hand, I am not heterosexual (and thus different); on the other, I am a student (and in many respects, no different at all from other students). No classification, no typology, will ever eliminate this paradox of developing as non-heterosexual (as a simultaneous center of a norm and a margin of another) while also developing as a student (itself centered and marginalized). I do not judge this inability to be precise when examining or conveying identity to be a liability. Instead, I view it as a queer job, both accepting and challenging the product of my efforts. I also perceive the typology I offered in this study as a method for further conversations and understandings about what happens when we identify, when we become "the same" while at the same time uniquely the other. As such, it is a beginning, rather than the end, of appreciating the lives of non-heterosexual male college students, "of trying to make sense of life as lived" (Clandinin and Connelly, 2000, p. 78).

Such an appreciation starts with an understanding of what those lives are like, of the phenomena and beliefs that individuals make sense. To do so in this project, I employed a compare/contrast approach to analyze the respondents' conversations with me. First, I compared the experiences, senses, and sensibilities the men conveyed to the other narratives; I subsequently grouped the respondents based upon their similarities. I compared those arrangements with the existing theories of identity development covered in chapter 2. From that consideration I developed the identity typology for non-heterosexual college males (see figure 1.1).

I chose to explain the theory through exemplary narratives for each type (as presented in Section II and contextualized in chapter 6). By providing multiple, extensive examples for each category, I strove to illustrate the richness of experience, sense, and sensibility of the individuals who participated in this study and who manifest the types. Although I designed the textual representation of the interviews in a formalist fashion, the research activities were truly grounded in narrative inquiry, to research non-heterosexual male collegiate experience "as expressed in lived and told stories" (Clandinin and Connelly, 2000, p. 40) rather than in theory.

As the narratives displayed, non-heterosexual collegians viewed themselves and their educational experiences as different from heterosexual students': as the typology summarizes, patterns of understanding those experiences and lives are evident. Figure 1.1 depicts commonalities of collegiate experience (although it certainly does not represent the entirety of possible experiences) of non-heterosexual men in each of the types.

Dealing with the topic of identity for a particular population of students unified by their self-identities (their senses, experiences, and sensibilities), I looked at what I problematically called "non-heterosexuals." I chose that term deliberately, to reflect a wide variety of identities that were formed in juxtaposition to heterosexuality, and with some reservation, reflecting my hesitancy to use a contrapositive term to label someone by what he is not. Among the outcomes of this project is the beginnings of a mapping of the various sensibilities and identities this campus population has displayed and deployed over the past fifty-five years; these identities were contextually based, fluid rather than fixed, formative rather than summative.

It stands to reason that if multiple non-heterosexual identities exist, if those identities are adopted, understood, and situated differently in contrasting contexts, then the identities of heterosexual students are also varied, fluid, and contextual, rather than monolithic (both as understood by the men in this project and as often portrayed in student identity development models). A logical extension of this work would, I hope, make use of the term "non-heterosexual" even more problematic, through a continued cartography of the lives and identities of this student population; perhaps, too, utilization of the concepts of identity I posited (senses, experiences, and sensibilities) would similarly problematize the concept of "heterosexual."

Observations for Theory and Practice

Moving from a narrative examination of the historical developments of non-heterosexual collegiate male identity of the previous chapter, I now briefly address six particular findings evident in the data (summarized in figure 7.1). How the findings are relevant to each type is depicted in figure 7.2. Each of the points reflects specific influences upon non-heterosexual identity for the collegiate males in this study, and each is rarely (if ever) addressed in either student development theories or gay identity development theories.

Campus Environments. The constraints and the opportunities of particular campus environments impacted non-heterosexual identity—positively and negatively. Men seeking other men—for sex, for companionship, for identification with others who are like themselves—found ways to do so in every campus community. In the 1940s, Walter knew of a "gay cruising area in a park," as well as private social gatherings in faculty members' homes. Sam related that, in private, a number of fellows on his campus "would try things," sexual things, with him. Chris found sex in the library bathrooms, Cliff found inspiration through sex at the urging of faculty members, Jim attempted to form a men's discussion group using his campus opinion board to find others who were "like" him, while Juan found sex in his fraternity house with someone who was both like Juan (a fraternity brother) and different from him (they disagreed on politics, management of the house, and company of friends).

The importance of these experiences for these men is more than just being in a context with other adolescents who might share their inclinations (although that certainly happened, as Chris, Sam, and many of the other respondents' stories convey), for through the experiences, the men discovered another aspect or quality against which to compare themselves and their identities. In Jimmy's words (from chapter 4), finding these relationships:

FIGURE 7.1: **Summary of Observations for Theory and Practice**

- **Campus Environments.** The constraints and the opportunities of particular campus environments did impact non-heterosexual identity—both positively and negatively.

- **Gay Student Organizations.** The formation of a gay student organization on campus provided some benefits to some non-heterosexual collegians, but simply having such an organization was not enough to provide all of the social and/or developmental opportunities needed for positive identity development.

- **Fraternity Life.** A sense of "common background and instant rapport" that enriched interpersonal relationships—albeit usually in non-overtly sexual ways—was a theme in the life stories of members of greek-letter organizations.

- **Sexual Activity.** Sexual activity was very important in the identity development of non-heterosexual male college students, more so than represented in either student identity development models or gay identity development models.

- **The Goals of Being "Normal."** Being "normal"—or at least considered by others as such—was a goal of many students who later identified as non-heterosexual.

- **Emotional Attractions.** While the physical act of sex with another man might be seen as a clear sign of not being heterosexual, often emotional attractions to other men were the first indications to non-heterosexual men of their difference.

- **Media Influences.** Media impacted non-heterosexual male collegian's views of non-heterosexual identity, and media (particularly film and television) impacted later respondents' self-identity.

was part of my coming to terms with my objectification of men as fuck objects. While I never dismissed my interest in pleasure, I did learn . . . that a gay man could be a friend as well.

Clearly, from the narratives, over the last half of the twentieth century, non-heterosexual students found more opportunity for social (not necessarily sexual) gatherings on college campuses in the United States. A number of respondents reported being a part of—either socially or as an active member—gay and lesbian student organizations, and historical reflections from nonmembers indicated a direct, positive attitudinal and climactic impact of such groups upon campuses.

This campus change from hidden alienation to public and political inclusion was neither comprehensive nor smooth. Court cases upheld the rights of students to gather for peaceful assemblies, even if campus administrators did not agree with the political (or personal) implications of the meeting, so long as the individuals did not advocate direct illegal activities (Harbeck, 1997; Kaplan, 1990). But such public endeavors were not the only forms of institutional socialization affecting non-heterosexual students. In many instances, the subcultural, clandestine activities engaged in by non-heterosexuals influenced how those non-heterosexuals pictured their identities, both personally and as members of campus. Gathering large numbers of post-adolescent males onto campuses with public "private" facilities fostered many opportunities to explore the physical side of non-heterosexual identities. As Chris stated in chapter 5, about being at the University of Illinois in the 1980s,

It was just a perfect situation for me to find the type of sex I enjoyed at the time, without feeling any guilt. . . . There's a lot of people who are jealous of my college experiences, because I had so much sex in college, and the type of sex and the type of guy I had sex with. U of I definitely enabled that, definitely allowed that to happen.

Secretive sex was engaged in not only by those who considered themselves "normal"; other types participated as well, as Dennis and Alec both discussed in chapter 5. The main point of this observation is that the combination of increased authority (of time and sexuality) and the institutional constructs related to public gatherings (including libraries, student unions, fraternities) aided non-heterosexuals' understandings of their sexuality and personal identities.

Those identities and concurrent activities were not without risk. Discovery

FIGURE 7.2: **Relevance of Findings to Identity Types**

	CAMPUS ENVIRONMENTS	STUDENT ORGANIZATIONS	FRATERNITY LIFE
Homosexual	Felt oppressed by campus	Rarely involved; rarely participated in social events, if at all	If a member, usually not out to other greek members
Gay	Challenged campus oppression; viewed campus as site for social inclusion	Formed student organizations and participated in existing campus activities	If a member, usually not out to other greek members
Closeted	Felt oppressed through campus institutions	Did not join or participate in social activities	If a member, usually not out to other greek members
Queer	Saw campus as site of public disruption for contesting social norms	Involved more in loose-knit social action groups, rather than traditional or gay student groups	Viewed as repressive, normalizing constructs
"Normal"	Campus viewed as nonpoliticized in public, but often very sexual in private or semipublic campus locales	Usually not involved in gay student or community organizations, as these students did not identify as non-heterosexual	Members often experienced homo-affectional and occasional homosexual experience with other fraternity members
Parallel	Campus seen only as a heterosexual (and homo-sexless) environment	Usually not involved in non-heterosexual campus or community organizations	If involved in greek system, separated sex from greek life; might experience homo-affections for other greek members
Denying	Did not often view or acknowledge homo-cultural aspects of campus	Did not participate	If a member, did not express any non-heterosexual senses

	SEX	"NORMALITY"	EMOTIONS	MEDIA
Homosexual	A private matter, even if conducted in semipublic places	Did not consider themselves normal	Did not display emotions publicly	Saw no role models; viewed representations of homosexuality as pathological and deviant
Gay	Viewed sex as less a private matter and more as a human right	Viewed themselves as virtually normal, differing only in gender of sexual partner and society's perceptions of them	Posited and displayed emotion in public, but not usually confrontationally	Self-identity influenced by increased media representation (both positive and negative); used media to posit equality to heterosexuals
Closeted	Rarely experienced, if at all	Tried to appear normal (i.e., heterosexual)	Felt homo-affections but did not reveal them to others	Felt media representations of non-heterosexuals were not positive
Queer	Publicly deployed sexuality to demonstrate social stigmatization	Normality seen as oppressive and opposite of queer	Emotions deployed in public to disrupt social norms	Used media to challenge or invert social norms through publicizing their sexuality
"Normal"	Viewed homo-sex as normal activity, not as signifying homosexuality (or gay or queer) as an identity	Viewed themselves as normal; experienced a disjuncture between homosexual acts and homosexual identity	Often no emotions involved in homo-sex relations; emtions often involved in hetero-sex relations	Viewed selves as not non-heterosexual, particularly in comparison to media representations of non-heterosexuals
Parallel	Homo-sex seen as separate from hetero-sex	Heterosexual aspects seen as normal, homosexual aspects as not	Experienced a disjuncture between homo-affections and self-identity	Impacted views of self-concept of non-heterosexual aspect of self
Denying	Did not engage in homo-sex	Did not view selves as not normal	Did not display homo-emotions	Media impacted lives only negatively ("I'm not that way")

of "personal, private" activity—either in "public, private" spaces on campus or in the privacy afforded most everyone (but not non-heterosexuals) off campus—jeopardized the students' careers and lives. Walter's depiction of the dismissal of two professors at the University of Illinois in the early 1950s, along with his subsequent expulsion, displayed the reality of this situation, as well as the institutional view of guilt by association. Bob's requirement to track, literally, suspected homosexuals at the University of Indiana in the early '60s is a prime example of the control (*in loco* or otherwise) that colleges and universities sought over non-heterosexuals, as is the earlier, the negative response of the campus psychiatrist at his religious undergraduate institution, who condemned Bob to hell, calling him "dirty" and "awful." This discrimination was a direct form of institutional control of sexuality, a prevalent theme through which to understand higher education of the times (cf., Bailey, 1999).

Not all administrative responses to non-heterosexuality was negative, even in the 1950s. Paul's school sent him to a "psychology professor who wisely wondered aloud with me if there was anything that would point me in that direction" of being homosexual. By the 1970s, some faculty and administrators were, if not encouraging, at least not discouraging of the political and public expressions of non-heterosexual identity (as shown in the stories of Jimmy and Cliff). Later still, the involvement in campus student organizations by non-heterosexuals (Duchess, Rad, and Pozzo, for example) did facilitate some development along the precepts of traditional student development theories and did facilitate relationships and friendships.

Gay Student Organizations. Gay student organizations operating on campus provided some benefits to some respondents, but this alone was not enough to provide the myriad social and/or developmental opportunities needed for positive identity development. Older respondents, having attended college before court rulings in the 1970s allowed non-heterosexual student organizations the right to assemble on campus, frequently mentioned their desire to have had such a group on campus. The creation of the organizations—and the concurrent resulting interpersonal and personal development for non-heterosexual students—provided opportunities for growth named on traditional student development models that, possibly, these collegians would not have had. While, as I noted earlier, non-heterosexual students involved in non-heterosexual campus organizations found some new friends and relationships, the majority reported having, on the whole, negative experiences with the student organizations. Even study participants who served as officers of such organizations reported these responses.

Gay student groups, by themselves, did not mitigate social stigmatization (as Pozzo's comments reflect, either within or without of the group) for non-heterosexual students. Indeed, Gene felt even more discrimination within the student organizations due to his ethnicity and national origin. Tim (a gay-type student from chapter 4) also found the gay student organization at California State University—Long Beach in the 1980s inhospitable: "I did try to [join] the gay and lesbian student union. . . . I found that really cliquish and not welcoming. I think I went maybe twice and didn't go back, because it was very insular."

Tim's encounter with gay campus organizations pointed out a discongruity in these organizations that many non-heterosexual men described: a conflict between personal goals (usually for socialization) and political goals (usually for inclusion of and equity for non-heterosexual students). Again, in Tim's estimation,

> They talked about [only] the business; I think that my interest in going was to meet people and to start to be part of some kind of group. I didn't know enough about the politics of the school or what they were trying to do.

Rad, a queer type (also from chapter 4), on the other hand, wanted to be active in efforts at social (political, yet still personal) change in the non-heterosexual student activities and organization at University of Southern California. He, too, found his time with the organization less than fulfilling; in his view, the efforts were not as "visible" or integrated with the other aspects of student life as he would have hoped them to be.

Whatever their motives for wanting to become part of the campus organizations for non-heterosexuals, clearly the students in this study did not find fulfillment of their needs or goals through such organizations. In this sense, their abilities to connect socially with other non-heterosexuals was as limited as that expressed by this student from the 1980s:

> I didn't really meet any other gay people in college—I mean there were other gay people I met, but it wasn't openly discussed (besides the gossip/speculation of other dorm members), so I didn't know they were gay. It wasn't like now, where sexuality brings a certain common background and instant (if not lasting) rapport.

Fraternity Life. A sense of "common background and instant rapport" that enriched interpersonal relationships—albeit usually in non-overtly sexual ways—was a theme in life stories of certain collegiate non-heterosexuals: members of greek-letter fraternities. Indeed, fraternity life greatly influenced the homo-emotional experiences of several narrators in this study. As Juan conveyed, he found during his years at Azusa Pacific University that his fraternity brothers were a source of companionship and friendship.

Chris also reported that being a fraternity member provided a sense of "fitting in" on campus; Peter echoed this and added that he viewed greek-letter life as an opportunity to be "very socially active," a personal goal for his collegiate experience after leaving community college. Bob's "very accepting, very supportive" fraternity friend helped Bob realize that the college psychiatrist's response to and judgment of Bob's fledgling homo-ideations was not universal; in this respect, Bob felt the fraternity brother "saved my life."

Not all individuals in greek-letter organizations had positive experiences, however. Malcom Boyd (1978), whom I classified as homosexual, was a fraternity member. In his autobiography, Boyd wrote:

> During the fraternity initiation rituals I felt especially a stranger. I was physically attracted to the lusty young men around me, yet was unable to reveal my feelings and emotions. . . . A homosexual person hiding my identity, I was compelled to play a constant role in fraternity life. One day an older brother who apparently found my behavior suspicious, and had been drinking heavily, shouted at me, "I'm going to take your pants down, beat the shit out of your ass, get your cock up, and see what's wrong with you." Another brother intervened and I was saved an ordeal and a beating.
>
> I wonder now at the bizarre self-deceit of it all. Those fraternity initiations were all very macho, and the participants would, for the most part, go on in life as firmly self-convinced straights, taking their roles in business or the professions, marrying and raising families, frightened or downright terrorized by any suggestions of deviance. Yet as a sexually mature gay, I can look back on those rites that took place in the privacy of the frat house and recognize them, under their cover of boisterous status assertion, for what they were—exercises in homosexual sado-masochism and voyeurism. (Boyd, 1978, pp. 46–48)

While these analyses of the benefits of greek life and its related social world are not novel, they are most striking when coming from non-heterosexual men. Interestingly, the respondents involved in non-heterosexual student organizations often reported alienation and isolation within those groups, while those who were members of greek-letter fraternities found camaraderie and friendship within those organizations (albeit while not publicly acknowledging their sexuality). This runs counter to the intuitive belief of the older non-heterosexuals in the study (as well as my own) that involvement in campus organizations would create better environments for establishing identities with non-heterosexual peers.

Sexual Activity. Some activities, did, though, form significant patterns in the development of non-heterosexual identities. Sexual activity was very important in the developmental processes, more so than represented in student identity development models or gay identity development models. A dichotomous discrepancy embodied this data, which, given the nature of queer analysis, was not all that surprising. Sex was crucial to the respondents, both in terms of their understanding their orientation and in much of their collegiate lives, as Chris's comments quoted earlier in this chapter convey. One student indicated sex "was important. At the beginning, I needed to know whether I was really gay. Then, it became an affirmation of self-worth." Some students hid from situations where they might be physically attracted to men, while others sought them out. Others engaged in activities with a great number of sexual partners, while others had no sexual activity during college. A few collegians believed that their sexuality was central to their identity, while others thought it was a "private, personal matter." "It was not intended to become a way of life— merely sidelines and detours. It was just something I did; it just wasn't me."

In contrast to this view, sexual activity was viewed by most of the respondents—particularly by those whose narratives I included as representative of the types—as important, even if they did not identify as an "other" type (say, *gay* or *homosexual*). Indeed, many of the respondents reported engaging in numerous sexual encounters and activities, even in repressive environments and contexts. For most of the respondents, sex was always available in college, if not on campus then close by (in what surely was never intended to be classified as "town and gown" relationships). But whether they were running from it or toward it, sex was a dominant concept affecting self-understanding (knowing one's self) and, consequently, self-identity (presenting one's self).

> Yes, it was important. At the beginning, I needed to know whether I was really gay. Then, it became an affirmation of self-worth. And as naive as I was, I thought for the longest time that this was how I could find a relationship.

The degree of importance, however, varied. To some non-heterosexual men, particularly those who were closeted or leading parallel lives, the impact and importance of the sex was relegated to a nonexistent role in their identity: "My homosexuality back then was just about sex, nothing more." Another student, classified as "normal," summarized his contemporary views of homosex: "In college, being gay meant just having sex with another guy." It certainly did not create a sense of identity for him.

But for men in the study who do not fit into the "closeted" or "homosexual" types, particularly those who attended college after the early 1970s, sex played a more primal role in their daily lives and in their self-concepts of identity. Many of them engaged in sexual activity at quite young ages; such early sexual activity has only recently begun to be addressed by gay identity development theorists (and not at all by student identity development theorists). Savin-Williams (1998) found that

> Perhaps counterintuitively, boys who had sex with other boys during childhood and early adolescence were not necessarily the same boys who readily recognized the meaning of their sexual behavior. Having sex with boys was not the same as being gay. (Savin-Williams, 1998, p. 56)

Such physical homo-expression without correlation to identity is certainly the case for the students classified as "normal." It's difficult for some to imagine, at the beginning of the twenty-first century, that such experiences would not clearly mean something about a particular identity for individuals; but neither the sense of desire nor the experience of genital gratification with someone of the same gender is the key determinant to identity. As one of the undergrads quoted in chapter 4 stated, "I remember having sexual thoughts about men as far back as eighth grade . . . I just never considered being gay."

How can we make sense of men who purport to be or to desire "straight-looking, straight-acting" men for relationships sexual and otherwise? Or men who consider themselves "normal" yet have clandestine sex with other men in public spaces—a stark paradox of "straight-conceptualized, gay-acting" identity? Or fraternity members, whose rituals are so sexually symbolic, whose social structures are often homo-social and erotically charged, and yet who do not engage in homo-sex? Or the straight undergraduate whose identity deployment includes baffling displays of homo-social and -sexual conversation and ideation; is he "just gay enough" for his identity to mean one thing to heterosexuals and something else to non-heterosexuals, while meaning perhaps something else entirely to himself? Identity, then, becomes a matter of meaning both within and beyond one's self, and where sex lies within that meaning is not always clear.

What constitutes "sex" is, as collegiate sexual health educators and anyone following the Clinton-Lewinsky scandal will confirm, always contested. To factor homo-sex into the sexual equation further confounds our comprehension. Is receiving a blow job sex or just fooling around? Does the gender of the participants matter? What about close physical contact, such as the initiation rites and behaviors of fraternity members, as Bob, Pete, and Juan conveyed?

Yes, the experiences matter a great deal, but not so much as the meaning made of those homo-sexual acts (experiences) and desires (senses). The acts appear to mean something particular to the man that relates to an interior understanding of identity ("I'm just like everyone else," for instance, or "I'm gay") that might not correspond to an exterior identity conveyed to others. In other words, although sexual acts can be part of the performative aspect of identity deployment, those behaviors alone do not constitute identity.

Still, some collegians who engaged in sex prior to college (or high school) made a direct connection between their (homo-) sexual behavior and their identity. As Tim's story conveyed, he felt different from his high school and college peers "maybe because I lost my virginity at a very early age." In Cliff's estimation, sex opened up ways of not only understanding himself but also allowed him "to become a good [theater set] designer." Another respondent agreed on the importance of sex upon his understanding of his identity:

> Yes! It was exploring and learning what sex was. It was a novelty. It was exciting. My first top, bottom, three-way, hustler, etc. It was all uncharted, new experiences. It was mostly fun, but a bit superficial. Something was always lacking; I think it was the romance.

For others, like Dennis, romance was sometimes evident, even if an ongoing relationship was not desired. In any event, though, sex—the thought of, the search for, the experience of, the consequences afterwards, the meanings the men made (or not) of homo-sex and homo-expression—profoundly affected the identities of the collegians in this study.

The Goals of Being "Normal." Sex was not the only objective of non-heterosexual collegians; in their quests for understanding "who" they were—and to whom they were similar—they also hoped to prove that they were like the majority of their peers (be they straight, homosexual, gay, or queer). Being "normal" was a goal of many students who later identified as non-heterosexual. Even if they were engaging in homo-sexual activity, the respondents perceived the identity formation process in relation to the societal norms of the time. That the norms favored heterosexuality and sanctioned against homosexuality was no surprise in the 1940s and 1950s. One e-mail respondent commented:

> Homosexual did not equate normal—and I wanted more than anything to be normal—one of the guys. Being gay or homosexual back then was still filled with the negative stereotypes of the limp-wristed, effeminate, lisping hairdresser. I wasn't that, so I decided I couldn't be a homosexual or gay. There weren't any images of regular homosexual men to refer back then. . . . For a long time—and certainly at that time—I considered the possibility of being homosexual to be a terrible curse—something evil had happened to me—and I was determined that it would go away if I denied it long enough. I wanted to be regular and normal. At that time, the idea that I could be gay and normal was an absurd thought.

Perhaps these feelings were the basis of the entire process of identity formation. As Mendelsohn (1999) pointed out,

> The English noun *identity* comes, ultimately, from the Latin adverb *identidem*, which means "repeatedly," . . . [and] is, in fact, nothing more than a reduplication of the word *idem*, "the same": *idem(et)idem. Same (and) same.* The same, repeated. . . .
> It seems odd, at first glance, that a noun that we associate with distinctiveness and individuality, with the irreducible uniqueness of each person, should derive from one that denotes (and even sounds like) nothing but mechanical repetition. But once you've given it some thought, the etymology of *identity* makes a kind of sense. At least one way of establishing what something is, after all, is to see whether it always remains itself, and nothing else, over and over again. This is also the case, presumably, for people: you are, endlessly and repeatedly, *you,* and not some other. (Mendelsohn, 1999, p. 41)

This paradox is the essential point of non-heterosexual college identity. One respondent viewed himself this way, as "Normal. All the kids in school were like me. At the same time, the idea that I could be gay and normal was an absurd thought."

The comparative process of one's experiences to the (perceived) identities of others was ongoing and extended to other non-heterosexuals as well as heterosexuals. This comparison between self and others, however, did not always bring about acceptance of one's sense of self as different. In the 1970s, as Arnie Kantrowitz (1977) helped to found the Gay Activists Alliance in New York, he finally felt he found other non-heterosexuals around whom he could feel comfortable: "Among them I could at last feel 'normal'" (Kantrowitz, 1977, p. 146). But simply being around other non-heterosexuals did not provide this feeling of solace. As an undergraduate at Vassar in the 1980s, Daniel Aibel's self-image contrasted the conflict of non-heterosexual men caught between paradigms of heterosexual and non-heterosexual.

> While I thought I might be gay, I seemed to have nothing in common with other gay people. I had no interest in being shocking, weird, or even fashionable. I spent most of my time alone; hoping, yet terrified, that someone would notice me. (MacKay, 1993, p. 119)

Emotional Attractions. For many respondents, such comparisons fostered behavior and ideation—at least for a time—that mirrored the closet or parallel types. "I was very uncomfortable with the idea and reality of being gay when I was in college. It was a burden then—something to hide," is a telling comment from one collegian. Also distinguishing is his perception of his sexuality in the absence of sexual activity. While the physical act of sex with another man might be seen as a clear sign of not being heterosexual, often emotional attractions to other men were the first indications to non-heterosexual men of their difference. He hid his "idea and reality" of being gay, and effected a facade of being "normal."

This identification as "normal" highlights the dilemmas of using gay identity development theories in the way educators use student development theory. Should the student development practitioner program activities and experiences for the "normal" student, or those in the closet or in denial, that challenge their concepts of their own sexuality, in the hopes of progressing that understanding to more closely align their sexual impulses or affections? On the other hand, should practitioners not address these issues through programming or advice, thereby perpetuating the feelings that form the closet and facilitate denial?

The issues are made more murky when one considers that, as the narratives corroborate, identity is neither stable nor fixed. How students conceptualized themselves (vis-a-vis their sexuality)—and how they allowed others to conceptualize them—fluctuated during their collegiate years. The parallel types formulated two almost disparate identities, based in relation to what was considered customary for different contexts; some students self-identified as "gay" while exhibiting qualities, behaviors, and sensibilities that are classified by others as "queer"; the homosexual students (like Duchess) made it clear that acting "too gay" was something they avoided, even though, in private, they might want to behave in those fashions.

Such is the untenable position student programmers and advisors find when confronted with counseling non-heterosexual male college students. Rather than progress through orderly stages of development, non-heterosexual male identity vacillates, adopting to suit the needs (and desires) of individuals to perform (or live) in contrasting environments. The sense of "normal, just like all the other kids" changes accordingly, as does the students' individual impressions of what is considered befitting the non-heterosexual identities.

Media Influences. The sense of what "all the kids in school were like" changed over the decades. The impact of media upon later respondents' self-identity—and ability to self-identify—is a clear pattern in the lives of the respondents and of other non-heterosexuals (Gamson, 1995, 1998). Moreover, this effect appeared closely tied to queer theory, because the representations in the media reflected changing social mores of acceptability as well as what was considered (and/or presented) as normal.

Sam (a closeted type from chapter 5) mentioned the few times in college career in the 1950s that someone in history or literature suspected of being homosexual was mentioned by fellows while studying, while Ralph bemoaned that his 1940s peers "were never informed of the great homosexual figures of the past; that could have meant so much to us." Ralph also regretted not having "the freedom and the encouragement by some role models to put myself into a gay relationship" during college. Indeed, for many of these men, their college years could be lonely; many believed, as Walter did in the 1940s, "there aren't many people like me." But by the 1980s, Gene saw lesbian characters on a soap opera; although the characters were going to commit suicide because of their sexual orientation, and despite his sister's declaration that homosexuality was "bad," Gene "automatically thought, *Oh, that's me.*"

Certainly, the progression of identities in the typology display an increase in role models and subjects of study on campus; if nothing else, there were other students to whom to compare and to contrast one's self—peer role models. But this change also reflects a greater emphasis on representing and examining those whose lives and identities were considered marginal.

Rick, another man closeted in college, relied upon movie imagery and stereotypes to impart the public image of openly non-heterosexual men in the 1950s: "The gay man of the time was a Clifton Webb-type—a fussy interior decorator or hair dresser." James's contemporary perceptions of his non-heterosexual colleagues in the theater in the 1960s repeat this stereotype, the "theater queen." Around the same time, James remembers seeing the (in)famous fourteen-page *Life Magazine* pictorial article (June 24, 1964) on homosexual subcultures in San Francisco: "they talked about men in tight white pants and cashmere sweaters. And I went, 'This is me, and I don't want to be that.'" Again, the contradiction between the recognition of one's non-heterosexual identity idea (in this case, as highlighted in media images and representations) did not match the man's sense of self highlights Mendelsohn's (1999) concepts of *men* and *de* in operation.

Within twenty years, though, those images had been replaced (or, at least, set beside) new portraits of non-heterosexual lives and lifestyles. Alec mentioned the movie *Cabaret* as metaphor for his self-awareness of his sexual identity; the movie, whose non-heterosexual characters were central to the plot, starred Liza Minnelli, the daughter of a gay icon, who was herself trying to establish an identity as "not Judy" while looking, sounding, and literally acting like her mother. It was to her image that Alec was drawn, her song that he performed in a moment where he finally felt complete in his non-heterosexual identity.

The increased public representations of non-heterosexuals were not confined to fiction, nor to films. By the 1980s, Juan witnessed "everyday individuals who were teachers, lawyers, couples" on Oprah Winfrey's television talk show. And Tim cited the influence of gender-bending artistic sexual outlaws David Bowie, Andy Warhol, and Lou Reed upon his thinking and self-conceptualization. The marginal identities had become the vanguard of popular media in the United States, and, in doing so, had become more mainstream than marginal. This process, while not totally alleviating the stigma of non-heterosexuality, did ameliorate some of the constrictions of the public concept of "normal" equating (only) to heterosexuality.

Some of the effects of publicizing non-heterosexual lives, however, were not positive. The earlier example of the kiss-in at the University of Kansas in 1992 (see photo 6.5) was photographed and reported upon in the campus newspaper. One of the participants, Patrick Davis (the young man on the right of the photo), was a sophomore at KU; Davis had not told his family that he was not heterosexual. Someone anonymously mailed a clipping of the photo to Davis's father, Herschel, in Wichita; when father confronted son, Patrick admitted he was gay. Herschel ordered Patrick home for medical and psychiatric testing, and informed Patrick he would not pay for Patrick to attend KU any longer, blaming "gay activism" at the university for influencing his son (Mansfield, 1993). Despite the changes made in self-identity from the 1940s, even fifty years later the potential for alienation from and subjugation to the norms of heterosexuality still existed, even if not from the institutions of higher education.

If the stories the men in this study tell of their college experiences emphasize one quality, in my estimation, their concepts of identity—along with the interpersonal behaviors and communications that deploy those concepts into practice—are far less static than the existing identity development models (both collegiate and gay) depict. While on the one hand most of the respondents depicted knowing, confidently, that they were truly non-heterosexual, on the other hand they often had difficulty conceiving how they could be non-heterosexual while being themselves. For them, it was not a process particularly of "unbecoming" straight, or of "becoming" gay or queer; rather, their paths to self-identity were (fairly) continuous negotiations of self and other, of straight and non-straight, of activities of varying meanings and meanings with varying activities.

During the years I was working on this project, a number of non-heterosexuals students (both current and former) told me they appreciated the "extremists," the extremely political and polemic queers; in the words of one,

> Compared to them, someone with my views is seen as a fairly moderate liberal. Not so long ago, I would have been considered extreme because of those same views. But as they keep expanding the boundaries of what is considered out there and edgy, my views become seen by the general public as more central.

This transition reflects changes in sensibilities of both the general (dominant, heterosexual) society's view of what is acceptable and "normal" and the (subordinate, non-heterosexual) subculture's conviction of what is permissible and customary. Non-heterosexual students found themselves a part of both worlds and are compelled by the values of both; who and how they can be are delimited by their dualistic position. A center cannot be central without margins; the margins cannot be marginal without a locus.

I find Mendelsohn's (1999) concept of the *men* and the *de*—the "on the one hand this, while on the other hand that" aspect of understanding non-heterosexual lives—important in understanding this construction and praxis of identity. Just as in the Greek language, neither portion of a sentence (the *men* or the *de*) can make sense without its pair, so too can these students' identities only be understood in relation to the "other" halves: they "move between two places" (Mendelsohn, 1999, p. 205), between the center and the margin, between the normed and the queered. In the context of collegiate non-heterosexual identities, on the one hand there is the individual's self concept, and on the other are the concepts of identity of (at all times) heterosexual and/or (at some times, in some contexts) homosexual, gay, queer, "normal," closeted, and parallel.

As individual students' understandings of the position of their identities within this schema evolved, so too did their perception of what value that position held to the center and the margins. Or, at least, that's what I eventually came to understand. Some students moved swiftly from one identity to another and remained fairly secure in their comprehension of their place in campus societies; they might engage in social and interpersonal communications and activities that placed them in opposition to the norms of heterosexuality, or they might remain publicly aligned with the center while trying to understand how they could feel disconnected that center. Others played (or frayed) at the margins, attempting to calibrate their sense of self with the views of others (both straight and non-straight).

A proponent of stage-model theories (which I confess I used to be) could argue that different ideations represented individual stages of progression through identity development; "queer," for instance, could be a phase of rebellion, an affectation of youth (or desired youth) to attempt to create change while on a "quest" or "journey" toward a normative concept of self-identity. A different form of disagreement might originate from an individual who subscribes to the idea of fixed identities; he might assert that whatever the reason for deviation of actions or motives, one is either homosexual or heterosexual (or perhaps bisexual), and the language used to describe the sensibilities and meanings individuals give to those actions and identities are semantics. The data from this study belies such polemics.

On the (In)Finality of Conclusions

I feel I have journeyed far from where I started, and yet I am oddly close to where I began. I know more about non-heterosexual identity, about how to understand what constitutes a non-heterosexual male college student. And yet so much about what might constitute identity remains unexamined in my construct: race, social background, economic status, geographic origins, interactions (or not) with women, the primacy of gender for males. In many aspects, I'm back at the beginning, ready to pose more questions to continue in my existential quest to determine "who are you? Who am I?"

Perhaps it's fitting that I now live not on the East Coast (where that night in Florida I first started talking to others about their queer lives) nor the West

Coast (where I learned at University of Southern California how to research, and discovered in Los Angeles just how extremely diverse the senses and experiences and sensibilities of non-heterosexual men are). No, I returned to the Midwest, to teach in a fairly rural university about one hundred miles from where I grew up, surrounded by again by forest and fields. A part of me feels complete in the locale; but on the other hand, there are times I wish I were back in the city, where, if the meanings men made of their lives were just as complex, at least there might be a greater mass of folks whose senses and experiences and meanings—of life, of identity, of sex, of what it means to be non-heterosexual—came close to mine. But then again, not being able to find such men prompted me to leave the West Coast. . . . *Men* and *de*, the struggle between two competing norms and desires, plays out in my life as much as in those of the men whom I've profiled in this book.

The classifications in my typology are neither prescriptive nor proscriptive; individuals might slide between classifications, based upon their own definitions of their sexuality, the specific actions they undertake, and (in instances) the motives behind both the definitions and the actions. As identity is neither fixed nor stable, the types are not based solely upon the essentialistic concept of identity determined by sexual activity with male partners (respecting the experiences and sensibilities of the "normals" and those, like Walter, Pozzo, and Tim, who identified as non-heterosexual at least to themselves before engaging in activity), nor exclusive because of the specific contemporaneous cultures of the individuals (a constructionist view of identity), nor just because of the terminology used during their college days to describe non-heterosexuality (a semantic perspective on identity complexities). As Alec noted of the early 1970s, "I don't think . . . there was much distinction" between the uses of the words gay and homosexual in normal parlance; "the words were synonymous."

I gave prominence, in assigning types to describe the college experiences of these men, to the actions (and the motivations) related to sexual identity. Consequently, some men were included with types whose labels might appear anachronous. For example, *homosexual* as a type applied to Duchess, who primarily used the term "gay" to talk about his sexuality in the 1980s. *Queer* pertained to Jimmy, whose childhood and collegiate experiences in the 1970s he now clearly views as "queer" (in the personal/political sense as well as the sexual sense). It is even possible to see the certain acts by non-heterosexuals (such as the womanless wedding at Baylor in the 1950s) as queer. The acts themselves were queer, and while they were engaging in them, the students adopted (and/or deployed) a queer identity; the image they understood to be project was queer, even if their own personal self-definition might not be.

Such a situation seems too implausible if we ascribe the values of queer that we now use, but less so if we utilize the concepts of queer theory to understand how an individual might publicly challenge the dominant social values and mores concerning sexuality. Just as performing particular sexual acts did not define one's sexuality, neither did committing queer acts make one queer. The identities were more fluid, based upon (on the one hand) the experience and (on the other) the meanings ascribed because of and to the experience.

Social changes over time—including due to media coverage of "others," increased research and study on non-heterosexual lives, and personal freedom to enact a praxis of identity apart from those considered "normal"—allow for new understandings of past experiences and sensibilities. This study and the resulting typology were not ahistorical or revisionist efforts on my part; rather, I crafted the types to challenge the dominant (and essentialistic) notions that one is either heterosexual or homosexual, and that the experiences (no matter what the "politically correct" term of the day) of each never change. These narratives simply do not allow those arguments: identity—both the process of discovery (or creation) and the resulting "product"—is far too messy. Like the concepts of *queer* and *queer theory*, the term cannot contain the contents we wish to understand. The best I could achieve in this study was to highlight how non-heterosexual male collegiate identity fit into the vessels of classification, along with the seepage and the spills.

The changes in identity (both those considered non-heterosexual and those considered "normal") over the past five decades are important, for they allowed non-heterosexual identifying men new ways to define themselves, interact with others, and effect social and personal change. College environments most certainly impacted both the process (ways and/or manners to self-identify) and the product (identity as label or term used for self-understanding and presentation to others) of these men: postsecondary institutions created environments (both positive and negative), provided structures for socialization and organization, gathered together like-minded peers, and offered the idea(l) of not only the prerogative to determine through college experiences whom one was but also, in time, the right to do so openly and publicly. This relationship has deepened within the last half-century, as witnessed by the increasing number of respondents who found not only their time in college easier in regards to their sexuality, but also encouraging (in ways intentional and not) of their examination of the possibilities of—and opportunities for—not being a heterosexual.

If history is about changes in people over time, one need look no further than the differences in experience between the homosexuals and closeted students on campus in the 1940s and 50s, and the gay and queer students of the 1980s and 90s. Analyzing those changes through the critical lens of queer theory, one can understand how and why non-heterosexual identities transformed. As conceptions of what was normal changed and society accepted divergent viewpoints and experiences, non-heterosexual experiences were examined more often, not only in relation to heterosexuality, and in light of the views of the examined (rather than only those of the examining).

As the position of the viewpoint of study (and media and self-representation) shifted to examine what had been at the margins, the sense of marginality and deviance of those not formerly in the middle changed. Identity development theories, however, did not keep pace with these metamorphoses; the existing stage-development models are still based upon a singular outcome (either for gay males or for college students). Any deviation from that theoretical norm is, indeed, a deviation.

The value of those existing theories is not nullified by this, however, just limited. If student identity development theories reflect the progressive process of self-understanding, that too is evident in the stories of the men in this study, particularly those who lead parallel lives and those who, at the time, thought of themselves as "just like everybody else." Finally, if the types represented in this theory of identity formation are accurate, then the understandings of higher education administrators, educators, researchers, practioners, and programmers who attempt to work with and/or understand "gay" students as a monolithic group must change to reflect the diversity of non-heterosexual lives and experiences. If their understandings of non-heterosexual student identities do not change, educators' (well-intentioned) efforts will be as incomplete as their concept of this student population.

A s a qualitative researcher, I am keenly aware of the need to be transparent about how and why I know what I know, of the importance of showing not only data but also methods of knowing and showing. To do so, I must provide background information about how I gathered the stories of these men's lives, and about how I analyzed and presented their experiences and identities. The first portion of this appendix, *The Interviews*, outlines the protocol of the interview project: the where, when, who, and how of the interview process. The second part, *Historical Analysis*, confronts the issues of validity and veracity in historical and identity research, and outlines the precautions I employed to assure that the individuals' answers to my questions, my analysis and representation of their lives into the typology were "real." The final part, *Narratives in Contexts*, conveys how I moved from the answers the respondents provided to the presentation and analysis of their narratives (Sections II and III of this book).

The Interviews

Where and When: Interview Solicitation. Between October of 1998 and December of 1999, I interviewed fifty-seven men who were undergraduates between 1945 and 2000. The interview respondents were solicited primarily through direct contact with key informants from academic, alumni, and/or social groups (chiefly graduate/faculty/staff groups at the University of Southern California and the University of California at Irvine), as well as from non-heterosexual social clubs (particularly the Phoenix, Arizona, chapter of Prime-timers, a national organization for senior gay men), academic conferences (including meetings at the University of California at Los Angeles and the University of California at Irvine, as well as the 1999 Annual Meeting of the Association for the Study of Higher Education in San Antonio, Texas), and establishments catering to non-heterosexual males (gay bars and restaurants in the Phoenix, Los Angeles, and San Diego areas).

I deliberately chose a range of ages of potential respondents, to provide access to informants who were students from across five decades. From those informants, I employed "snowball" or "network" techniques of recruiting interview respondents (Glesne and Peshken, 1992, p. 27; Merriam, 1998, p. 63; Patton, 1990); Snowballing, coupled with the response from initial respondents in the Los Angeles and Phoenix areas, helped narrow the focus of the in-person interviews to those two metropolitan areas.

I also placed advertisements in local publications with target audiences of gay men who would be of an age to have attended college from the 1940s (including chapter newsletters of the Primetimers organization in Palm Springs, California, and Phoenix, Arizona). Finally, I utilized postsecondary institutions' gay/lesbian/bisexual student and/or alumni electronic list-servs (primarily at the University of Southern California and Arizona State University, although, given the distributive nature of electronic communication, respondents replied from other lists, both private and public).

Who: Respondents Profile. The interviews did not concentrate on any single period of time, but rather represent fairly equally each year of the fifty-five year period. Of the fifty-seven respondents, three primarily attended institutions outside of the United States for their undergraduate education (as opposed to attending as part of a study-abroad or exchange program); the remaining fifty-four attended more than fifty different institutions (some attended more than one institution to complete their undergraduate education), located in twenty-two states across the United States. The states were: Arkansas, California, Connecticut, Illinois, Indiana, Kansas, Kentucky, Louisiana, Maine, Maryland, Massachusetts, Michigan, Missouri, Nevada, New Jersey, New York, Ohio, Oregon, Pennsylvania, Tennessee, Texas, and Wisconsin. The schools the men attended include public and private, religiously-affiliated and state-supported, smaller liberal-arts institutions, and larger research universities. Within the data chapters, I group each type and then arranged the narratives chronologically, to show changes over time in the concepts of identities and within experiences and sensibilities that comprise the individual identity types as well.

How: Interview Profile. The in-person interviews were, for the most part, conducted privately, one-on-one. Although I prefer to interview in this method, which allows for more concentrated analysis from the respondent and richer data, in some instances the practicalities of the lives of the respondents did not allow this. Five of the interviews were of couples who had been living together for varying numbers of years, and another was of a couple whom had just recently met. Interviewing these men together, as pairs, brought out new challenges (giving attention to detail and follow-up to both respondents within a limited amount of time) while presenting distinct benefits (having someone as part of the interview who could act not only as a source of validity and veracity for the respondents but also as a sounding board for reflections about college experience and identity ideation). In addition, I conducted one small focus group of three friends. I did not conduct all of the interviews in person: six of the interviews were conducted via electronic mail, and consisted of two or three sets of questions posed to the informants.

The single-meeting interviews lasted between forty-five minutes and three hours, depending upon the number of respondents being interviewed at the time, their time available for the interview, and the depth of our conversations. The interviews were semi-structured, ethnographic interviews designed to elicit each respondent's life story (delimited, usually, to the time from their entering high school to graduating and/or leaving postsecondary institutions). Given the comfort, interest, and experiences of the individual respondents, the interviews often deviated from the protocol, but always focused on the men's self-concepts, concepts of sexuality, and college memories.

The protocol questions were crafted to elicit personal oral histories (Denzin, 1995), focusing on the issues of sexuality, identity, and how experiences during the college years (and, to a lesser extent, the high school and immediate post-graduation years) impacted both. Although I did not ask every question in every interview, the questions I posed were a balance of close-ended (*Where did you attend college?*) and open-ended (*When you went to college, how did you define yourself in terms of your sexuality?*), as well as the different types of ethnographic questions Spradly (1979) outlines, including descriptive (*Please tell me what a typical Tuesday night of, say, junior year, was like: what would you be doing?*), structural (*What words or terms did you use to refer to someone you might be dating?*), and contrasting (*Can you tell if someone is not heterosexual? How?*).

The in-person interviews I tape-recorded for later transcription. I also took field notes during the interviews and drafted interview summaries immediately following the interviews. For those men I interviewed via e-mail, I edited the interview protocol to two sets of questions. Initially, I e-mailed the first set of questions; when the respondents returned that set, I forwarded them the second (utilizing recent research methods for electronic research [cf., Goldman-Segall, 1995; After receiving their second set of answers, I conducted a brief content analysis, and followed up, in the third and final collection of questions, on their first two sets of responses. That set of questions included inquiries of veracity as well as questions chosen to probe for deeper, more analytical responses to the first sets of questions, utilizing recursive and compare/contrast techniques.

In each of the interviews, I used a variety of styles of posting queries. Most often I employed a recursive questioning technique—a model of interpersonal communication I crafted to address sensitive, potentially confusing, or distant events, approaching the topics from through a number of redundant questions and varied vantage points—to probe a respondent's memories of his collegiate experience, his concepts (both past and present) of his identity and sexuality, and his analysis of the meanings and/or importance of each. This style is a variant of both the respondent validation and compare/contrast techniques: not only was I repeating respondents' terms and stories back to them for confirmation (and at times clarification), I also compared their beginning ideas and ideations about their identity with apparent changes (evident from their responses) that occurred during college (or, for a very few, soon after college).

Further, in some interviews I employed a constant/comparative approach to the interview subjects' identity formations and analyses of those formations, particularly after I began to discern the actual identity types. Utilizing this method I compared the respondents' ideations with those of other interview subjects, theories of gay and/or student development, and/or other published research. For other interviews, I adopted a life-history approach (Atkinson, 1998; Dollard, 1935; Linde, 1993; Mandelbaum, 1973; Rosenwald and Ochberg, 1992) to better understand (and later, convey) changes that the individual felt concerning his ideation of himself and his collegiate experiences. Each of these styles of eliciting data works within Garmezy's (1974) retrospective method of data collection. I attempted, though, to adopt a conversational style of interviewing that best elicited narratives from the respondents.

When speaking with the men, I also utilized tenets of queer theory, juxtaposing the memories and identities that the men recalled against a variety of "norms," including the concepts of student identity and related development models, gay identity development models, and other cultural markers, both within higher educational systems and the broader society as a whole.

Historical Analysis: Validity and Veracity

Using retrospective data collection methods requires one to address two issues of truthfulness: Did the data (in this case, college experiences and self-ideations) provided by the respondents actually happen, or occur as the researcher presented it (*veracity*, or what can be proven to have occurred)? Second, did the respondents' analyses, as well as the researcher's, represent truthfully the data (*validity*, or what can be said to be true or relevant). Researchers who mine other people's memories for data should obviously do so with a plan for why and how they will gather the information. Menneer (1978) proffered guidelines for assessing memory-based data:

- Is the subject matter sensitive to time errors?
- If so, will the errors be important to the study?
- Can erroneous data be corrected by comparing it to data from other existing sources?
- Can other, more mechanical (i.e., less human) methods be used to collect the data?

In planning this project, I determined that the understanding of changes in non-heterosexual male identities in the latter half of the twentieth century was not highly dependent upon respondents' perceptions of single events; rather, I examined patterns, through the culmination of experiences, of ideas about the respondents' self-identity. The project was consequently less vulnerable to distortion of respondents' experiences in college, for the interview questions could be answered with reference to events over time, rather than in specific instances. As the data in chapters 3 to 6 reveal, some respondents represented themselves as quite sexually active, even promiscuous, before and during college; such a respondent's current concept of himself has tells us not only about his understanding of his collegiate experiences but also how his concept of himself in college changed—or did not change—because of those experiences and sensibilities. Moreover, the typological model is less susceptible to such distortions, as it based upon how a number of individuals experience the same kinds of events, emotions or ideations, creating patterns of development; such patterns would, by design, not exist if multiple men did not have similar (and thus verifiable) experiences.

Several factors can, however, limit the availability, as well as veracity and validity, of retrospective data. Social norms, guilt, respondents' levels of interest in the subject, and, perhaps most of all, memory error pose serious threats against respondents' abilities to provide accurate information (Menneer, 1978). Memory error (whether it be forgetting what occurred or a "false consciousness" of what did happen) is an uncontrollable potential fallacy of any work utilizing retrospective methods, for

It appears that our actual memories change over time, and that we tend to "reconstruct" rather than "recover" them as details fade or become lost. In short, we automatically seem to be remolding our past to fit our present circumstances or emotional needs and to maintain a consistent personal narrative. (Ludwig, 1997, p. 22)

As Gandara (1995) pointed out, "there is considerable evidence that the reporting of general attitudes and factual information is relatively stable over time" (1995, p. 20); she cited Gutek (1978) and Haaga (1986) as sources refuting most of these inhibiting factors.

The respondents in this study were, for the most part, extremely interested in the project. Most of them expressed a desire to see the finished product; several of them indicated that not only did they enjoy the process of the interview, they appreciated remembering events and emotions and thanked me for allowing them "the opportunity to review their lives in such a nonthreatening forum" (Gandara, 1995, p. 21). In this regard, some of the men were remembering, in the words of McLaren and Tadeu da Silva, "in a critical mode . . . in Freirean terms, to confront the social amnesia of generations in flight from their own collective histories" (1993, pp. 73–74).

As another non-heterosexual man, I was viewed by the respondents as an "insider" who shared many of the same formative questions of self-identity as the respondents; this helped to increase their levels of comfort and insight, since neither the respondents nor I had to confront layers of difference between us because of differing social norms (Coffey, 1999; Denzin, 1989; Fontana and Frey, 2000; Gergen and Gergen, 2000; Glesne and Peshkin, 1992; Merriam, 1998; Warren, 1998). I feel this identification engendered a sense of trust and openness in the responses of most of the men, causing them to feel less inhibited and less likely to "reinterpret" their experiences or ideas into a heterosexual context. Further, as each respondent had advanced to postsecondary education (and all but one graduated with at least a bachelor's degree), these respondents were "uniquely predisposed to accuracy in reporting" (Gandara, 1995, p. 21), and, as highly educated respondents, their retrospective reporting and analyses were probably more accurate (Haaga, 1986).

Memory, though, is still a confounding issue when dealing with retrospective qualitative research. I have used the terms "memories" and "experiences," or variations thereof, relying upon a common understanding of the concepts. To understand memory better—and to address its relation to this project—I shall clarify the terms. Experiences are actual (verifiable) events that occur in a person's life: an incident that occurred at a particular time, in a specific place.

Memories on the other hand, are placed [contextually] in the time they are remembered, narrated, reinterpreted, sometimes rejected and often forgotten. Recollections are immediately experienced. Memory makes a critical difference to these: in being remembered an experience becomes a memory. (Hastrup, 1995, p. 102)

Consequently, I faced a Janus-like dilemma in this project: several of the respondents had been in college so recently that they had not gained the time and perspective with which to place those experiences into the realm of memory; conversely, many of those I interviewed were so distant from the experiences—had remembered, narrated, even reinterpreted the meanings of those experiences to their identities and lives—that the opportunity for their misremembering the experiences (the development of a false consciousness) confounded my ability to verify the veracity of what they told me (how true their memories were to their experiences) and the validity of what they told me (how true—or applicable—their collective memories were to the experiences of others).

Perhaps it is unavoidable, as Proust might have cautioned us, to reflect upon our past without recoloring it in hues less harsh and more bright than the light of the times allowed us to see. This is a problem in a field that is situated in the social sciences; as Stoll chided those of us who work with others' memories, "Factuality is a legitimate issue for any narrative" (1999, p. 273). It is not enough that we avoid improprieties in our questions, our data, our analyses, our presentations of the three; we must avoid the *appearance* of impropriety. In this case, the one impropriety that I cannot disprove is the potential for respondents' faulty memories.

Accordingly, it is not enough simply to repeat (even in edited format corresponding to the standards of the field, as the narratives that follow this chapter do) the stories these men have told me; I—the researcher, the theorist, and the writer—must simultaneously accept and question what I am told. One challenge, then, to the ethnographer, to the historian, to the theorist, is to find multiple sources of data, both apart from and within the individual narrators. The addition of sources of information outside of the study participants allowed greater historical perspectives of the social and educational climates, provided insight from college students who wrote of their experiences and sensibilities prior to this study, and offered non-"professional" observations of participants and reporters of social change in the United States during the twentieth century. In the vernacular of qualitative research, this is called "triangulation of data" (Denzin, 1988). My multiple sources of information, which I used to check against the others to determine validity of the information, included:

1. interviews with non-heterosexual men who attend college in the United States between 1945 and 2000;
2. study of memoirs written by non-heterosexual men who attended college in the United States between those same years;
3. study of historical documents from selected postsecondary institutions, concerning the activities and politics of non-heterosexuals on campuses (particularly University of Kansas, Stanford University, Pennsylvania State University, Rutgers University, and University of Michigan);
4. study of journalistic accounts of non-heterosexuals (on campus and off, both historic and contemporary);
5. study of other histories of the lives and experiences of non-heterosexuals in the United States, 1945 to 2000;
6. study of other research projects on identity formation for non-heterosexuals;
7. study of other research projects on identity formation for college students;
8. archival research at the University Archives of the University of Kansas in January of 2002.

I also utilized multiple methods of recording the data (Merriam, 1998; Rossman and Rallis, 1998; Warner, 2002). Making notes while tape-recording the interviews allowed me freedom to comment to myself connections within the context of the conversation I was having with the respondent as well as to other men's comments and my (then current) thoughts on the identity typologies. More formal field notes after each interview also provided different forms of insight and connections. Having the tapes of the interviews allowed me to listen and to transcribe, which both clarified the data and confounded what it was that I thought when making the interview and field notes.

To further safeguard for veracity of the respondents' narratives and experiences, I invited the respondents in this project to provide a "member check" (Kushner and Norris, 1980/1981; Lather, 1986; Lincoln and Guba, 1985; Rossman and Rallis, 1998), by reviewing and commenting upon the first draft of the manuscript of the data. I posted the data section of the project (chapters 3, 4, and 5) on a website I maintained at the University of Southern California. The pages were not listed on the homepage of the site, but they were accessible to the respondents who entered the complete page address, which I provided via e-mail, into their web browsers.

Multiple sources helped to clarify the validity of the data, but the veracity of individuals' memories was another matter. The second challenge to someone attempting something as nebular as a "typological history" is to find multiple ways of asking individual interview subjects to express their recollections and analyses of their collegiate lives. I had to question, and re-question, what meanings they made of their collegiate experiences, both while in college and later. Consequently, I conducted the interviews using the recursive method I mentioned earlier in this appendix, along with the contrast method of questioning outlined by Spradly (1979) coupled with life history (Atkinson, 2002) and in-depth (Holstein and Gubrium, 1995; Johnson, 2002) approaches to structuring interviews to elicit data.

History shows changes in people over time; a typological history shows changes in how people identified (or were identified, or were identifiable). If history can rely upon facts (or at least the assumption of facts), identity typologies can rely only upon the larger perspectives of the patterns of those memories of our subjects, upon our analyses of those memories.

Narratives In Context

> Ethnography is an act of memory. . . , [and] Memories are individual and collective, the result of shared experiences and individual quests. (Coffey, 1999, p. 127)

As I noted earlier, I endeavored throughout this project to avoid determining the types of identity I would find (or was finding)—based as they are, on memory and experiences—until after I finished my conversations with the informants. I wanted to nullify, to the extent possible, biasing the study with my own memories, ideations, and experiences. In addition, typologies present to (and from) researchers views of patterns of individuals' lives. "The biographer should let his material form its own shapes: lives do form patterns, but patterns accumulate one piece at a time" (Reid, 1990, 6). However, the patterns in non-heterosexual lives are not always linear; as Gale wrote,

> the trouble with homosexual biography is that it tends to fall into overlapping narratives rather than an easily assimilated line. Where even a philandering straight subject will tend to have a succession of mistresses or a succession of wives, gay lives, especially gay lives before the mid-1970s, tend to be lived several at a time. Official lovers, rough

lovers, family, non family, those who know, those who don't; the mere fact of the subject's alternative sexuality causes narrative fractures. (Gale, 1999, p. 7)

In my representation of the collegiate experiences and influences upon the respondents' identities, I have attempted to smooth out, as much as possible, the *men* and *de* (Mendelsohn, 1999) of the lives of the narrators, as well as to be, as Reid (1990) implores, "decently selective rather than drudgingly inclusive," sparing "the truly trivial" while "not fear[ing] to find certain small things significant" (1990, p. 6).

The construction of the narratives—choosing what passages from a particular interview to include, to combine with other statements to make sense and convey meaning (both that the interview respondent intended and that I, as the researcher, found)—is a complex process (Polkinghorne, 1988) in which transcription and analysis overlap (Kvale, 1996); indeed, "Analysis cannot be easily distinguished from transcription" (Riessman, 1993, p. 60). The narratives I produced from the transcriptions, the audio tapes, and my field notes were filtered through my analysis of the totality of all three.

In the data section, I present those narratives constructed from interviews with informants whose experiences and stories convey key aspects of each type of identity for non-heterosexual collegiate men. I have structured our conversations chronologically, with two main components to guide the reader: *early college* and *later college*. Most of the narratives begin with a section on *adolescence*, and a few conclude with *post-college* experiences that illuminate the collegiate sensibilities formed from the narrators' experiences and senses.

The accounts comply, for the most part, to Labov's (1972, 1982; Labov and Waletzky, 1967) schematic for structuring narratives: each provides an orientation to the narrative (time, place, setting), a complicating action (the sequence of the relevant events), at least partial evaluation (the respondent's meaning and significance of the experiences conveyed), the resolution (what finally happened; in this case, how they adopted/accepted/ integrated a non-heterosexual identity), and, for a few, a coda returning the narration to a present-day perspective (particularly necessary for some of the men, whose identity—while impacted during college—they did not accept or declare as non-heterosexual until after college).

Some of the informants for this project wished to remain anonymous. While I agree with Becker's (1997, p. 354) charge to historians to reflect that "history is made by real people possessing real names" and not pseudonyms, I respect the complexities of the lives of the interview respondents. Anonymity, in this case, assured greater detail of collegiate experiences, increased freedom to share ideas and experiences of a sexual nature, and opportunities for me to strive for deeper and more evocative data. I have provided pseudonyms for the individuals who chose not to use their true names—as well as for all persons named within respondents' narratives (who obviously did not provide consent to use their names).

The reader will find little of my experience (either as researcher or conversationalist) in the data section of this project, which contains the three chapters explaining the details of the typolgoical categories, focusing upon the narratives of twenty-one respondents. While this might appear to support a belief in "objective" reporting of data, that is not my intent; fully cognizant of the criticism inherent in omniscient narration, I chose to remove as much as possible of myself from the respondents' narrations. I did so because their individual collegiate experiences, senses, and sensibilities form the basis for the typology. Additionally, I crafted the conversations we had during the interviews (and e-mailings) into cohesive narratives that attempted to convey, accurately and vividly, their stories. Further, the chronological narrative structure imparts clearly and tellingly how each individual fits into the typological classification. To be sure, my voice is in each paragraph, in the restructuring of conversational and interview speech into cohesive narratives that address the issues of identity and collegiate experience, in the analytical lives that contextualize the men's stories. I hope this style conveys the understandings of the lives of these men, presents the meanings they have made in (and because of) postsecondary contexts, in their own words.

BIBLIOGRAPHY

"100 in N.Y.U. sit-in charge bias against homosexuals." (1970, September 21). *New York Times*, p. 26.

"400 in 'gay' protest dispersed by police." (1970, September 26). *New York Times*, p. 30.

Abelove, H. (1995). The queering of lesbian/gay history. *Radical History Review, 62*, 44–57.

Alexander, J. (1993). *Jeb and Dash: A diary of gay life, 1918–1945*. Boston: Faber and Faber.

Allyn, D. (2000). *Make love, not war: The Sexual Revolution, an unfettered history*. New York: Little Brown & Company.

Astin, A. W. (1993). *What matters in college? Four critical years revisited*. San Francisco: Jossey-Bass.

Atkinson, R. (1998). *The life story interview* (Qualitative Research Methods Series, Vol. 44). Thousand Oaks, CA: Sage.

Atkinson, R. (2002). The life story interview. In J. F. Gubrium & J. A. Holstein (Eds.), *Handbook of interview research* (pp. 121–140). Thousand Oaks, CA: Sage.

Baily, B. (1999). *Sex in the heartland*. Cambridge, MA: Harvard University Press.

Becker, M. (1997). When I was a child, I danced as a child, but now that I am old, I think about salvation: Concepcion Gonzalez and a past that would not stay put. *Rethinking History, 1*(3), 343–355.

Beemyn, B. (Ed.). (1997). *Creating a place for ourselves: Lesbian, gay, and bisexual community histories*. New York: Routledge.

Berlant, L., & Freeman, E. (1992). Queer nationality. *Boundary 2, 19*(1), 149–180.

Berube, A. (1990). *Coming out under fire: The history of gay men and women in World War II*. New York: Free Press.

Blair, R. (1972). *Student personnel services and homosexuality: A national review of provisions and opinions of deans of students, directors of counseling, and homosexual college students* (The Otherwise Monograph Series, No. 2). New York: National Task Force on Student Personnel Services and Homosexuality.

Blasius, M. (Ed.). (2001). *Sexual identities, queer politics*. Princeton, NJ: Princeton University Press.

Boyd, M. (1978). *Take off the masks*. New York: Doubleday.

Bravmann, S. (1997). *Queer fictions of the past: History, culture, and difference*. Cambridge, England: Cambridge University Press.

Britzman, D. P. (1995). Is there a queer pedagogy? Or, stop reading straight. *Educational Theory, 45*(2), 151–165.

Britzman, D. P. (1997). The tangles of implication. *International Journal of Qualitative Studies in Education, 10*(1), 31–37.

Brown, L. S. (1995). Lesbian identities: Issues and concepts. In A. R. D'Augelli & C. J. Patterson (Eds.), *Lesbian, gay, and bisexual identities over the lifespan* (pp. 3–23). New York: Oxford University Press.

Browning, F. (1993). *The culture of desire: Paradox and perversity in gay lives today.* New York: Crown.

Browning, F. (1996). *A queer geography: Journeys toward a sexual self.* New York: Crown.

Carlson, D. (1998). Who am I? Gay identity and a democratic politics of the self. In W. F. Pinar (Ed.), *Queer theory in education* (pp. 107–119). Manwah, NJ: Lawrence Erlbaum Associates.

Cass, V. C. (1979). Homosexual identity formation: A theoretical model. *Journal of Homosexuality, 4*(3), 219–235.

Cass, V. C. (1983/1984). Homosexual identity: A concept in need of definition. *Journal of Homosexuality, 9,* 105–126.

Cass, V. C. (1984). Homosexual identity formation: Testing a theoretical model. *Journal of Sex Research, 20*(2), 143–167.

Chan, C. S. (1989). Issues of identity development among Asian-American lesbians and gay men. *Journal of Counseling & Development, 68,* 16–20.

Chandler, K. (1995). *Passages of pride: Lesbian and gay youth come of age.* New York: Times Books.

Chauncey, G. (1994). *Gay New York: Gender, urban culture, and the making of the gay male world, 1890–1940.* New York: Basic Books.

Cheseboro, J. W. (1981). Views of homosexuality among social scientists. In J. W. Cheseboro (Ed.) *Gayspeak: Gay male and lesbian communication* (pp. 175–188). New York: The Pilgrim Press.

Chickering, A. W. (1969). *Education and identity.* San Francisco: Jossey-Bass.

Chickering, A. W., & Reisser, L. (1993). *Education and identity* (2nd ed.). San Francisco: Jossey-Bass.

Clandinin, D. J., & Connelly, F. M. (2000). *Narrative inquiry: Experience and story in qualitative research.* San Francisco: Jossey-Bass.

Clark, B. R., & Trow, M. (1996). The organizational context. In T. M. Newcomb & E. K. Wilson (Eds.), *College peer groups: Problems and prospects for research* (pp. 17–70). Chicago: Aldine.

Clendinen, D., & Nagouring, A. (1999). *Out for good: The struggle to build a gay rights movement in America.* New York: Simon & Schuster.

Coffey, A. (1999). *The ethnographic self: Fieldwork and the representation of identity.* Thousand Oaks, CA: Sage.

D'Augelli, A. R. (1989). Lesbians' and gay men's experiences of discrimination and harassment in a university community. *American Journal of Community Psychology, 17*(3), 317–321.

D'Augelli, A. R. (1991). Gay men in college: Identity processes and adaptations. *Journal of College Student Development, 32*(2), 140–146.

D'Augelli, A. R. (1994). Identity development and sexual orientation: Toward a model of lesbian, gay, and bisexual development. In E. J. Trickett, R. J., Watts, & D. Birmans (Eds.), *Human diversity: Perspectives on people in context* (pp. 312–333). New York: Oxford University Press.

D'Augelli, A. R., & Rose, M. L. (1990). Homophobia in a university community: Attitudes and experiences of heterosexual freshmen. *Journal of College Student Development, 31*(6), 484–491.

Davies, P. (1992). The role of disclosure in coming out among gay men. In K. Plummer (Ed.), *Modern homosexualities: Fragments of gay and lesbian experiences* (pp. 75–83). New York: Routledge.

de Monteflores, C., & Schultz, S. (1978). Coming out: Similarities and differences for lesbians and gay men. *Journal of Social Issues, 34*(3), 59–72.

D'Emilio, J. (1983). *Sexual politics, sexual communities: The making of a homosexual minority in the United States, 1940–1970.* Chicago: University of Chicago Press.

D'Emilio, J. (1990). The campus environment for gay and lesbian life. *Academe, 76*(1), 16–19.

D'Emilio, J. (1992). *Making trouble: Essays on gay history, politics, and the university.* New York: Routledge.

D'Emilio, J., & Freedman, E. B. (1988). *Intimate matters: A history of sexuality in America.* New York: Harper & Row.

Denzin, N. K. (1989). *Interpretive biography* (Qualitative Research Methods Series, Vol. 17). Newbury Park, CA: Sage.

Dilley, P. (1999). Queer theory: Under construction. *International Journal of Qualitative Studies in Education, 12*(5), 457–472.

Dilley, P. (2000). Student organizations (U.S.). In G. E. Haggerty (Ed.), *Gay histories and cultures* (pp. 847–849). New York: Garland Publishing.

Dilley, P. (2002). 20th century postsecondary practices and policies to control gay students. *The Review of Higher Education, 25*(4), 409–431.

Donaldson, S. (1967, December 3). Letter to the editor, *New York Times*. Quoted in D. Allyn (2000), *Make love, not war: The sexual revolution, an unfettered history* (p. 152). New York: Little, Brown.

Doty, A. (1993). *Making things perfectly queer: Interpreting mass culture.* Minneapolis: University of Minnesota.

Duberman, M. (1991). *Cures: A gay man's odyssey.* New York: Dutton.

Due, L. (1995). *Joining the tribe: Growing up gay and lesbian in the '90s.* New York: Anchor Books.

Duggan, L. (1992). Making it perfectly queer. *Socialist Review, 22*(1), 11–31.

Duggan, L. (1995a). The discipline problem: Queer theory meets lesbian and gay history. *GLQ: A Journal of Gay and Lesbian Studies, 2,* 179–191.

Duggan, L. (1995b). History's gay ghetto: The contradiction of growth in lesbian and gay history. In L. Duggan & N. D. Hunter (Eds.), *Sex wars: Sexual dissent and political culture* (pp. 144–154). New York: Routledge.

Duggan, L. (1995c). Queering the state. In L. Duggan & N. D. Hunter (Eds.), *Sex wars: Sexual dissent and political culture* (pp. 178-193). New York: Routledge.

Edelman, L. (1995). Queer theory: Unstating desire. *GLQ: A Journal of Lesbian and Gay Studies, 2*, 343-346.

Erickson, E. H. (1968). *Identity: Youth and crisis.* New York: Norton.

Erickson, E. H. (1980). *Identity and the life cycle.* New York: Norton.

Escoffier, J., & Berube, A. (1991). Queer/Nation. *OUT/LOOK: National Lesbian and Gay Quarterly, 11*, 267-319.

Espin, O. M. (1987). Psychological impact of migration on Latinas: Implications for pyschotherapeutic practice. *Psychology of Women Quarterly, 11*(4), 489-503.

Esterberg, K. G. (1997). *Lesbian and gay identities: Constructing communities, constructing selves.* Philadelphia: Temple University Press.

Ettinger, M. (1992). The Pocahontas paradigm, or will the subaltern please shut up? In L. Garber (Ed.), *Tilting the tower: Lesbians teaching queer subjects* (pp. 51-55). New York: Routledge.

Evans, N., Forney, D. S., & Guido-DiBrito, F. (1998). *Student development in college: Theory, research, and practice.* San Francisco: Jossey-Bass.

Evans, N. J. (1996). Theories of student development. In S. R. Kmoives, D. B. Woodard, Jr., & Associates (Eds.), *Student services: A handbook for the profession* (3rd ed., pp. 164-187). San Francisco: Jossey-Bass.

Evans, N., & Levine, H. (1990). Perspectives on sexual orientation. In L. V. Moore (Ed.), *Evolving theoretical perspectives on students* (New Directions for Student Services, Vol. 51, pp. 49-58). San Francisco: Jossey-Bass.

Fassinger, R. E. (1998). Lesbian, gay, and bisexual identity and student development theory. In R. L. Sanlo (Ed.), *Working with lesbian, gay, bisexual, and transgender college students: A handbook for faculty and administrators* (pp. 13-22). Westport, CT: Greenwood Press.

Fellows, W. (1996). *Farm boys: Lives of gay men from the rural Midwest.* Madison, WI: University of Wisconsin Press.

Fontanta, A., & Frey, J. H. (2000). The interview: From structured questions to negotiated text. In N. K. Denzin & Y. S. Lincoln (Eds.), *Handbook of qualitative research* (2nd ed., pp. 645-672). Thousand Oaks, CA: Sage.

Foucault, M. (1978). *The history of sexuality, volume 1: An introduction.* (R. Hurley, Trans.). New York: Vintage Books.

Gair, C., Toy, J., & Blair, R. (1972). *Gay peer counseling at Michigan* (The Otherwise Monograph Series, No. 9). New York: National Task Force on Student Personnel Services and Homosexuality.

Gale, P. (1999). *Armistead Maupin.* Bath, England: Absolute Press.

Gamson, J. (1995). Do ask, do tell: Freak talk on TV. *American Prospect, 23*, 44-50.

Gamson, J. (1998). *Freaks talk back: Tabloid talk shows and sexual nonconformity.* Chicago: University of Chicago Press.

Gandara, P. (1995). *Over the ivy walls: The educational mobility of low-income Chicanos.* Albany, NY: State University of New York Press.

Garmezy, N. (1974). Children at risk: The search for the antecedents of schizophrenia. Part 1, Conceptual modes and research methods. *Schizophrenia Bulletin, 8,* 14–90.

Gay Alliance of Students v. Matthews, 544 F2d 162 (4th Cir. 1976).

Gay And Lesbian Students Associations v. Gohn, 850 F.2d 361 (9th Cir. 1988).

Gay, Lesbian, and Bisexual Concerns Study Committee (1993). *The final report to the Executive Vice-Chancellor from the Gay, Lesbian and Bisexual Concerns Study Committee.* Lawrence, KS: The University of Kansas.

Gay Lib v. University of Missouri, 588 F.2d 848 (8th Cir. 1977).

"Gay student body president elected." (1978). *Midwest Gay Academic Journal, 1*(3), 3.

Gay Student Organization of the University of New Hampshire v. Bonner, 506 F.2d 652 (1st Cir. 1974).

Gergen, M. M., & Gergen, K. J. (2000). Qualitative inquiry: Tensions and transformations. In N. K. Denzin & Y. S. Lincoln, *Handbook of qualitative research* (2nd ed., pp. 1025–1046). Thousand Oaks, CA: Sage.

Glesne, C., & Peshkin, A. (1992). *Becoming qualitative researchers: An introduction.* White Plains, NY: Longman.

Goldman-Segall, R. (1995). Configurational validity: A proposal for analyzing ethnographic mulitmedia narratives. *Journal for Educational Multimedia and Hypermedia, 4*(2–3), 163–183.

Gose, B. (1996, February 9). The politics and images of gay students. *The Chronicle of Higher Education,* pp. A33–A34.

Greenberg, D. F. (1998). *The construction of homosexuality.* Chicago: University of Chicago Press.

Gustav-Wrathall, J. D. (1998). *Take the young stranger by the hand: Same-sex relations & the YMCA.* Chicago: University of Chicago.

Gutek, B. (1978). *Accuracy of retrospective data from the Malaysian family life survey.* Santa Monica, CA: The RAND Corporation.

Haaga, J. (1986). *Accuracy of retrospective data from the Malaysian family life survey.* Santa Monica, CA: The RAND Corporation.

Halperin, D. M. (1995). *Saint Foucault: Towards a gay hagiography.* New York: Oxford University Press.

Harbeck, K. M. (1997). *Gay and lesbian educators: Personal freedoms, public constraints.* Malden, MA: Amethyst Press and Productions.

Hastrup, K. (1995). *A passage to anthropology: Between experience and theory.* London: Routledge.

Helms, A. (1995). *Young man from the provinces: A gay life before Stonewall.* Boston: Faber and Faber.

Hendreson, A. (1984). Homosexuality in the college years: Developmental differences between men and women. *Journal of American College Health, 32,* 216–219.

Herdt, G., & Boxer, A. (1993). *Children of Horizons: How gay and lesbian teens are leading a new way out of the closet.* Boston: Beacon Press.

Hertick, E. S., & Martin, A. D. (1987). Developmental issues and their resolutions for gay and lesbian adolescents. *Journal of Homosexuality, 14*(1/2), 25–43.

Hesford, W. S. (1999). *Framing identities: Autobiography and the politics of pedagogy.* Minneapolis: University of Minnesota Press.

Higgs, D. (Ed.). (1999). *Queer sites: Gay urban histories since 1600.* London and New York: Routledge.

Hocquenghem, G. (1978). *Homosexual desire.* London: Allison & Busby.

Holland, J. L. (1958). A personality inventory employing occupational titles. *Journal of Applied Psychology, 42,* 336–342.

Holland, J. L. (1959). *A theory of vocational choice.* Waltham, MA: Blaisdell.

Holland, J. L. (1966). *Vocational preference inventory (VPI): Professional manual.* Odessa, FL: Psychological Assessment Resources.

Holland, J. L. (1992). *Making vocational choices: A theory of vocational personalities and work environments* (2nd ed.). Odessa, FL: Psychological Assessment Resources.

Holleran, A. (1997). My Harvard. In J. R. Schneider (Ed.) *The best of The Harvard Gay & Lesbian Review* (pp. 4–19). Philadelphia: Temple University.

Holstein J. A., & Gubrium, J. F. (1995). *The active interview.* Thousand Oaks, CA: Sage.

"Homosexuality in America." (1964, June 26). *Life Magazine,* pp. 66–74.

Honeychurch, K. G. (1996). Researching dissident subjectives: Queering the grounds of theory and practice. *Harvard Educational Review, 66*(2), 339–355.

Horowitz, H. L. (1984). *Alma mater: Design and experience in the women's colleges from their nineteenth-century beginnings to the 1930s.* New York: Knopf.

Horowitz, H. L. (1987). *Campus life: Undergraduate cultures from the end of the eighteenth century to the present.* Chicago: University of Chicago Press.

Howard, J. (1999). *Men like that: A southern queer history.* Chicago: University of Chicago Press.

Howard, K., & Stevens, A. (Eds.). (2000). *Out & about campus: Personal accounts by lesbian, gay, bisexual, & transgendered college students.* Los Angeles: Alyson Books.

Jacobsen, J. R. (1998). Queer is? Queer does? Normativity and the problem of resistence. *GLQ: A Journal of Lesbian & Gay Studies, 4*(4), 511–536.

Jagose, A. (1996). *Queer theory: An introduction.* New York: New York University Press.

Jay, K. (1999). *Tales of the Lavender Menace: A memoir of liberation.* New York: Basic Books.

Jenkins, K. (1991). *Re-thinking history.* New York: Routledge.

Jenness, V. (1988). Lesbian generations, communities, and lives: Continuities and changes in identities, sexualities, and narratives. *GLQ: A Lesbian & Gay Journal, 4*(3), 477–485.

Jenness, V. (1992). Coming out: Lesbian identities and the categorization problem. In

K. Plummer (Ed.), *Modern homosexualities: Fragments of lesbian and gay experiences* (pp. 65–74). New York: Routledge.

Johnson, J. M. (2002). In-depth interviewing. In J. F. Gubrium & J. A. Holstein (Eds.), *Handbook of interview research* (pp. 103–119). Thousand Oaks, CA: Sage.

Jung, C. G. (1923/1971). *Psychological types* (H. G. Baynes, Trans.) (Vol. 6 of *The collected works of C. G. Jung*). Princeton, NJ: Princeton University Press.

Kaiser, C. (1997). *The gay metropolis, 1940–1996*. New York: Houghton Mifflin.

Kameny, F. E. (2001). Foreward. In J. T. Sears, *Rebels, rubyfruit, and rhinestones: Queering space in the Stonewall South* (pp. ix-xi). New Brunswick, NJ: Rutgers University Press.

Kantrowitz, A. (1977). *Under the rainbow: Growing up gay*. New York: William Morrow.

Kaplan, W. A. (1990). *The law of higher education*. San Francisco: Jossey-Bass.

Katz, J. (1976). *Gay American history: Lesbians and gay men in the U.S.A.* New York: Thomas Y. Crowell Co.

Katz, J. N. (1995). *The invention of heterosexuality*. New York: Dutton.

Kaufman, M. T. (1973, January 28). Homosexuals organize at universities. *New York Times*, p. 46.

Kolb, D. A. (1984). *Experiential learning: Experience as the source of learning and development*. Englewood Cliffs, NJ: Prentice Hall.

Kolb, D. A. (1985). *The learning style inventory*. Boston: McBer.

KU News Bureau. (1970, September 5). Press release. In D. D. Barney (Ed.), *Gay and lesbian history at the University of Kansas* (1992, p. 21). Lawrence, KS: Student Assistance Center, The University of Kansas.

Kushner, S. & Norris, N. (1980/1981). Interpretation, negotiation, and validity in naturalistic research. *Interchange on Educational Policy, 11*(4), 26–36.

Kvale, S. (1996). *InterViews: An introduction to qualitative research interviewing*. Thousand Oaks, CA: Sage.

Labov, W. (1972). The transformation of experience in narrative syntax. In W. Labov (Ed.), *Language in the inner city: Studies in the Black English vernacular* (pp. 354–396). Philadelphia: University of Pennsylvania Press.

Labov, W., & Waletzky, J. (1967). Narrative analysis: Oral versions of personal experience. In J. Helm (Ed.), *Essays on the verbal and visual arts* (pp. 12–44). Seattle: University of Washington Press.

Lather, P. (1986). Research as praxis. *Harvard Educational Review, 56*(3), 257–277.

Levine, H., & Evans, N. J. (1991). The development of gay, lesbian, and bisexual identities. In N. J. Evans & V. A. Wall (Eds.), *Beyond tolerance: Gays, lesbians, and bisexuals on campus* (pp. 1–24). Alexandria, VA: American College Personnel Association.

Lichtwardt, R. (1992a). A stroll down Gayhawk Lane: 1976–1986: The dance & go to Sambo's years. In D. D. Barney (Ed.), *Gay and lesbian history at the University of Kansas: Lawrence Gay Liberation Front: 1971–1975, Gay Services of Kansas, 1976–1980* (p. 1). Lawrence, KS: Student Assistance Center, The University of Kansas.

Lichtwardt, R. (1992b). A stroll down Gayhawk Lane, part II: "Private activities, habits, or proclivities." In D. D. Barney (Ed.), *Gay and lesbian history at the University of Kansas: Lawrence Gay Liberation Front: 1971–1975, Gay Services of Kansas, 1976–1980* (pp. 2–4). Lawrence, KS: Student Assistance Center, The University of Kansas.

Lincoln, Y. S., & Guba, E. G. (1985). *Naturalistic inquiry.* Beverly Hills, CA: Sage.

Linde, C. (1993). *Life stories: The creation of coherence.* New York: Oxford University Press.

Loiacano, D. K. (1989). Gay identity issues among Black Americans: Racism, homophobia, and the need for validation. *Journal of Counseling & Development, 68,* 21–25.

Louganis, G., with Marcus, E. (1995). *Breaking the surface.* New York: Random House.

Loughery, J. (1998). *The other side of silence: Men's lives and gay identities: A twentieth-century history.* New York: Henry Holt.

Ludwig, A. M. (1997). *How do we know who we are? A biography of the self.* Oxford, England: Oxford University Press.

MacKay, A. (Ed.). (1993). *Wolf girls at Vassar: Lesbian and gay experiences, 1930–1990.* New York: St. Martin's Press.

Mandelbaum, D. G. (1973). The study of life history: Gandhi. *Current Anthropology, 14*(3), 177–206.

Mann, W. J. (2001). *Behind the screen: How gays and lesbians shaped Hollywood, 1910–1969.* New York: Viking.

Mansfield, S. (1993, May). Gays on campus. *Redbook,* pp. 124–127, 140, 142.

Marcus, E. (1992). *Making history: The struggle for gay and lesbian equal rights, 1945–1990: An oral history.* New York: HarperCollins.

Marotta, T. (1983). *Sons of Harvard: Gay men from the class of 1967.* New York: Quill.

Martin, A. D., & Hetrick, E. S. (1988). The stigmatization the gay and lesbian adolescent. *Journal of Homosexuality, 15*(1/2), 163–183.

McCrea, R. (1978). Madison gay purge. *Midwest Gay Academic Journal, 1*(3), 25–30.

McGarry, M., & Wasserman, F. (1998). *Becoming visible: An illustrated history of lesbian and gay life in twentieth-century America.* New York: Penguin Studio.

McLaren, P., & Tadeu da Silva, T. (1993). Decentering pedagogy: Critical literacy, resistance, and the politics of memory. In McLaren, P., & Leonard, P. (Eds.), *Paulo Friere: A critical encounter* (pp. 47–89). New York: Routledge.

Mendelsohn, D. (1999). *The elusive embrace: Desire and the riddle of identity.* New York: Alfred A. Knopf.

Menneer, P. (1978). Retrospective data in survey research. *Journal of Marketing Research, 20,* 182–195.

Merriam, S. B. (1998). *Qualitative research and case study applications in education.* San Francisco: Jossey-Bass.

Miller, N. (1995). *Out of the past: Gay and lesbian history from 1869 to the present.* New York: Vintage.

Moore, L. V., & Upcraft, M. L. (1990). Theory in student affairs: Evolving perspectives.

In L. V. Moore (Ed.), *Evolving theoretical perspectives on students* (New Directions in Student Services, Vol. 51). San Francisco: Jossey-Bass.

Myers, I. B., & McCaulley, M. H. (1985). *Manual: A guide to the development and use of the Myers Briggs Type Indicator.* Palo Alto, CA: Consulting Psychologists Press.

Myers, I. B. (1987). *Introduction to type: A description of the theory and applications of the Myers-Briggs Type Indicator* (4th ed.). Palo Alto, CA: Consulting Psychologists Press.

Nardi, P. M.; Sanders, D., & Marmor, J. (1994). *Growing up before Stonewall: Life stories of some gay men.* New York: Routledge.

Neiberding, R. A. (1989). *In every classroom: The report of the President's Select Committee for Lesbian and Gay Concerns.* New Brunswick, NJ: Rutgers University.

Nelson, M. (1992, Winter). Alumni/ae profile: David H. Stout—Pushing the frontier. *KU GALA Update, 4,* pp. 5–6.

O'Connor, A. (1995). Who gets called queer in school? Lesbian, gay, and bisexual teenagers, homophobia, and high school. In G. Unks (Ed.), *The gay teen: Educational practice and theory for lesbian, gay, and bisexual adolescents* (pp. 95–101). New York: Routledge.

Pascarella, E. T., & Terenzini, P. T. (1991). *How college affects students: Findings and insights from twenty years of research.* San Francisco: Jossey-Bass.

Penn, D. (1995). Queer: Theorizing politics and history. *Radical History Review, 62,* 24–42.

Polkinghorne, D. E. (1988). *Narrative knowing and the human sciences.* Albany, NY: State University of New York Press.

"Princeton students vote." (1977, March 3). *New York Times,* pp. 71.

Pronger, B. (1990). *The arena of masculinity: Sports, homosexuality, and the meaning of sex.* New York: St. Martin's Press.

Read, K. (2001). *How I learned to snap: A small-town coming-of-age coming-out story.* Athens, GA: Hill Street Press.

Reid, B. L. (1990). *Necessary lives: Biographical reflections.* Columbia, MO: University of Missouri Press.

Reinhold, R. (1971, December 15). Campus homosexuals organize to win community acceptance. *New York Times,* pp. 1, 47.

Reisser, L. (1995). Revisiting the seven vectors. *Journal of College Student Development, 36*(6), 505–511.

Renn, K. A. (1998). Lesbian, gay, bisexual and transgendered students in the college classroom. In R. L. Sanlo (Ed.), *Working with lesbian, gay, bisexual, and transgendered college students: A handbook for faculty and administrators* (pp. 231–238). Westport, CT: Greenwood Press.

Renn, K. A., Dilley, P., & Prentice, M. (forthcoming). Identity research in higher education: Commonalities, differences, and complementaries. In W. G. Tierney (Ed.), *Higher Education: Handbook of Theory and Research.* Bronx, NY: Agaton Press.

Retzloff, T. (1991). Outcast, miscast, recast: A documentary history of lesbians and gay men at the University of Michigan. In Study Committee on the Status of Lesbian and Gay Men, University of Michigan, *From invisibility to inclusion: Opening the doors for lesbians and gay men at the University of Michigan* (pp. 110–134). Ann Arbor, MI: Affirmative Action Office, University of Michigan.

Rhoads, R. A. (1993). *The cultural politics of coming out*. Paper presented at the annual meeting of the Association for the Study of Higher Education. Pittsburgh, PA.

Rhoads, R. A. (1994). *Coming out in college: The struggle for a queer identity*. Westport, CT: Bergin & Garvey.

Rhoads, R. A. (1997a). Crossing sexual orientation borders: Collaborative strategies for dealing with issues of positionality and representation. *International Journal of Qualitative Studies in Education, 10*(1), 7–23.

Rhoads, R. A. (1997b). A subcultural study of gay and bisexual college males. *Journal of Higher Education, 68*(4), 7–23.

Riessman, C. K. (1993). *Narrative analysis* (Qualitative Research Methods Series, Vol. 30). Newbury Park, CA: Sage.

Rosenwald, G. C., & Ochberg, R. L. (Eds.). (1992). *Storied lives: The cultural politics of self-understanding*. New Haven, CT: Yale University Press.

Rossman, G. B., & Rallis, S. F. (1998). *Learning in the field: An introduction to qualitative research*. Thousand Oaks, CA: Sage.

Sadownick, D. (1996). *Sex between men: An intimate history of the sex lives of gay men, postwar to present*. San Francisco: Harper San Francisco.

Savin-Williams, R. C. (1990). *Gay and lesbian youth: Expressions of identity*. New York: Hemisphere Publishing.

Savin-Williams, R. C. (1998). *". . . And then I became gay": Young men's stories*. New York: Routledge.

Sears, J. T. (1992). Researching the other/searching the self: Qualitative research on [homo]sexuality in education. *Theory Into Practice, XXXI*(2), 147–156.

Sears, J. T. (1997). *Lonely hunters: An oral history of lesbian and gay southern life*. Boulder, CO: Westview Press.

Sears, J. (2001). *Rebels, rubyfruit, and rhinestones: Queering space in the Stonewall South*. New Brunswick, NJ: Rutgers University Press.

Seidman, S. (1991). *Romantic longings: Love in America, 1830–1980*. New York: Routledge.

Seidman, S. (1995). Deconstructing queer theory or the under theorization of the social and the ethical. In Linda Nicholson & Steven Seidman (Eds.), *Social postmodernism: Beyond identity politics* (pp. 116–141). New York: Cambridge University Press.

Sidel, R. (1994). *Battling bias: The struggle for identity and community on college campuses*. New York: Viking.

Signorile, M. (1993). *Queer in America: Sex, the media, and the closets of power*. New York: Random House.

Signorile, M. (1997). *Life outside: The Signorile report on gay men: Sex, drugs, muscles and the passages of life.* New York: HarperCollins.

Slagle, Ra. A. (1995). In defense of Queer Nation: From *identity politics* to a *politics of difference. Western Journal of Communication, 56,* 85–102.

Solon, S. (1992, April 10). About 40 "kiss-in" for noon audience. *University Daily Kansan,* p. 3.

Spencer, C. (1995). *Homosexuality in history.* New York: Harcourt Brace & Company.

Sprung, J. (1972). *Rutgers conference on gay liberation.* New York: National Task Force on Student Personnel Services and Homosexuality.

Stanley, W. R. (1983/1984). The rights of gay student organizations. *Journal of College and University Law, 10*(3), 397–418.

Steffan, J. (1992). *Honor bound: A gay American fights for the right to serve his country.* New York: Villard Books.

Stoll, D. (1999). *Rigoberta Menchu and the story of all poor Guatemalans.* Boulder, CO: Westview Press.

Student Coalition for Gay Rights v. Austin Peay State University, 477 F. Supp. 1267 (M.D., Tenn., 1979).

Study Committee on the Status of Lesbian and Gay Men, University of Michigan. (1991). *From invisibility to inclusion: Opening the doors for lesbians and gay men at the University of Michigan.* Ann Arbor, MI: Affirmative Action Office, University of Michigan.

Talburt, S. (1999). Open secrets and problems of queer ethnography: Readings from a religious studies classroom. *International Journal of Qualitative Studies in Education, 12*(5), 525–539.

Talburt, S. (2000). *Subject to identity: Knowledge, sexuality, and academic practices in higher education.* Albany, NY: State University of New York Press.

Task Force on Lesbian and Gay Concerns, University of Oregon. (1990). *Creating safety, valuing diversity: Lesbians and gay men at the university: A report to the president of the University of Oregon.* Eugene, OR: The University of Oregon.

Teal, D. (1995). *The gay militants: How gay liberation began in America, 1969–1971.* New York: St. Martin's Press.

Thomas, R., & Chickering, A. W. (1984). Education and identity revisited. *Journal of College Student Personnel, 25*(5), 392–399.

Thompson, M. (Ed.). (1994). *Long road to freedom: The Advocate history of the gay and lesbian movement.* New York: St. Martin's Press.

Tierney, W. G. (1997). *Academic outlaws: Queer theory and cultural studies in the academy.* Thousand Oaks, CA: Sage.

Tierney, W. G., & Dilley, P. (1998). Constructing knowledge: Educational research and gay and lesbian studies. In W. F. Pinar (Ed.), *Queer theory in education* (pp. 49–71). Mahwah, NJ: Lawrence Erlbaum Associates.

Troiden, R. R. , & Goode, E. (1980). Variables related to the acquisition of a gay identity. *Journal of Homosexuality, 5*(4), 383–392.

Tsang, D. (1997a). Gay Ann Arbor purges. *Midwest Gay Academic Journal, 1*(1), 13–19.

Tsang, D. (1997b). Gay Ann Arbor purges: Part two. *Midwest Gay Academic Journal,
1*(2), 11–13.

Walters, D. M. (1972a). *Homophiles of Penn State* (The Otherwise Monograph
Series, No. 14). New York: National Task Force on Student Personnel Services and
Homosexuality.

Walters, D. M. (1972b). *Student teaching and gay liberation* (The Otherwise Monograph
Series, No. 10). New York: National Task Force on Student Personnel Services and
Homosexuality.

Warner, M. (1993). *Fear of a queer planet: Queer politics and social theory.* Minneapolis:
University of Minnesota Press.

Warren, C. (1974). *Identity and community in the gay world.* New York: John Wiley &
Sons.

Warren, C. A. B. (1988). *Gender issues in field research* (Qualitative Research Methods Series, Vol. 9). Newbury Park, CA: Sage.

Weinberg, M. S., Williams, C. J., & Pryor, D. W. (1994). *Dual attraction: Understanding
bisexuality.* New York: Oxford University Press.

Windmeyer, S. L., & Freeman, P. W. (Eds.). (1998). *Out on fraternity row: Personal accounts of being gay in a college fraternity.* Los Angeles: Alyson Books.

Windmeyer, S. L., & Freeman, P. W. (Eds.). (2000). *Secret sisters: Stories of being lesbian
and bisexual in a college sorority.* Los Angeles: Alyson Books.

Witt, L., Thomas, S., & Marcus, E. (Eds.). (1995). *Out in all directions: The almanac of gay
and lesbian America.* New York: Warner Books.

Zemsky, B. (1996). GLBT program offices: A room of our own. In B. Zimmerman & T.
McNaron (Eds.), *The new lesbian studies: Into the twenty-first century* (pp. 208–214).
New York: Feminist Press at the City University of New York.

INDEX